75 60 45 30 15 0 15 30 45

75

Intercepted
Dec. 25, 1916

60

45

30

Gladys Royal Jan. 9, 1917

Lundy Island Jan. 10, 1917

Pinm

ish Yeom

Rochefo

15

0

15

30

er

inzessin

Chile

45

e Hor

30 45

The Cruise of the
SEA EAGLE

The Cruise of the SEA EAGLE

THE AMAZING TRUE STORY OF IMPERIAL GERMANY'S GENTLEMAN PIRATE

Blaine Pardoe

THE LYONS PRESS
GUILFORD, CONNECTICUT
AN IMPRINT OF THE GLOBE PEQUOT PRESS

The Lyons Press is an imprint of The Globe Pequot Press.

10 8 6 4 2 1 3 5 7 9

ISBN 1-59228-694-1

Printed in the United States of America

Library of Congress Cataloging-in-Publication Data

Pardoe, Blaine Lee, 1962-
    The cruise of the Sea Eagle : the amazing true story of imperial Germany's gentleman pirate / Blaine Pardoe.
        p. cm.
    Includes bibliographical references and index.
    ISBN 1-59228-694-1 (trade cloth)
    1. Seeadler (Ship) 2. Luckner, Felix, Graf von, 1881-1966. 3. World War, 1914-1918—Naval operations, German. 4. Germany. Kriegsmarine—Officers—Biography.
    5. Ship captains—Germany—Biography. I. Title.

    D582.S44P37 2004
    940.4'5943—dc22
                                                                  2005040747

CONTENTS

CONTENTS

PREFACE

In writing this book, I tried to find at least some semblance of the truth. The Lowell Thomas book, *Count Luckner, The Sea Devil*, is considered by some the best English-language version of the story. Numerous mistakes crept into the Lowell Thomas work, most being unintentional, and it can really only be relied on as a source for conversations and some of von Luckner's early years. Other books were written over the years, but these were simply retellings of the same misinformation. Others yet were just fanciful stories that von Luckner added for color.

Other sources of dialogue in this book came from the numerous prisoner transcripts from the *Seeadler*'s cruise and articles in magazines that granted the former prisoners interviews. The words you read are from actual accounts; they are their words, not mine.

The myth of von Luckner has been fed by books such as *Seeteufel*, von Luckner's own published account, and *The Sea Devil*. The myth was part of the struggle of this book. It was my intent to write a truthful account of Count von Luckner and the events that led to his fame. I only leveraged his accounts for such things as dialogue and for those elements where no other sources were necessary. In writing this book, I found myself dissecting the story I had grown up with—the Lowell Thomas account of the cruise.

What I found instead is that von Luckner had shortchanged himself. The reality, the true story, was just as gripping—if not more than his own version of events. I'm not an historian, though I wish I was. This book turned me into a detective of sorts. I discovered possible villains that I never knew existed in the count's own crew. I found heroes aboard the *Seeadler* that none of us ever got a chance to know until now. There is tragedy, daring, and honor to be found in this story.

If you think you know the story of Count von Luckner you will find new details and new stories here that may change your perspective as well. I don't want you to forget what you may have read before. I want you to look at it in a new light.

A number of legitimate sources, archival and otherwise, were brought to bear against the myth. Interviews with prisoners and crewmen, the war diary of the *Seeadler*, and the intelligence reports of various governments—these provide the best glimpse into the reality of what occurred during the cruise of the *Seeadler* and in the years that followed.

I also discovered that the story of the *Seeadler* didn't end when the war was over. The legend that is Felix von Luckner reaches much further than I ever expected. His struggle against the Nazis, his saving of a Jewish woman's life, and his role in the preservation of his hometown from destruction at the hands of the American army in World War II are simple glances into the man that I came to know during the writing of this book.

Why write this book now? First off, access to archival evidence has never been better on von Luckner or the raid of the *Seeadler*— and this account will hopefully correct some of the previous errors that have been printed. Secondly, there are at least two generations of people who have been denied this story in all of its laughs, its excitement, its adventure, its grandeur, and its chivalry. Who am I to deny people a chance to thrill to such an adventure?

—Blaine Pardoe
Amissville, Virginia
November 2004

INTRODUCTION

The odds against the crew of the *Seeadler* (Sea Eagle) succeeding in their mission, let alone surviving, were staggering.

The most likely scenario the crew faced was being captured a few hours after leaving port and sent to a prisoner of war camp. Their worst-case scenario was facing the Royal Navy in battle. If not for their captain, Count Felix von Luckner, they didn't stand a chance.

Ultimately, it becomes impossible to separate the *Seeadler* from the story of Count von Luckner. The two are hopelessly intertwined. If he had never taken command of the ship, he still would have made his mark on the world. The fact that he did lead the ship and the "Seeadlers" on their trek of over 30,000 miles is even more incredible.

They don't make men like von Luckner anymore. Today a celebrity like Count Felix von Luckner would be dissected by the media and a cynical public. His story is too big for us to believe. Our heroes today are sports figures and movie stars, shallow money-makers rather than individuals who have earned the right to be placed on our society's pedestal. In many ways the word is not worthy of a man like Von Luckner, not anymore. Perhaps that is part of the reason we're drawn to him and his story.

So who was Count Felix von Luckner?

At age thirteen he ran away from home, leaving the lap of luxury to become a merchant sailor. He eventually returned home at the age of twenty-one as an officer in the German Navy. He took part in the largest naval battle of the First World War.

In 1916 he took command of a three-masted sailing ship, a windjammer named the *Seeadler*. The cruise of the *Seeadler* defined what we know about von Luckner.

The ship's mission: sail through the British blockade and raid the shipping lanes. The *Seeadler* was a captured American windjammer—a relic of another age squaring-off against steam-powered, armor-plated warships. Posing as a neutral ship, he lured in merchants and captured them with daring and guile. It was the last time a major government sent a sailing ship into combat. In many respects he was a privateer, a throwback to an age of swashbuckling and daring that had long passed. His crew epitomized bravery and took risks in the mission that bordered on heroic. The crew battled the elements, the Royal Navy, armed enemies, treachery, scurvy, shipwreck, and—eventually—each other.

Von Luckner was also a storyteller, a braggart, and a person who made his living selling the one product that he knew and believed in, himself. People such as Lowell Thomas who wrote his story never validated his account. Instead they took him at his word. In some cases, von Luckner lied and in others his memory failed him. Much like an old man telling his grandchildren stories of what he did during the war, his public appearances and speaking engagements became a chance for the story to grow and change over time. Each time it was told, it was a little different, a little bolder, a little more incorrect.

Count von Luckner has been called a fraud, a liar, a spy, a pirate, a killer, an adventurer, a magician, a simple merchant sailor, captain, a chivalrous "knight of the sea," a romantic, and a hero. Some of these titles are just plain wrong, others are fairly close to who the man was. The reality is that there are few words that can convey such a complex man and series of events as the cruise of the *Seeadler*.

Part of the mystique that surrounds the man is that he represents something in all of us, something we all aspire to. There isn't a boy out there who doesn't at one point or another think of running away from home. There isn't a child out there who doesn't admire a pirate. Von Luckner was a bad boy, a diamond in the rough; yet at the same time he showed courtly manners and grace. He had a willingness to face risks that most of us would never consider. He was an easy man to admire. It is not hard for anyone to imagine what it would be like to stand with him on the deck of his windjammer, running the Royal Navy's blockade or cutting through the storms at Cape Horn.

There are those who say the voyage of the *Seeadler* had little impact on the Great War, that von Luckner's cruise and his life as a whole are mere footnotes in history. It is true: the *Seeadler* did not change Germany's fate in the First World War. His purpose was to show inspiration. To an entire generation of Germans, Felix von Luckner, the Sea Devil, the captain of the *Seeadler*, represented what an individual could do if he applied himself. Von Luckner represented hope, a future, daring, and even a reminder of a more chivalrous time.

To understand the great success of the cruise of the *Sea Eagle* you must understand the era it took place in. Before the outbreak of the Great War, the creation of the HMS *Dreadnought* changed the way the world saw naval warfare. The steel behemoth was built around steam turbine engines and massive guns that were anywhere from eight to fifteen inches in diameter and capable of tossing explosive shells miles away. The shells themselves weighed anywhere from 275 to 850 pounds, armor-tipped with explosive fuses that set them off deep in the bellies of their targets. Thick armored belts protected the waterline.

Dreadnought-type ships made other vessels obsolete. They were strategic weapons, a way for a country to impose its will on another. Having dreadnought-type ships in your fleet was the 1916 equivalent of possessing a nuclear weapon. These deadly massive weapons platforms were the vision of power for any nation.

At the onset of the Great War, the two rival German and British navies tangled a few times in minor battles; but in May of 1916 the two fleets engaged in the Battle of Jutland. The fighting was horrific. Some of the ships sunk in a matter of minutes, blown apart from the inside out as their powder magazines exploded. Other ships were more lucky and were pounded so many times that their decks resembled junkyards more than warships. Thousands of men died over two days for a stalemate. For sailors, death on the high seas was often not quick and painless. Explosive shells could rend a body, twist it inside out, tear off arms or legs. Explosive cannon shells could disembowel their vessel in a matter of seconds. Broken steam pipes and explosive powder could scald a sailor, searing his flesh instantly. If your ship was hit, your survival could only be measured in a matter of moments in the icy waters of the North Sea or the Atlantic. Both sides claimed a bloody victory in the Battle of Jutland yet neither really held the upper hand.

The Royal Navy shifted to a pure blockade strategy against Germany. The North Sea was patrolled to intimidate the German High Seas Fleet from leaving port. Naval mines, a new invention to warfare, were planted in the icy waters to make the passage of ships even more risky.

Germany responded to the blockade with a new and deadly pairing of weapons: torpedoes and submarines. Where Britain used her submarines to augment patrol lines of the blockade, Germany used her submarines, U-boats, to hunt the Royal Navy and merchant ships supplying the British Isles.

Sailing ships were still in use during the Great War but their era was waning. Most navies maintained at least a single commissioned sailing ship as a training vessel. These arcane training ships were often throwbacks to a bygone era. The remaining sailing ships that plied the seas were merchant ships. Most sailing ships were several decades old and new merchant sailing-ship construction was no longer happening on any scale. The construction of steam-powered ships had replaced the sailing ship as the most common merchant vessel on the oceans. Within two decades windjammers and barques had all but been replaced with steamships. The days of men working under billowing canvas sails was disappearing rapidly as technology overcame their eloquence.

The stalemate of the fight in the North Sea left the Germans to consider another tactic, employing merchant raiders. Merchant raiders consisted of civilian merchant ships being mounted with hidden guns or other weapons. They would sail under a neutral country's flag and would wage war on the high seas against merchant ships that were supplying the enemy. Much like the U-boats, the hope was that the use of such raiders could strangle the island nation of Britain.

To serve on such a ship was dangerous duty. Running the Royal Navy's blockade of the North Sea was not a task for the timid. There were several lines of destroyers and heavier cruisers. Merchant ships armed with deck cannons and manned by naval officers and marines

INTRODUCTION

called auxiliary cruisers were added to the Royal Navy's might. There were lines of naval mines, hundreds of pounds of explosives that could be set off at the slightest contact. These risks were faced in a converted merchant ship not built for combat. Any encounter with an armed enemy was almost certain death for a crew.

This was the world of war the *Seeadler* crew faced.

Christmas Morning, 1916

The entire crew was exhausted. Even the men hidden in the concealed holds of the ship were weary. Some of the exhaustion stemmed from the churning of the gale they had sailed through for the last few days. The risks of floating sea mines added tension, and there had been little chance for the crew to relax. They had sailed in a winter storm into the middle of the British blockade. The tension was only heightened with the knowledge that only a madman would attempt to sail an antique windjammer past the might of the British fleet.

The risk of the Royal Navy finding them and boarding them prevented every man from sleeping. Even the smallest patrol craft that the British put to sea was more than a match for Captain Felix von Luckner's sailing ship. So far they had been very lucky, even though the storm had nearly done them in.

But today was Christmas. It was a day for miracles. Von Luckner felt that for a brief moment, he might be able to relax. Besides, they were past Iceland and moving into the North Atlantic. Any time now they might spot their first victim.

A call came from the lookout that shattered that intermission, "Steamer ahoy!"

Captain von Luckner went to the deck railing and pulled out his binoculars, scanning off in the distance where the lookout was pointing. He saw it. It was not a merchant ship. He knew those lines and they could spell an end to his mission. It was an auxiliary cruiser. A *Royal Navy* auxiliary cruiser. More importantly, it was heading straight at the *Hero*, apparently under full steam. Black coal smoke twisted and gnarled into the air as the ship closed on his windjammer. He made out the signal flags and for a moment, his heart raced.

The signal was clear. Stand by or we fire.

His mind danced. "Hustle, you non-Norwegian chaps. Get below deck." Weary crewmen suddenly had a burst of energy and scampered for the lower decks. Then he called out for Schmidt. Seaman

Schmidt needed to get on his dress and assume the role of Josefeena, von Luckner's rather homely wife. He ordered the chief engineer to kill the auxiliary diesel engine. The engine had proven problematic already but the last thing he needed was black diesel smoke billowing up. Something would have to be done about the exhaust fumes in the lower decks. Diesel had a distinct aroma. Sailing ships like his proud windjammer were not supposed to have modern diesel engines.

Von Luckner glanced at the guns. Good, they were still hidden under their soaked tarps. With the rails up, they would appear like nothing more than pigpens. If he wanted to slug it out with the auxiliary cruiser, they would be needed—but mostly as a futile gesture. It was more important that they remain concealed. After all, what would a Norwegian lumber transport need with two naval cannons? Best to maintain the disguise.

As the ship got closer he could make her lines out. This was a warship not to be trifled with. He had prepared for five months for this moment—now he would learn if British spies had figured out the truth behind the *Hero*.

The sea-water soaked ship's log was in his cabin where he had laid it out to dry days before. He glanced at the Norwegian chronometer that hung in the chart room and noted the time. The time had finally come to see if all of the training, practicing, and guile they had mustered would work. Despite the layers of woolen clothing and the thick oilskin gloves, the days of cold left his fingers numb as he watched the ship approach. Everyone aboard his ship was freezing, cold but alive. If they remembered their roles and duty, there was still a chance of beating the Royal Navy, beating them without firing a shot.

It was 0939 on Christmas morning.

I

THE RIGHT SHIP

Summer 1916–December 1916

The *Pass of Balmaha* was a ship that appeared to be from another era, a ghost from another century. An American vessel, she was a windjammer but was often referred to as a Yankee Clipper ship. Clipper ships tended to be three-masted vessels like this one, but she had a composite hull like most windjammers. Her lines were sleek like a clipper, but her hull was made of steel ribs lined with thin steel plating and she lacked the fourth mast that most windjammers had. English hewn oak and hard teak made up her decks and superstructure. She was American on paper, but British in composition.

Although her registry was American and she was owned by the River Plate Shipping Company of New York, she had been built in Glasgow in 1888 by the Robert Duncan & Company shipbuilders. At first she was just a number, Yard No. 237. Until ownership was taken, ships were named by the number assigned to them in the construction yard. It was the first of a number of names that she would bear over the years. The *Pass of Balmaha* was a transport vessel, one of a dying breed. In this era of steam-powered merchant ships, only a few sailing ships still plied the sea lanes carrying their cargos from port to port.

The age of sailing transports was quickly evaporating with the start of the war in 1914. A single shell from a U-boat deck gun or from an auxiliary merchant could penetrate up to five inches of hardened steel. The composite steel and wooden hulls of a windjammer of the period were equal to just a sixteenth of an inch of unarmored steel, at best. Armor plating such a ship was not practical given the shape of the hulls, the impact on the handling of the ship, and the costs. New windjammers were not being built, not for use as merchant transports. Insurance rates on these older vessels were tolerable, but they were increasing as more of these ships were relegated into the attic of history as icons of another century.

The *Pass of Balmaha's* sleek lines gave a glimpse of the power she still possessed. Her length was just over 245 feet, with a mixed hard oak and teak deck nailed to the thin steel braces and ribs underneath. Her poop deck on the rear was all teak-covered. Fully loaded with cargo, she drew just under 23 feet of water. Unloaded, she was recorded at 1,571 tons; when fully loaded, she could top out at 4,500 tons. Her speed was set by the wind in her sails and the skill of her crew. The masts of the *Pass* were steel and wood, over 100 feet tall. When fully rigged, she had over 9,000 square feet of canvas that could pull the ship. Depending on her load and the breeze, she easily could top between seventeen to twenty knots, though that was pushing her to the limit. Normal cruising speed was six to fourteen knots.

Windjammers were the epitome of the evolution of large sailing craft. Their rigging was not the ropes of old, but steel cables that were mounted in place. Unlike her predecessors, the clipper ships, the *Pass of Balmaha* and her sister vessels did not rely on crews to manually hoist sails with block, pulley, rope, and sweat. Small donkey engines would do the work that took a dozen men in the past.

That's not to say these were automated vessels. They required crews that knew how to handle them. You couldn't take a normal steam sailor and put him on a windjammer with any hope that he could just master the art of sailing. Handling a large fast ship on the high seas, especially dangerous waters like those of the combat zones of World War I, required very skilled sailors—almost artisans. They were becoming fewer in number each year, but necessary for ships like the *Pass* to stay in business. A typical crew size ranged between fifteen and thirty-five men.

She was an American vessel—and in 1916, America was neutral to both sides in the war. Her captain, a man with the last name of Scott, was a burly, bearded, seasoned sailor who had no interest in the war other than its impact on his profit margins. Wartime needs generated business with merchants; as long as he flew a neutral flag, Captain Scott knew he had nothing to fear. Accidental attacks did happen on neutral ships, but they were very rare. No country wanted to violate the law of the high seas.

In 1915 the Russians were in need of cotton, so the *Pass of Balmaha* loaded up with cotton in New York in June of 1915. Her goal was to sail to Archangel, Russia, and sell her load at an inflated wartime price. The route would take the vessel through the midst of the British naval blockade on the North Sea. The Russians and the British were allies and with his declared neutrality, the captain did not worry about the blockade. What would they do? Let him pass—they had no choice. And if he encountered the Germans, they would let him go as well. Scott and his American vessel were neutral to the fighting in Europe.

The voyage was uneventful until the ship arrived in the North Sea. Even in the middle of summer, the waters there were cold and rough, and it was not the kind of place that any ship or crew savored. Off the coast of Norway a British armored cruiser spotted the sailing ship and ordered her to heave-to. With the increase of merchant raiders, the British were not taking any chances with any ships, even those flying neutral flags. Captain Scott made sure the Stars and Stripes was hoisted and brought the *Pass* to a halt.

The British cruiser sent a boarding party on a small launch to come and inspect the ship, her paperwork, and her crew. Such boarding parties were usually led by the first mate or the captain himself, and given that the armored cruiser was not threatened by the tiny sailing ship, the captain of the cruiser came aboard.

The boarding party did their work thoroughly. They inspected the cotton bales to make sure that no contraband was being smuggled. Because of the size and number of the cotton bales loaded, several of the lower deck hatches were not reachable by the boarding party, but this was not entirely uncommon with merchant ships. The paperwork of the ship and her log were read and cross-referenced by the boarders to make sure the ship was who she claimed to be and was heading where she was supposed to. It was a process that took time, but Captain Scott showed patience. After all, he was a neutral and the Russians were allies of the British.

The captain of the British cruiser turned to the American captain and told him that he had suspicions regarding the ship. He ordered

Captain Scott to turn the *Pass of Balmaha* around and make for Kirkwall in the Orkneys. Kirkwall was a northern British port. Once there, the windjammer would be more thoroughly inspected and their story confirmed.

Turning around and sailing back was going to take time. The northeast wind was against such a trip and it would take almost two weeks to tack to Kirkwall and make port there. Captain Scott angrily confronted the British captain, warning him that the Russians were British allies. They would be months late in delivering their cargo to them, even if their stay at Kirkwall was short. "Are you chaps trying to win a war or lose one?" he demanded.

The Royal Navy officer was unshaken. And perhaps driven by the gruff attitude of the Yank, he insisted that he was going to leave behind a boarding party to make sure that the *Pass of Balmaha* did exactly as he commanded. One officer and six marines would remain on the vessel. Captain Scott was furious, but he also knew there was little he could do. The cruiser belched out a thick blanket of black coal smoke and took off while he turned the *Pass* around and headed back toward the northern British Isles. The young British naval officer left in command of the ship drew up a schedule of watches with his marines to ensure that Captain Scott did not alter the course of the ship on its trip to Kirkwall. The ordeal was humiliating and infuriating to the American captain.

It was not likely tense aboard the American ship as much as it was frustrating. The captain and crew were being made to feel like criminals. By Captain Scott's account of the affair, the young British officer was arrogant toward him and his men. As the *Pass of Balmaha* turned back toward the British Isles, everyone on board came to the realization that it could be a very long voyage.

Matters were made worse when the young officer ordered that the American flag be lowered and the British Union Jack be raised. Captain Scott bluntly refused. The officer, backed by his rifle-armed marines, ordered the job done. His logic was simple: as a British officer, he was temporarily in command of the vessel, thus he was entitled to change her colors to the British flag. In doing so, Captain Scott realized that the ship was no longer seen as a neutral vessel, but a British one. With bitter reluctance he obeyed the order from the young officer. Scornfully he spat back at the brash young Brit, "I wish the Germans would come."

The next morning, they did.

The *U-36* surfaced off of the side of the *Pass of Balmaha* during the first watch. She flag-signaled the seemingly British windjammer to heave-to and prepare to be boarded. The once-arrogant British officer suddenly found himself in need of a friend in Captain Scott. His requests quickly turned to pleas with the Yank, who blamed him for the German's appearance. "Serves you right! If the Stars and Stripes were up there, they wouldn't bother us." The British officer realized that he and his men were facing a long time in a German prisoner of war camp—and Captain Scott realized that his ship would be impounded by the Germans if they were discovered.

More out of his own preservation than any desire to help the Brits, he had his men hide them in the holds below and quickly replaced the Union Jack with his own American flag. Given the similarity in colors, he was hoping the Germans might believe they had made a mistake. The German boarding party that climbed aboard the windjammer was not convinced, however, demanding to know what had happened to the British flag they had seen. They had not seen the switching of the flags, however. For at least a few seconds, it seemed that Captain Scott's luck had held. The boarding party searched the vessel just as the British had done before, checking her logs and cargo.

What remained was suspicion. Captain Gräfe of the *U-36* was convinced he had seen the Union Jack flying over the windjammer. He met with Captain Scott and told him that he was going to order the *Pass of Balmaha* to sail to the German port of Cuxhaven. He would leave behind an ensign to make sure they reached their destination. Once in port, German Navy authorities would be able to verify what had taken place.

Having been captured and had two prize-crews assigned to his ship in two days, Captain Scott agreed. The *Pass* turned again with the wind, this time facing toward Germany. The *U-36* set off on its own ill-fated voyage, destined to be sunk in battle with a British Q-ship a few days later.

The ensign left behind was armed and experienced. He stuck close to the captain for the remainder of the day and that night hung a grenade by its pin on the cabin door of the captain's quarters, where he planned on bedding down. He informed Captain Scott that if there was any disturbance or anyone attempted to open the door and overpower him, both he and the captain would be blown up. The ensign suspected something was wrong and told the captain he would be at his side, day and night, until they made port. It was not a threat, but the mark of a sailor who knew he was outnumbered on a ship on the high seas. One didn't survive in the U-boat service without a high degree of caution.

Fearful that the British officer might foolishly attempt to retake the ship with his six marines, the captain managed to smuggle word to his own crew to make sure the Brits remained where they were. His crew went one step further, locking the British marines in their dark hold. Their loyalty was to their captain, not to the surly upstart officer who had seized their ship and gotten them into such trouble.

Captain Scott really didn't have a plan. After several days of travel, he knew the British were not going to be able to retake the ship; it was too far from their patrol lanes. Going into a German port, he knew his only real chance was to convince the Germans that he was not supporting the British war effort. When they reached the German port of Cuxhaven, a small ship was sent to meet them and the Germans sent aboard a larger boarding party. When he was convinced that the Germans had superior numbers aboard his ship, he pulled aside the ensign who he been so glued to his every move.

"You wanted to know what was wrong here? All right, I'll show you." Leading the armed Germans belowdecks he took them to the hold where the British were locked up. The hold hatch was small, and when he opened it the Royal Navy officer stuck his head out and demanded to know where they were. He blinked his eyes, having been stuffed into the darkness for several days, unsure of the images he saw towering over him. When he did focus, he saw German marines with rifles aimed at his head and the bearded face of Captain Scott scowling down at him.

"You're in Germany. If you'd left my flag alone you'd be alright, but now you're prisoners!" He stormed away and left the officer and marines to the Germans. No one has recorded the reactions of the young U-boat ensign who was outnumbered for several days, seven to one, by the Royal Navy; but he had to have felt relieved that his suspicions were proven correct. The British prize crew was arrested and the *Pass of Balmaha* sailed into port under the watchful eyes of the German Navy.

The ship was caught in something of a legal quandary. She had not flown the Union Jack on her own accord; she was forced to do so by the British, who had essentially seized the vessel. Maritime law allowed the Germans to seize the vessel as spoils of war since it was flying the British flag when captured. Captain Scott and his men were more bitter toward the British than the Germans, but they still did not want to lose their ship and cargo. It was decided that the Americans would be released to a neutral country, but their ship would become a possession of the German Navy.

But what would the Germans do with a twenty-eight-year-old 'jammer? Her usefulness seemed limited other than as transport, and even then she was not much of a test for the British blockade. For most, it seemed that the *Pass of Balmaha* was destined to spend the rest of the war rotting and rusting in a slip at Cuxhaven harbor, banished to the elements and time.

Her destiny seemed lost and her fate bleak, until a reserve officer at the port came up with an idea and submitted it to the Admiralty. Rather than let the ship rot on the wharf, could she be used as a raider instead? Was it possible to arm such a vessel? Would a windjammer be able to slip past the ever-tightening Royal Navy blockade better than a steamship? There would be no need for precious recoaling stations or ports—a clipper ship could remain at sea for long weeks at a time, if not longer.

The risks were obvious and the odds seemed long at best. For now, it was an idea that needed more fleshing out—and perhaps the right men to try it.

✠ ✠ ✠

In late summer of 1916, Alfred Kling was a lieutenant in the German Naval Reserves assigned to Cuxhaven when he received word he was going to take a ship to the port in Hamburg for refitting. Kling was a skinny man with a lean face and a well-maintained mustache. For him, the assignment was welcome relief. When he saw the ship was a sailing vessel, the *Pass of Balmaha*, it was even more pleasing.

Lieutenant Kling was a reserve officer—not a true commissioned officer of the German Navy. His rank might be the same as full-time officers, but there was a distinct difference. Reservists were often seen as second-class sailors. More often than not, they got land-based assignments or small ship duties while commissioned officers got true high sea assignments on the larger battle cruisers and dreadnoughts. He was happy he was going to sea, and even more happy he was going on the large windjammer.

Kling had experience with sailing ships. In 1913 before the outbreak of the war, he had served with Doctor Filchner's South Pole expedition where he got experience on sailing ships in some of the worst weather on the planet. At one point Kling had assumed command of the ship used on the expedition—exerting his leadership potential. His only combat assignment since the start of the war had been a posting to a small torpedo boat, the *D4*. With the fleet not engaging the British head-on, most of his time was spent performing meaningless tasks in port.

The lieutenant had reason to believe he might get the ship. After his boring posting at Cuxhaven he learned about the *Pass of Balmaha* and of her story of how she had come into Germany's hands. He suggested in writing to his commanding officer that the ship might be a candidate for converting to a surface raider, believing the British might not suspect a windjammer as a raider. The actual letter itself has disappeared from the records; but what is known is that his commanding officer forwarded it up the chain of command—along with his own endorsement. Half a dozen initials and blurred signatures were attached to the recommendation. For the immediate time being, during her refitting as a raider, Alfred Kling was to take temporary command of the vessel.

For Kling, the assignment to take the *Pass of Balmaha* down to Hamburg offered some potential to break the monotony of port duty. He knew that few of the regular navy sailors had expertise with large sailing ships. There was a hope that the Admiralty might be planning to put the old ship to sea. If they were planning on it, there was a good chance that *he* might get the full command of the ship at some point later on. Lieutenant Kling had no idea that the Admiralty was already considering another commander.

His orders were to pick a skeleton crew to take with him. He leapt at the chance to prove his skills—choosing men who, like him, had sailing experience.

Upon his arrival in the port of Hamburg, the old windjammer was moved by tug into a narrow drydock. Lieutenant Kling reported, as per his orders, to the harbormaster at Hamburg, Captain Langkopf. He expected that he would either be told he was in command of the old windjammer or he would be sent back to Cuxhaven. He was surprised to find neither. Captain Langkopf told the reserve lieutenant that he was temporarily assigned to the *Pass of Balmaha* and that he was to oversee her refit. In fact, his first assignment was to paint over her stern and bow names and replace the American names with her temporary name—the *Walter.*

Was he going to be the new commanding officer of the ship? No. The Admiralty had found another man to assume the role of captain of the *Walter.* He was let down but knew that if he performed his duties well, he would probably get to remain on board the ship. Like all good officers, he quickly buried himself in his assignment, overseeing the tasks that Captain Langkopf ordered him to do until the new captain arrived.

The man chosen for the command of the *Walter* was Count Felix von Luckner. How he had been selected for that command was something that would plague his mission from the start.

Count Felix von Luckner felt as if he had the world at his command. A few months earlier he had received a posting that any rising star in the German Navy would envy. The raider *Möwe* had punched through the British blockade and had returned home months earlier.

She was being outfitted for another run and he had been chosen by Captain Count Dohna-Schlodien as her new gunnery officer. While the High Seas Fleet remained at port, he was getting a chance to take on the enemy.

The *Möwe*'s raid was legendary. Posing as a merchant ship, her 1914–1915 cruise had shaken up the Royal Navy and had driven the insurance rates from Lloyd's of London through the ceiling. Her infamous history and press coverage made assignment to her a plum choice for an up-and-coming officer.

Lieutenant Commander von Luckner met with an old friend and a ship owner named Hans Dalström during a summer evening in 1916 when he was interrupted by a courier. He was ordered to the Admiralty in Berlin. A train ticket was waiting for him and he was to pick up his personal belongings from the ship.

It was not a good sign. Such an order usually was an indication that you were going to be transferred or assume a new set of duties. Von Luckner had been looking forward to his cruise on the *Möwe*, and the trip to Berlin seemed to be putting an end to that.

The next day he arrived in the German capital and was taken to the Imperial Headquarters to face an admiral whose name is lost to history. The meeting was short and to the point. "You are to take command of a vessel. We want you to run the blockade and raid enemy commerce. Since we have no coaling stations, a sailing ship will be the best. Do you think you can do it?"

The normally talkative von Luckner was stunned. After a pause, he finally spoke. "Yes sir! I'd like nothing better."

Von Luckner asked why he had been chosen for the mission. The admiral didn't flinch. A search of the command-level personnel in the German naval records showed that only Lieutenant Commander Felix von Luckner had experience under sail on the high seas. In short, he was the only one qualified for the mission.

"What should you consider the greatest importance for the venture?"

Von Luckner didn't hesitate. "Luck."

Apparently the answer was the one the admiral was looking for. "All right then, take the *Pass of Balmaha*. She has already carried

British prisoners to us. She has been lucky for us once and may be lucky for us again."

And so Lieutenant Commander von Luckner left the meeting as a captain.

On September 29, 1916, the Admiralty sent formal orders marked MOST SECRET to the Beermanne Hotel where the count was staying. They were short and to the point: Count Luckner was to assume command of the ship known as the *Pass of Balmaha* for use as a merchant raider. He was to complete the outfitting of the ship and take her to the Indian Ocean.

The orders were so vaguely written they could be interpreted in a number of different ways, but he was going to need a high level of discretion for the mission he was undertaking.

To convert the *Pass of Balmaha* to the raider *Seeadler* required a great deal of modification to the old windjammer. Workers conducted the heavy drydock labor in the port of Hamburg in the late summer of 1916 under the watchful eyes of Lieutenant Kling as first officer and his new commanding officer, Captain von Luckner.

A surface raider needed provisions for staying at sea for an indefinite period of time. The *Seeadler* posed some interesting challenges in that she was a windjammer. This meant that she could only maneuver when there was a wind. For a merchant that was fine, but there might be times when as a raider she would need maneuvering capabilities, so one of the first tasks was to fit her with auxiliary engines. It wasn't to make her fast, but to enable her to move without the aid of nature if she had to.

Most vessels of the period were steam powered with coal-fired boilers, but the *Seeadler* was to have a single 900–1,000 horsepower diesel engine. The diesel was a relatively new engine and their use for marine vessels was limited. The Admiralty looked into a small two-cylinder engine, but it was deemed too small. The larger German-built Burnmeister & Wain engine would have been the prime choice—but these tended to be custom built, many being used for the zeppelin engines. Attempting to acquire one of these would attract a great deal of unwanted attention.

Eventually, the shipyard was able to locate a four-cylinder two-stroke engine built by the Belgium firm of Usines Carels Freres SA of Ghent. It was not exactly what Captain von Luckner or Lieutenant Kling would have chosen—but it would have to suffice. With a single propeller on the modified rudder, the speed was not overly impressive, only nine knots; but it was designed to augment the *Seeadler's* sails, not replace them.

Dropping such an engine and running a propeller shaft to the stern of the windjammer was no small engineering task. If done incorrectly, the vibration would literally shake the old ship apart. Lieutenant Kling oversaw the placement of storage tanks for over 480 tons of fuel and oil.

Other modifications were extensive as well. While she could gain some supplies from those ships she captured, the *Seeadler* was intended to operate like most other German surface raiders, with long stretches at sea with no resupply. Concealed cargo holds deep in the ship stored nearly two years' worth of provisions, not just for the crew, but for many more men who would hopefully be her prisoners.

Workers fitted the ship with holds for 480 tons of sweet water used for drinking and cooking. Standard rations were not the only food on board. Captain von Luckner insisted that the ship not just

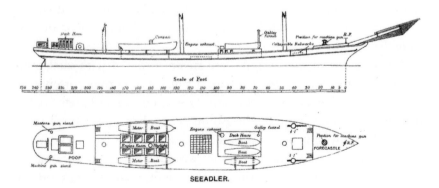

After interviewing several of the *Seeadler's* former prisoners in Rio, the U.S. Navy prepared this deck plan configuration. *Source: U.S. National Archives.*

have sea rations, but also a full stock of Norwegian food supplies in the galley. If they were inspected, he wanted every detail to appear as if the *Seeadler* was a Norwegian windjammer. A Norwegian ship would give the raider the looks of a neutral vessel, and the Norwegians were on the North Sea and made extensive use of sailing ships.

Most sailing ships of the day relied on exterminators with fumigation gear at port; insects and rats were commonplace, depending on the cargo hauled. The *Seeadler* was not planning on making port during her raid. A fumigation plant was installed in the forecastle so that prisoners and their luggage could be thoroughly deloused.

Merchant captains had little use for the crow's nest on a windjammer. But for a surface raider, this perch would be more important than any other post on the ship. Lieutenant Kling, at von Luckner's bidding, oversaw the installation of two very comfortable padded seats in the crow's nest. The padding would be needed by the men who would be spending days at a time there.

The *Seeadler's* complement numbered sixty-four sailors, though this was far more than was needed on a standard merchant ship. As such twenty-nine Norwegian-speaking crewmembers played the role of Norwegian merchant crewmen. The rest of the crewmembers were marines, machinists, gunners, and gunnery mates. They were quartered on the same deck deeper in the ship. The officers had more private cabins. The extra crew quarters were hidden belowdecks in concealed compartments.

They would also need quarters for crewmembers of the ships they would capture on the raid. First Officer Kling oversaw the outfitting of concealed compartments that could house upwards of 400 bunks, made out of pipes with stretched stark-white canvas for bedding and a limited amount of privacy. The aisle between the rooms was only wide enough for a single person to go through at a time, to prevent a large rush of prisoners out of the hold. If there was an uprising of some sort, it would be a slow and cumbersome venture.

Von Luckner insisted that the captured captains have some degree of personal privacy, so a suite of private cabins was outfitted for captive captains. Each of these had two bunks but more could be added while at sea.

Security was a problem on the docks. A steady stream of carpenters, mechanics, pipefitters, and other workmen came aboard the *Walter* every day for work. None knew they were outfitting a merchant surface raider, and von Luckner wanted to keep it that way. At his direction, First Officer Kling hung up signs to play along with the guise of the *Walter* being a training ship. Some of the signs placed in the holds were marked "150 Cabin Boys," "80 Apprentice Seamen," "Teacher's Stateroom," and "Study Room for Ship's Boys." To anyone coming aboard the ship, it would appear she was being configured to take young men out and turn them into sailors.

Von Luckner seemed to go out of his way to drive the quartermaster insane with his special requests. The captain's galley was specially designed. The entire room was built on a hydraulic elevator and was designed to deal with a boarding party situation. If a landing party came on board, von Luckner could invite them to dinner in his saloon. He would pass a verbal signal to his crew by saying, "Cookie, serve up the best we've got." This was the signal to his marines to arm themselves and assume positions on the lower deck.

Once his "guests" seated themselves, von Luckner would casually rise and hit a button on the wall behind the barometer in the adjacent chart room. The floor in the galley would drop the entire room to the deck below, and the enemy boarding party would find itself surrounded by armed German marines pointing their Mauser rifles at them.

The ship itself was outfitted with an array of hidden compartments, fake wood panels, concealed crawlspaces, and hatches where Kling hid grenades, rifle ammunition, guns, dynamite, and fuses. The crew was trained to arm themselves in a matter of minutes on command.

The Admiralty did not want any raider, including the *Seeadler*, to fall into the hands of the Royal Navy. It would prove to be a propaganda coup if the British seized one of these feared ships. From an intelligence standpoint, they could take it apart and learn how and where things were hidden and what to look for—so keeping a raider out of enemy hands was crucial. As such, explosive charges were planted on the keel of the ship in three places. If the ship was to be captured, von Luckner had orders to blow up his own ship. The crew all knew about the charges and their function.

A wireless set was installed on the ship, a rarity for such sailing ships at that time, which the *Seeadler* crew would use to listen to enemy wireless messages. The antenna, usually easily spotted, was hidden by being wrapped around the base of the mast. It was invisible unless someone knew exactly what to look for.

Before the *Seeadler* was ready to sail, other refinements had to be made—such as rerigging the masts and inspecting and replacing the sail canvas. The crew needed a way to unload cargo and provisions from captured ships. The solution was to equip the ship with two large gasoline-powered launches. The launches were perfect for sending sizable armed boarding parties to take their prize vessels. The fact that these were powered might raise suspicion, and while they had canvas pegged over their tops, the propellers would be a dead give-away. The solution: the mounting blocks that held the launches in place were positioned to perfectly conceal the propellers.

The final touch to the ship was her main armament. The deck was cut down on the foredeck at the bow. Two modified 4.2-inch (105 mm) SK L/40 cannons were installed on the lowered deck. Additional bracing was installed so if they were fired, they would not pop all of the rivets loose on the hull. One was mounted on each side for broadside coverage. Four hundred rounds of ammunition for the cannons were loaded as well. The guns were of the same type used on U-boats—with shortened barrels, they didn't stick out. The solid steel plated rails concealing the guns could be lowered quickly, giving the guns a broad field of fire. Covered with tarps, they were disguised to look like covered deck equipment—such as a converted pigpen, a common sight on a sailing vessel. The crew even hung some laundry there when weather permitted, just to make the area seem less suspect.

The cannons were not the only armament she carried. The *Seeadler* carried two machine guns as well. To provide the machine guns with a stable firing base, workers made two special mounts on the poop deck to the port and starboard sides. Similar mounts were placed at the bow of the ship, another deck mount was placed. The

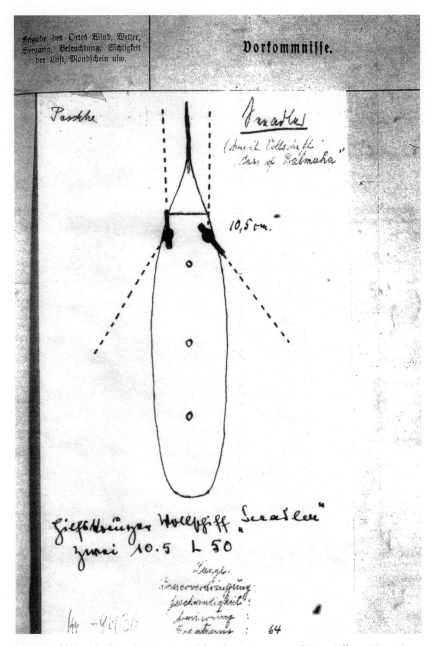

Never published before, this image and handwritten notes of First Officer Kling show the gun placements from the war diary of the *Seeadler*. *Source: U.S. National Archives.*

ship carried two hundred explosive charges to be used to scuttle captured vessels.

Von Luckner added some personal touches. Pictures of the king and queen of Norway and of their relative, King Edward VII of England, were placed in his quarters along with a small library of Norwegian books.

The unique supplies and gear required for the refit of the *Seeadler* proved to be a point of difficulty between her new captain and the quartermaster. Some of the supplies secured were not what Von Luckner demanded and were sent back. Many of the pieces of gear had to be inspected to ensure they were exactly what he had requisitioned. Everything, even the ship's oil, was a matter of suspicion. At times it was as if the captain were fighting his own navy as well as the British.

A ship's log is an incredibly important piece of documentation. It is the life story of the vessel it is attached to. It covers mundane details, such as who was sick and how much fresh water is on board. It addresses cargo, ports of call, ships encountered—everything. Creating a fake ship's log that would pass any sort of detailed inspection would be difficult, if not impossible. The number of details that could be checked and verified under inspection were so numerous that any chance of using a fake log to pass off a ship was almost impossible.

In the fall of 1916, the Admiralty made the decision to send the *Walter* raiding on the high seas. Her name would be changed eventually to *Seeadler*, but a name change alone would not get her past the British blockade: she would have to pass herself off as a neutral ship. Chances were very high that the British would put a boarding party on the ship. They would need to appear to be another ship, in every way possible. If the Royal Navy was anything, it was thorough.

Von Luckner sought a windjammer from a neutral country that was similar to the *Seeadler*, which at that time bore the name *Walter*. During this period, Captain von Luckner hung around the docks disguised as a marine customs inspector named von Eckmann. Mingling with other crews and workers, he learned of a ship in Copenhagen named the *Maleta* that might serve his purposes. The guise of an inspector helped him work around the Hamburg docks without attracting attention to himself, and to obtain information that wouldn't attract British spies.

If he could disguise the *Walter/Seeadler* to be the *Maleta*, and perhaps even have the ship's log from that ship, he might be able to fool the Royal Navy if he was stopped. They would check Lloyd's Registry and discover that the *Maleta* was a real ship, a windjammer similar to his own. With some good acting performances on the part of his crew, they might be able to pull it off.

Von Luckner almost didn't get to go to Copenhagen to check out the ship. The chief inspector for the docks became suspicious when word of von Eckmann reached him from several locals. There was no record of such a man, but inquiries about the mysterious von Eckmann raised a number of eyebrows and finally von Luckner was traced to the Beermanne Hotel. Von Luckner was registered, but not the mysterious von Eckmann. A suspicious captain from the docks followed the inspector to the hotel and was surprised to see that the man now donned a German captain's uniform. Only one kind of man traded disguises so freely: a spy. One of the hotel employees tipped off the German shore patrol that the alleged German officer was at the Trocadero, a night club.

He was confronted openly in public in the club and produced papers showing him to be an officer in the German Navy, which was the truth. That was not enough for the crowd that began to gather. In their mind, this was what a spy would do. There was a risk of a public lynching on the spot, one man calling out, "Kill the spy! Kill him!" But Von Luckner was escorted from the night club and his true identity was eventually revealed.

Von Luckner's intent was simple: steal the log of the *Maleta* and refit his *Seeadler* to become that ship. He traveled to Copenhagen where the *Maleta* was supposed to be in dock for refit through November and December. For the German captain, his trip had to stir up old memories. He went under the name of a dockhand named Phelax Lüdicke, the name he had used in his youth. In Copenhagen he blended in perfectly with the local dock workers and was able to get close to the *Maleta* and study how she was protected.

The *Maleta* was tied to the dock fore and aft, and the watchman was posted near the captain's cabin. Von Luckner cut the rope on the bow line almost all of the way through. The pull of the tide and the breeze was enough for it to snap a short time later, swinging the ship loose in the dock. The watchman sprang to secure the ship at the bow; no one noticed von Luckner jumping aboard on the aft end of the ship.

The search for the ship's log took a long time, but he eventually found it stuffed under the captain's mattress. As the skeleton crew resecured the *Maleta* to the dock, Phelax Lüdicke made his way off the ship with the precious logbook.

The *Walter*'s disguise was that of a training ship, at least that was what the dockhands in Hamburg had been told during her refit. The hull had been painted a dull gray, the kind of gray that every ship of the German Navy wore. It was repainted a black and faded tan color.

Thanks to the recovered log, the crew that von Luckner had selected could begin to assume their new identities as members of the Norwegian ship's crew. He chose some of the men for the raid not just for their experience under sail, but for their ability to speak Norwegian. If and when the British came aboard, they would have to convince them that this was the *Maleta* and this was her crew from Norway.

The ship had to be refit as a Norwegian merchant. Ship's furniture from Norwegian manufacturers was brought aboard. With blessings from the Admiralty, von Luckner employed both the Admiralty and the Ministry of Foreign Affairs to write letters to the fictitious crewmembers, all placed in envelopes with stamps from Norway and postmarked there as well. Pictures were procured from studios in Norway and provided to the crew so that their personal effects, if searched, would bear up the story of the *Seeadler/Maleta*.

Clothing with marks from Copenhagen tailors were purchased for the crew. When they fought, they would don the uniform of German sailors in accordance with maritime law. However, when attempting to pull off their ruse, they would appear as commercial sailors from Norway. Seaman First Class Heinrich Hinz described the garb: "The crew dressed like Norwegian seamen with Träsko wooden shoes, thick woolen Icelander sweaters, and blue shipmen's caps and carried Norwegian tobacco, Skraa chewing tobacco, and above all Norwegian identification papers. Many all of a sudden got fiancés in Norway who wrote letters full of longing. We let our beards grow and took Norwegian names." Von Luckner even had Captain Knudson's name of the *Maleta* sewn onto his own clothing tags.

Captain von Luckner locked horns constantly with the quartermaster over his ship. He successfully argued that having German provisions in his galley would tip off the Brits and insisted that authentic foods be procured. The real *Maleta*, according to the log, was installing a new donkey engine for hoisting and lowering her sails. He wanted the exact same model of engine installed on the *Seeadler/Maleta*. He knew that this was the kind of simple detail a British boarding party could verify. These were not easy requisitions to fill and only served to cause the quartermaster to begin to chafe at the requests from von Luckner.

There had been a large number of modifications already done to the ship to prepare her for raiding, but her captain wanted things that would complete her ruse. A load of lumber was needed—Norwegian lumber of course, properly stamped from lumber mills in Norway. This fake cargo was supposedly going to be delivered to Australia—and false shipping documents were drafted to validate this ruse. The quartermaster found some but did not arrange to bring it to port. If von Luckner wanted it, he and his crew could sail out to the barge that had it and load it themselves.

The *Walter*, as the *Seeadler*'s name still was at the time, used the chance to turn the mission into a short training cruise. The lumber was important in getting through the blockade. Stacked on the deck, it could cover some of the hatches that led to some of the more deadly secret modifications done to the sailing vessel. His men worked hard to transfer the wood to the *Walter/Seeadler*. Von Luckner also ensured that the wood was mentioned in the logbook stolen from the *Maleta*.

The officers drilled the crew not only on their seamanship, but on their false backgrounds and identities. What is your hometown?

What is your mother's name, your sisters? What ships have you served on? The crew attended Norwegian classes aboard the ship. Those crewmembers who could not speak the language would be hidden in the ship's secret holds, where hopefully the British wouldn't discover them.

The British blockade was not a single imaginary line to be crossed in the North Sea. In reality, it was three sets of lines, each heavily patrolled. Because of the successful cruise of the German raider *Möwe*, the Royal Navy patrolled the waters between Scotland and Iceland and all along a line from England to Norway. Their patrol ships worked in small groups. Any vessel, even Allied, was stopped and searched. They conducted constant surveillance for U-boats as well.

In the late fall of 1916, the blockade went on a heightened state of alert. The reason was that the Germans had sent a merchant submarine, the *Deutschland*, to the neutral United States for supplies. The cruise of the *Deutschland* had been something of a thorn in the side of the Royal Navy. It had slipped through the blockade and made it to New York with no problems. American newspapers played up the arrival of the sub, and the British felt that the integrity of their blockade had been called into question. If they did not sink the *Deutschland* on the way back to Germany, there was a genuine fear that the Germans might create a fleet of merchant submarines that could simply slide under the might of the Royal Navy. It was an unrealistic threat, but high motivation for the British ships at sea.

Von Luckner was ready to go at the end of November, but the Admiralty held him at anchor outside of port. With the Royal Navy on such high alert, he had to delay setting sail until the *Deutschland* made port.

The submarine *Deutschland* was not the only reason the Admiralty was holding the *Seeadler* from starting her raid. What von Luckner did not know was that the Admiralty had given the go-ahead to two other raiders—the *Wolf* and his former vessel, the *Möwe*—to begin their cruises. There was concern that sending three raiders out at the same time might triple the risk they would be captured. The risks of sending out even one alone seemed very high, given the heightened sensitivity by the Royal Navy to capture the *Deutschland*. So each went out one at a time, separated by several days to a week.

Germany was directly challenging the strength and resolve of the British blockade and was counting on the fact that at least one of the raiders would get through. None of the ships would be aware of the other until later in the war. The Admiralty did not inform either captain of the other ship out of fear that capture might result in the information reaching the British.

It took two weeks for the ship to arrive in port—but then word came to him that threatened his entire mission. The *real Maleta* had left Copenhagen. By now, it had already crossed the British blockade line. If he took off now, his ruse would almost certainly be exposed: the Royal Navy would know that a ship of the same name had already passed the blockade.

Months of hard work seem to have been wasted. Von Luckner asked for help searching for another windjammer and found the *Kalliope*. It too was in Norway, and for some time he hoped they would be able to alter the stolen log from the *Maleta* so it matched that of the *Kalliope*. That task proved difficult if not impossible for German intelligence. Removing the name *Maleta* from the paperwork proved relatively easy; putting in a new name proved much more difficult. The variety of inks and the paper quality in the log showed obvious signs of tampering when they tried to make the necessary alternations.

Matters were made worse when German agents learned that the *Kalliope* had been intercepted by the British blockade in the first weeks of December and was on its way to Kirkwall for inspection. The news appeared as a small article in British newspapers, tipping off the Germans. Now there would be no chance to use that name to slide past the British: they would know something was amiss.

Von Luckner's greatest chance of sliding through the blockade was the fact that no one would suspect a sailing vessel of such a mission. If word leaked out that a windjammer would be used as a raider, there was no chance of getting past the Royal Navy. To preserve that risk, he kept his crew on the ship outside of the port so a slip of the tongue would be nearly impossible.

Then came the gale. With it, there was hope he might just slip by in the fury of the storm. He wanted to name the ship the *Irma*, after his fiancé, but was worried that it might tip his hand with the British if they received word from their spy network that he was the captain of a new raiding ship. All he needed was a fake name, one that might mimic that of another ship. Count von Luckner chose *Hero* for his ship, at least until they cleared the blockade. Given the nature of their cruise, the crew endorsed the new name for their ship openly.

That only left the vital evidence of the paper trail. Von Luckner decided he would rather ruin the ship's log than attempt to tamper with it and give any prize crew reason to be more suspicious. Soaking the logbook, he could always explain the kind of damage that a storm could wreck on an old sailing ship. Additional paperwork and manifests were produced listing the vessel as the *Hero*, and they were all carefully placed in the chart room and captain's quarters. These forgeries were soaked in sea water as well and left out to dry.

2

THE RIGHT CAPTAIN

December 1916

The German Admiralty had learned some important lessons when it came to raiding operations by late 1916, thanks mostly to the cruise of the *Möwe*. There were key elements to the success of a merchant raider, and they were simple and critical.

The right ship: It needed to be armed, fast, capable of getting past the blockade, and had to pass as a merchant so as to lure in its victims. It had to be equipped to take merchant crews as captives and hold them for extended periods of time.

Stealth: Once a raider was launched, it did not contact anyone—even their peers in the German Navy. Part of what made a merchant raider successful was that no one knows that it even exists. Both sides had ships and shore stations monitoring wireless radio traffic and knew each other's codes.

The right crew: Raider crews had to be independent thinkers. If boarded by the enemy, they had to be great actors to pose as the crew of a neutral ship. In a battle, they had to behave like any other German sailor in a fight.

The right captain: Men who commanded raiders had to be able to operate beyond the chain of command, using only the resources they could salvage or capture. Independent thought and action were the hallmarks of a good raider captain. Someone who wanted to know what the Admiralty thought of his next actions was the wrong man for the job.

Merchant raiders were not a revolutionary concept during the First World War. After the Battle of Jutland, the Germans switched naval strategies. Up until Jutland, they hoped to engage the British Grand Fleet in a massive Trafalgar-like battle. At Jutland the two fleets had tangled at close range, but true victory for either side had proven elusive and dangerous.

After the battle, the general consensus was that the kaiser did not want to risk his precious fleet in a massive battle. In his mind, Jutland was not the victory the newspapers made it out to be and he had the ships relegated to light raiding and patrols. There were sorties, but none of the grand battles anywhere near the scale of Jutland.

His admirals agreed to a certain extent, albeit with some degree of reluctance. Even Vice Admiral von Scheer of the German High Seas Fleet wrote, "Even the most successful result of a battle on the high seas will not compel England to make peace." This helped solidify the thinking of the kaiser. Why risk the fleet if victory would not cripple the British?

The German Admiralty resorted to two new ways of fighting the British. The first was their U-boats, the predecessors of Hitler's Wolf Packs. The U-boat submarines of the Great War were often death traps all on their own; but they were effective at sliding past the British blockade. Once in the sea lanes, they could strike at merchant ships, pinching off British supply lines on the seas. The threat of a U-boat in an area was enough to divert shipping lanes and force the British fleet to send out a squadron of ships to find and destroy them, draining force away from their blockade.

The other way the Germans fought the British was by using merchant raiders. The idea for using raiders came from a junior lieutenant in the Admiralty named Theodor Wolff who wrote a paper in October 1915 suggesting this tactic as a way to strike at British merchants. Using tramp steamers, outfitted with extra coal bins and weapons, they could overtake merchants on the high seas and sink them. The concept of privateers was far from new, but applying the principles to twentieth-century maritime law was original. Admiral von Pohl began to explore ways of implementing it.

Raiders were merchant ships that were secretly armed. Deck guns would be hidden under false crates or bogus superstructures on their decks. They would fly flags of neutrality and attempt to pass as neutral vessels to slip through the British blockade. Once on the high seas, they would attack, sink, and capture merchant vessels of the British and her Allies.

Most raiders were not fighting ships, but merchant ships that were given enough teeth to fight if they had to. More often than not they had to bluff and intimidate ships into surrender. They were not pirates, as much as the propaganda machines of the Allies tried to paint them as such. Pirates robbed for the profit of the plunder. They were privateers, sanctioned by the German government and manned with German sailors.

There were several such raiders that had already slid past the British and driven the Lloyd's of London insurance rates through the roof. The *Möwe* had proven to be a deadly foe—punching through the blockade twice, once when leaving and once when returning to port. The *Emden*, a cruiser turned surface raider, had led a successful cruise as well. They were hated names by the British, feared by Allies, and revered heroes in the eyes of the Germans.

The Royal Navy had two things working to its advantage in dealing with the surface raider threat. The first was that its fleet of ships, augmented with auxiliary cruisers, was large enough to patrol the entire world. The British had another advantage: coaling stations. By 1916 all of the German raiders that had put to sea before the *Seeadler* needed coal for fuel, and the British had numerous ports around the world where their navy could refuel. The Germans had never been a true globe-spanning empire and were limited to a handful of neutral ports to get coal to keep their raiders at sea. More and more, the British tightened their patrols of such ports—strangling the capability to put raiders to sea. For a raider to survive, it had to capture a coaling ship or steal coal from the vessels it captured. Coal was the lifeblood of a steam-powered raider. But the *Seeadler* did not need coal.

Free from the need to scavenge coal to remain at sea, the *Seeadler*'s only limitations were the vague areas of international maritime law. A ship on the high seas could fly any *neutral* flag it wanted until it went into battle. To fire its guns or otherwise attack, it had to fly the flag of its nation. Its sailors had to wear the uniforms of the navy they served, and in the open. As long as this letter of the law was obeyed, the mock-Norwegian windjammer became and acted like a vessel of the German High Seas Fleet.

✠ ✠ ✠

Felix von Luckner was born the first of two sons of Count Heinrich von Luckner. The von Luckner family was well known in Prussian circles. Felix's great grandfather Nicholas was said to be something of a wild child and his parents sent him to a monastery at a young age in hopes that the monks would teach him discipline. Predictably, it didn't work. As a young teenager, Nicholas ran away from his life at the monastery to join the Turks in their war with the Austrians. He spent two years learning cavalry fighting and tactics from the Turks and all that he could about the military before he returned to his homeland and joined the Prussian Army under Frederick the Great as a lieutenant in the cavalry.

Leveraging his family's funds and landholdings, he formed his own regiment of cavalry known as Count Luckner's Hussars. It was the convention for royals to raise their own regiments and to offer their services to the highest bidder as renowned mercenaries. The distinct brown and green uniforms and fighting prowess of Count Luckner's Hussars were highly regarded. Their expertise was so desired that the king of Hanover offered to purchase the unit for his own burgeoning military. Nicholas was willing to sell them under one condition—that the unit would retain its name.

Nicholas confronted the king and was rebuffed. He tossed his uniformed mantle into the fire and stormed off, vowing to fight against the king from that time forward. Nicholas threw his lot with the king of France and eventually became the commander of the army on the Rhine. After securing a string of important victories in Belgium, he was made a marshal of France. When his soldiers were not paid, he led the army to Paris to demand their wages. Instead, he was seized and guillotined. With that stroke, the Luckner family's commitments to the affairs of France ended.

Nicholas started the great cavalry tradition in the von Luckner family. Felix's grandfather and father were both seasoned and highly decorated cavalrymen. But horsemanship was not Felix's passion. Born June 9, 1881, Felix von Luckner was raised to a life of royalty. He was fond of telling the story that as a baby he was coddled by Queen Victoria on a visit—though the evidence of this is anecdotal at best. His parents took trips on sailing ships; for the young boy, these were some of his happier childhood memories. For young Felix, his true love was not mastering equestrian prowess, but handling a ship on the ocean.

Felix brought up his naval desires with his father but was snubbed bluntly. Von Luckners were cavalrymen—not sailors. The young boy's interest in traveling the oceans did not fade. The one thing father and son did see eye-to-eye was a sense of duty to Germany. No matter what, Felix von Luckner would wear the uniform of the emperor in service of the country.

Young Felix was not a good student at all. It was not that he wasn't smart: he seemed to lack focus. His grades were never good and were a source of tension between Heinrich and his son. His father tried to tutor him personally, but he became more frustrated than pleased. Felix was transferred several times to other schools, all with the same effect. His grandmother took on the boy as her own pet project, tutoring the young count. She even went so far as to attempt to pay him for good grades—but the wily child lied to her about his class rank to earn the money rather than study to earn his seat in class. As time went on it became increasingly clear that Felix simply was unable to perform to his father's satisfaction in school.

Felix was caught in the classic vicious circle. The more frustrated his father became, the more his father put pressure on the young boy. The more pressured he became, the worse he performed. He reached a point where he no longer wanted to even try. At the age of thirteen, he stole his father's best boots and coat, borrowed money from his younger brother, and ran away from home. Felix purchased a train ticket to Hamburg. He was determined to board a ship and learn everything he could to become a good sailor.

Once in Hamburg he made his way to the seaport area of Sankt Pauli. At each of the massive sailing ships, the young boy stopped and offered his services as a cabin boy. At each ship, he was told that he needed his father's permission. Dejected, he found an old sailor working a small rowboat ferry named Peter Bömer, "Old Peter" to those who knew him in Sankt Pauli. The old sailor was seasoned and grizzled, but he was not going to leave a young boy alone on the wharf. He took Felix in and was stunned to find out he was harboring a royal runaway.

Peter tried to convince Felix that the last thing he wanted was to go on the high seas, that he should simply go home and knuckle down with his studies. Felix would hear nothing of it. Peter finally consented to help young Felix find a ship.

The ship he found was the Russian barque *Niobe*. The deal that Peter had arranged was not well negotiated. Felix could go as a cabin boy, but since he did not have the proper permission, the captain of the *Niobe* refused to pay him. To Felix, the money did not matter: he was finally getting to go to sea. Peter helped the boy take what money he had left to purchase supplies he would need—oilskin coat and boots, a knife, warm clothing, and a pipe. Old Peter gave the young count his own sea chest and as much advice as he could. His most pointed words of advice were critical for the young Felix's hope of survival on the high seas: "My boy, always remember: one hand for yourself and one for the ship."

His final advice was to change his name. The Luckner family was well known and Peter suggested he take on a name more apt for a sailor. His true motivations were probably more attuned to the fact that the von Luckners had the money and reach to look for the boy; he would be harder to find if he used an alias. Felix came up with his new alias: Phelax Lüdicke. The last name, Lüdicke, was his mother's maiden name, and for over five years it would be his own.

Life aboard the *Niobe* was not the glamorous life on the high seas that he had envisioned. The ship was crewed by Russian sailors who did not speak German, and he could not speak Russian. The count, a boy who had lived life on a plush estate, found himself with an entirely different breed of men. The Russians did not bathe. They carried with them a roaring stench. The men did not wear socks, but simply wore their boots barefoot. Covered with weeks of sweat and grime, the boots themselves were soaked in porpoise oil, which only served to add to the aroma. Felix would learn over time that the men occasionally had clean hands—only when the skin on their hands peeled, taking with it a layer of dirt and grime.

The forecastle of their ship where they lived was a tight dark space whose walls were covered with stuffed flying fish. For the Russian sailors, most of whom were from the steppes, the flying fish were an oddity and were kept as souvenirs for family and friends back at home. They were not cleaned but were painted with thick coats of shellac to keep their form and color. But the men lacked basic taxidermy skills and tools, so the rotting fish on the walls only added to the reek of the ship.

The captain of the *Niobe* was not a friendly man. He had no love of the Germans and had no use for Phelax. The only person that Phelax could speak to at all was the helmsman of the ship, who along with Phelax spoke a little English. The helmsman acted as an interpreter for the boy and the crew. His first day out, the helmsman asked him what his father did. Phelax blurted out that his father was a farmer.

The helmsmen smiled. "Well then, it would be just the right thing if I appoint you Chief Inspector."

Phelax was excited at the new title, which sounded like a position of responsibility. In reality, the chief inspector was the crewman in charge of cleaning the pig sty on the ship, home to half a dozen hogs. It was filthy work in dark and stifling conditions. In the tight confines, the pigs constantly rubbed against him and their waste was so deep that it sloshed over the tops of his shoes. When Phelax complained, he was also appointed as the Superintendent of the Starboard and Larboard Pharmacies. On a sailing ship, "pharmacy" was slang for latrine. Not only did he get to slop and clean the pig sty, but he was also responsible for cleaning and emptying the latrines.

He learned one Russian word—голубь, meaning "pig." The crew called him that and would kick him as he came by. Phelax learned that he was not entitled to food as a normal cabin boy in the crew. Instead, he was only allowed to eat what the other sailors left on their plates, which was usually the scraps of heavily salted meat, stale bread soaked in vodka, or assorted fish leftovers.

There was a way out of the sty, and that was to demonstrate a use elsewhere on the ship—namely in the rigging. Phelax was worried about the height of the masts and was nervous about falling. Other cabin boys and members of the crew seemed to dance on the masts, but for him it was a harrowing experience. Eventually he got more comfortable with the heights, but not enough to get out of his role in the latrines and sty.

When the *Niobe* rounded Cape Horn it was caught in rough weather common in the region. Phelax, wanting to show the crew that he could be of use and was not afraid, climbed the rigging to help set the topsail. A gust of wind caught the sail and knocked the young boy loose. He fell ninety feet and into the sea. When he broke the surface it was in the wake of the fast moving ship. In a panic he shed his oilskin boots and heavy coat to attempt to stay afloat. The *Niobe* continued on without him.

Several albatrosses circled him as he attempted to tread water in the rough seas. The birds thought that the drowning boy might be a source of food. One swept low and he grabbed onto one of its legs. The massive white bird beat its wings to try and fly away; when that didn't work, it began to stab its beak into Phelax's hand to try and break free. His right hand bore the scars from the encounter for the remainder of his life.

A few minutes later, he found himself coming to on the deck of the *Niobe*. The old Russian captain was furious with the boy. In the crew's efforts to go after him, they had lost the topsail. The helmsman told Phelax later that the captain had threatened the crew to not rescue him, at the point of a harpoon. The captain was under no obligation to rescue the boy if the maneuver placed other members of the crew at risk. They finally convinced him to put a boat in the water and managed to get Phelax a line before he died.

The captain was irate. He poured vodka into the boy's mouth in hopes of invigorating him, but it only served to make him sick. When he did come around and was too sick to do his duties, the captain beat him severely.

The sheer isolation of being aboard a ship of strangers who hated him was his salvation. He could not run away from his situation, nor was it going to change to accommodate him. But Phelax did love the sea, and he was proud of the fact he was overcoming his fear of heights in the masts and learning the ways of sailing a large ship on the high seas.

Weeks later the *Niobe* arrived in Fremantle, Australia. The boy who arrived in Fremantle was not the same one who had climbed aboard the *Niobe* weeks before. Once in port, Phelax decided he needed to be on a different ship. Jumping ship was serious business for a paid crewman because fines and jail time were not uncommon outcomes. As such, Phelax laid out his plans for escape carefully. He met some fellow German sailors in the shipyards who helped him smuggle Old Peter's sea chest off the *Niobe*. He worried that he was going to be caught by the *Niobe*'s captain, and only realized in later years that the old man had not even bothered to look for him.

Phelax had not lost his love of the seas: he was ready for a new sailing ship to test himself on.

Adapting to new circumstances and a variety of people was a skill that Count von Luckner had honed over the years. Despite years on the high seas as a ship's mate, he found that his return to the Royal Court was a challenge. Wilhelm II, Kaiser of Imperial Germany, found von Luckner to be an anomaly. His rough edges lacked the savoir faire of a privileged upbringing and formal education. His life of adventure in the real world—a realm that most royals were kept far away from—and the stories he told made him a favorite of the kaiser.

On many occasions, he was forced to deal with different characters in different situations. In 1913, as a young lieutenant in the navy, the kaiser invited the officer to attend a formal ceremony with the king of Italy. The reception was to be held on the dreadnought *Kaiser* and was attended by a wide range of Europe's royal families.

Von Luckner was well known for his stories and his slight-of-hand magic and parlor tricks. The kaiser told him he wanted to see a magic trick performed, and the young count prepared carefully. When presented to the king of Italy, the kaiser asked him to perform a trick to impress the visiting monarch.

The count took an egg and produced an old red sailor's handkerchief. He stuffed the handkerchief into the egg in his hand to make it disappear. Then he asked the kaiser to reach into his coat pocket and produce the handkerchief. Reaching in, he pulled out the red rag. The kaiser wanted to make the kerchief appear in another pocket. Von Luckner once again stuffed it into the egg to make it disappear. This time he produced the handkerchief in the pocket of the Italian king.

At the start of the reception, Lieutenant von Luckner had taken a handful of identical red handkerchiefs and had the valet hide them in most of the guests' pockets. Hiding his own in a fake egg, he was able to make the handkerchief appear in anyone's pocket where he had placed a false one prior to the reception.

The trick had nearly backfired. The kaiser told him that a week later the empress had discovered one of the red handkerchiefs in the kaiser's pockets and had become immediately suspicious as to the origins of the rag and who it had come from.

Three years later in late November, 1916, the summons had come from Kaiser Wilhelm II's aide rather than from the emperor himself. The weather in Berlin was moderate compared to most years. In another port at that time, Alfred Kling pondered if he would get command of the *Walter*. That determination had already been made, and this meeting would solidify it.

The thirty-five-year-old von Luckner wore his full dress uniform that day, a Kapitänleutnant, or captain. He stood out in a crowd, but that was because most naval officers were much shorter than he was: he topped off at over six feet in height. He was a strong man; his neck muscles were thick and the dress shirt collar strained under them. For an officer, this was out of the ordinary. His skin was darkened from spending years outdoors in the sunshine. His jawline was stern and his smile was as warm as his voice was loud and booming.

The captain of the *Seeadler*, formerly known as the *Pass of Balmaha*, was a man who had almost as many different names as the ship he commanded.

Although he had met with the kaiser many times before he was nervous about the meeting. The kaiser was intrigued by von Luckner's years on the high seas and by the stories that he told. Despite that, he was concerned about the meeting because he was convinced they were going to take his ship away from him. Rumors against him circulated in the Admiralstab for some time. It appeared that political-minded officers sought to undermine him.

He knew he had enemies, not the kind that one sought out, but the kind that feared for their own positions. This made the refitting of the *Seeadler* even more complicated. There were enemies in the Admiralty who thought it was a waste of resources to even attempt such an act—sending a sailing ship out against the might of the British dreadnoughts and cruisers. There were enemies in court that resented the fact that the kaiser liked the young officer and treated him like a protégé, helping his career along.

The kaiser entered the room in the greeting chamber of the palace, and the officers—including von Luckner—snapped to attention. The older man wasted no time, cutting to the chase.

"Well, Luckner, at the Admiralty they now tell me it is madness to attempt the blockade in a sailing ship. What do you think?"

His infectious grin took over. "Well your majesty, if our Admiralty says it's impossible and ridiculous, then I'm *sure* it can be done." He paused for a moment and allowed himself a quick glance to his superior officers. While no one has recorded their reactions to his comments, it is safe to assume some red faces rose at his words.

Von Luckner, however, wasn't done. "For the British Admiralty will think it's impossible also. They won't be looking out for anything so absurd as a raider disguised as a harmless old sailing ship."

Kaiser Wilhelm II looked back at his officer and returned the smile. "You're right, Luckner. Go ahead! And may the hand of the Almighty be at your helm." With those words the emperor turned and left the room.

Count von Luckner had played his hand and won. His opposition in the Admiralty would hear of this meeting. They wouldn't like it, but they would know that to stand in his way or the mission of the *Seeadler* was to cross the kaiser himself. He also knew that he had burned his last bridge with his superiors. If he failed, no one would stand to defend him in the Admiralty.

3

THE RIGHT CREW

December 1916

Captain von Luckner interviewed his crew personally months before. His first officer, Lieutenant Alfred Kling, had already done the initial recruiting; but the count had a broad depth of discretion in the choices. He had obtained permission to recruit any personnel he chose for his crew, and he recruited and picked his men carefully. Some were in the navy and naval reserve, some were artillerymen, and two had served aboard zeppelin service. For the most part he chose men with sailing experience who would be assets in handling the windjammer. There are no records of him rejecting any of the experienced men Kling had found; in fact, the count added at least one of his own.

Naval experience under sail was important, but so was the character of the men. They were going to sea just like those sailors in the German patrol squadrons, facing exactly the same risks that their fellow sailors were facing. The only difference with assignment to a raider was that it would be at sea for an indefinite period of time. When von Luckner interviewed candidates for his crew, he never told them the type of mission that they would be undertaking. He concentrated instead on their character and whether they had the right personalities for an extended operation such as a raid.

Count von Luckner fully understood the key roles he needed to fill. That of his second in command, his executive officer, had already been addressed by the Admiralty. A boatswain, carpenter, and a cook—the heart and soul of any sailing vessel—would be important roles that needed the right men for the job. He was going to need a good medical officer and gunnery officer. The *Seeadler* had auxiliary engines to propel her, so a mechanic/engineer was important as well. All of the men filling these positions needed to have sailing expertise at sea.

One of the most important jobs to be filled was that of the man who would lead his boarding parties. Going on a boarding party was a raider's most dangerous duty. They would be going aboard a potentially hostile ship—and no matter what, the odds were against them if a crew turned angry and decided to turn the tables.

For that role, he needed brute force and size. He had run into an old acquaintance on the docks in Hamburg, a lieutenant he had gone to school with and sailed with once before. Lieutenant Richard Pries was a large man who surpassed von Luckner's own six foot height and muscled bulk. He had a round mustached face and the thick muscles of a wrestler. In the photographs, his uniforms always appeared to be straining against his size. Von Luckner knew that the six-foot-four brawler would be more than able to take care of himself if problems arose. He had the right attitude as well.

"Is it one of those trips that is likely to send you to heaven?" Pries asked when presented with the chance to join him.

"Yes," von Luckner replied.

"Then I'm with you!"

An atmosphere of paranoia raged in the dockyards about possible Allied spies, and Captain von Luckner heeded those fears. His men trained in their new roles; but with the exception of the officers, he didn't inform them of their mission. As he waited to sail in his attempt to run the blockade, von Luckner was worried that sooner or later, enemy agents might learn of his true intentions. At the end of November, he put his officers aboard the *Hero* and sent the ship to the mouth of the Weser River outside of Hamburg.

Von Luckner passed word to the crewmembers to meet him at midnight at the docks. There he had them climb aboard a small navy steamer and ferried them out to the ship they knew as the *Walter*. The newly renamed vessel, the *Hero*, was flying the Norwegian flag. The crew was ordered aboard the ship and told where to report to put their personal belongings. In the holds of the ship, they found all of the signage in Norwegian and pictures of Copenhagen and other scenes of Norway hung in the hallways.

Now that they were isolated from the mainland, he could explain their true mission. "Boys, the British say that not even a mouse can get through their blockade. But we will show them by Joe, and under full pressure of sail. Then, once we reach the high seas, we will sink their ships, by Joe. Can we do it?"

To the man, the crew shouted out their support—not just for the mission, but for their captain. They remained sequestered aboard the *Hero* until the morning of December 17. A German torpedo boat, S-128, pulled up alongside of the windjammer and an officer came aboard with orders. They were hand-delivered to prevent the British from monitoring wireless traffic and perhaps interpreting the intent of the message.

The time had come for the *Seeadler* to begin her hunt.

The *Hero* pulled away from the port entrance as the stiff December winds buffeted the distant Hamburg docks. The vessel had been anchored in that location for weeks, only hoisting anchor for short training cruises. This was the start of a storm, a full-blown northern gale on the North Sea in December. There were more miserable places to be on Earth, but not many. This gale was just starting—and it was already showing signs of being a fierce storm. The rigging and canvas for the *Hero*'s three masts were still tied down as her auxiliary engine did all of the work, moving her along at a plodding five knots. Waving in the breeze over the ship was the Norwegian flag.

The ship was not really the *Hero* at all, but no one other than her crew knew that for sure. In reality, it was the *Seeadler*. While every other ship was lashed to the Hamburg docks two miles distant to ride out the storm, her captain was lifting anchor and putting to sea.

The gale that blew along the North Sea that December was far from a mild and passing storm. It had started on the 21st of December, and weather watchers predicted that it would last for a week. Records show that it was one of the worst storms of the decade in terms of wind speed, and definitely the worst storm of the Great War on the North Sea. Taking a sailing vessel into such a gale was a calculated risk. Captain von Luckner saw it working to his advantage two ways.

First was the fact that the British Grand Fleet blockaded the North Sea. In weather this foul they were less likely to intercept his ship. Since the *Seeadler* was about to become the first merchant raider that was a sailing vessel, he had good reason to want to avoid the blockade.

The second reason that the storm worked to his advantage was the fact that the Royal Navy had laid a large number of mines in the North Sea shipping lanes. The *Seeadler* drew less water than a steamship, even when fully loaded. But under full sail and tilted so her keel was not flat to the water's surface, she was at even less risk.

Mines were tricky business. The British commonly used a sea mine known as the H II Class Mine. It was a essentially a copy of a German mine and consisted of a metal frame that acted as an anchor, a cable or chain to hold the floating mine, and the spherical mine it-self—with 320 pounds of explosives, usually guncotton, packed in. The mine's depth was set by the length of the cable holding it to the sea floor where the metal frame would come to rest once deployed. The mine was covered with Hertz Horns, contact probes that stuck out all over the surface of the mine. Each contained a thin glass vial filled with acid. When bumped, the glass broke and released the acid, allowing for a chemical electric reaction that provided the battery in the mine with enough charge to set it off.

Before von Luckner ordered full sails up, there was another task. He turned the helm over to First Officer Lieutenant Kling and asked that the ship's carpenter, Gustav "Chips" Dreyer, and boatswain Ernst Dreyer join him in his quarters. Once there, he tossed the ship's log from the windjammer *Maleta* out on the floor. The two men joined him shortly and he gave them their new assignments.

"Come on Chips, I'm going to make you admiral of the day. Get an ax and smash all the bull's eyes, portals, windows, and everything," the captain ordered.

Turning to the boatswain, he gave out his second set of commands. "Half a dozen men with buckets of sea water. Throw it around. Soak everything."

For a long moment the men must have thought him mad, but von Luckner smiled. He grabbed one bucket from one of the men, then took the ship's log from the *Maleta* and dunked it in good and deep. The pages would be ruined.

The sailors went to work immediately, smashing portals, dumping buckets of water everywhere—in every cabin and accessible hold. Crewmen broke chairs and some of the oak railing sections. Sailors drenched their own clothing and hammocks knowing that in the weather they faced there was little hope of them drying out for days. In a matter of a few minutes, the *Hero* looked as if she had been through hell itself. Captain von Luckner tracked down the ship's carpenter. "Now repair everything you have smashed, Chips. Nail it all back up. Repair it as if you had done it on the high seas."

The repair work took much more time and effort than the breaking. If the crew wondered if their captain was mad before, they now wondered if he was insane or simply had a grudge against the ship's carpenter. Von Luckner smiled and ordered the ship to prepare to raise full sail. Above and around him the dark gray and purple skies of the storm seemed to reach down to the *Hero* and shove it north toward the waiting British blockade.

Sailors, especially those who sail the seas under stretched canvas, are a hearty lot of men. Merchant seamen spend most of their lives at sea, and like many captains, Captain Knudson of the *Maleta* took his wife Josephine with him on long voyages. The wives of sailing captains are not exactly known for their beauty, but more for their devotion and "rugged" good looks. Captain von Luckner knew that if he had a woman on board posing as his wife, the good-natured British might believe he was the *real* Captain Knudson.

There was an issue in the fact that Captain Knudson was supposed to command the *Maleta*, not the *Hero*. Von Luckner decided that he and his crew would maintain their fictitious identities. If they were discovered, it would be because of the ship, not because of the duplication of names.

The count had no intention of taking a real woman on his raid, but he checked his crewmen for someone who might pass as "fair"— hopefully fair enough so when in drag, he might pass for a captain's wife. The best candidate was Seaman Hugo Schmidt. His face was the cleanest when shaven and when covered with a little rice powder, his skin appeared feminine. He was shorter than most of the seamen. Unlike most of the men, he was skinny and did not have a thick muscled neck. His sparkling blue eyes certainly must have helped.

There were two primary problems with Schmidt playing the role. One, despite lessons, he did not speak convincing Norwegian. Second, his feet were incredibly large. Von Luckner dug into his bag of tricks and came up with a long dress, long enough to cover the huge feet of the seaman-in-drag. The seaman's language problem was solved with a face wrap and a wad of cotton in his mouth. Posing as a woman with a painful toothache, she would not be expected to speak well, if at all.

Seaman Schmidt was a good sport. He donned a dress complete with fake breasts and practiced his role like every other member of the crew. While there is no record of him taking any verbal jibes from his fellow crewmates, his fortitude and courage must have been great to take on such a role.

Once clear of the harbor, von Luckner ordered full sails. In normal winds, this was a good move for speed. In the gale's buffeting fifty mph winds, the *Seeadler* took off recklessly to the north. The captain's plan was to follow the general route the *Möwe* had taken earlier in the year in her raid. Rather than attempt to go through the English Channel, he would take his ship to the north to Scotland and then head west between England and Iceland and out into the Atlantic.

The crewmembers posing as Norwegians were the only ones the captain wanted out on deck. The rest of the crew retreated to the secret compartments in the bowels of the ship. Those sent to the darkness of the ship were pitied: it was a rough place to ride out a bad storm. However, they turned out to be the ones who had it easy. Those fighting to keep the *Hero* intact faced a much harder test of their endurance.

By noon the storm had reached force 10, with sixty mph winds. Von Luckner still did not order the sails reduced. Speed was something he was hoping to turn into his ally, perhaps sailing past British patrols that had pulled back to port to ride the storm out.

It became clear after the first day that the storm was no normal gale. Waves broke over the bow of the *Seeadler* constantly, despite her speed. Her aft was riding a little low in the water. If they struck a mine it would be the stern that suffered the most damage. But by day two, mines were the smallest risk the ship and crew faced. The storm showed no sign of weakening, and von Luckner ordered the crew (including himself) to don their life vests. Lookouts were posted in pairs to protect each other on the watch. When not on deck, the men used porpoise oil to treat their boots and keep them waterproof from the icy water. Most captains would have pulled their canvas in a storm, but von Luckner could not afford such a course of action. It sent a subliminal message to the crew; one way or another, the *Hero* was going to continue forward.

By the next day the strain on the masts was starting to show. The captain ordered the royals and gallants pulled down, still leaving a lot of canvas propelling his ship. The barometer continued to drop as the *Hero* turned north by northwest and started the stretch around Scotland. Von Luckner recorded her speed as over fifteen knots. At night, to avoid detection, he ordered no lights at all. The *Hero/Seeadler* ran dark, caught between the fear of the gale and the British fleet.

Two members of the *Seeadler*'s crew huddled in the forecastle, hiding on their small bed. The ship's dogs, Piperle and Schnäuzchen, curled up on their floor bed to ride the storm out. Piperle was usually the most friendly of the two schnauzers, but even this energetic dog had begun to cower under the force of the storm.

Ice began to take hold on the *Hero*. Her rigging cables became encrusted in a thick coating of ice from the North Sea spray. The hawsers and mooring lines froze in place. The idea of taking down any canvas became impossible with each passing minute. The stacked lumber on the decks was so heavily coated in ice that the individual planks were invisible. The wind continued to take the ship north. Despite the captain's attempts to tack against it, they were being blown further in that direction.

Von Luckner had been in this kind of weather before and broke out the oxygen torches, sending some of the crew up the icy rigging to try and free the lines up in the blocks. They unfroze the lines—but a few minutes later, they froze up again. The deck had become a sheet of thick ice: even the anchor and chains were frozen solid in place.

For all of his and Lieutenant Kling's meticulous planning for the voyage, they had not packed arctic gear—not enough for the entire crew. The lower holds where some of the German crew hid turned into freezers. Many of the crew started to show signs of frostbite, keeping the ship's surgeon busy doing what he could. He tried to crank up the small cooking stoves in the galley, but these were not as much for heat as for cooking.

A trip into the water meant death in a few short minutes. There was a real risk the ship could be blown to the polar regions and become trapped, and perhaps crushed by the ice floes. The sails, laden with iced canvas, hung heavy on the frigid masts. A gust might even capsize the vessel. Each new gust of wind made every piece of teak and oak on the ship creak, and the hull seemed to groan under the strain. The crewmembers could not pull the sails down and there was concern that they would be shredded, or that the ship would be dismasted and left only to its engine.

The 1,000-horsepower auxiliary diesel engine on the *Seeadler* had been broken in on several of the training cruises the ship had taken when it sailed as the *Walter*. It had performed very well on the relatively short training cruises, but now the engine was starting to exhibit problems. Engineer Krause, the engineer and mechanic on the ship, had to stop it for service.

Getting inside the large diesel engine was not a quick or easy undertaking in the hold of the windjammer. It required dismantling the engine itself, a costly process in terms of time and the loss of propulsion cherished in the storm. Once inside the massive diesel, Krause came across the problems.

While diesels had been installed before on ships, they had not been installed on a sailing ship like the *Seeadler*. The commercial diesel engine was still relatively new technology. Most installations were on small freighters with wider hulls—ships that used the engines as their sole means of propulsion. In this configuration they ran generally in a level position. But on the *Seeadler*, running with full sails in a gale, the ship was tipped constantly in the breeze and the oil was not lubricating all of the vital engine parts.

The other problem was the oil itself. First Officer Kling had made sure the quartermaster's materials were of good quality; there had been problems with some materials and von Luckner had Kling follow up with the quartermaster. It was a bureaucratic struggle and Kling had generally prevailed—but bad oil had apparently gotten past both Kling and Engineer Krause. The oil didn't hold its viscosity after running the engine for long periods of time. There was no way to easily test the oil before departure, and now that the culprit had surfaced nothing could be done.

Krause rebuilt the engine and changed the oil, but it was a patch-fix at best.

4

SEASONING

1903–1916

In 1903 young Phelax Lüdicke signed on as a ship's mate aboard the *Caesarea*, a German sailing merchant ship in Australia. He sailed aboard the ship for the better part of two years—sailing the Pacific, around Cape Horn up to New York, and even back to Germany. After his experiences aboard the *Niobe*, serving with fellow Germans was a pleasant change of pace. The captain of the *Caesarea* was something of a skinflint, skimping on food as much as possible to make his trips more profitable. It was never easy sailing on a trip aboard the *Caesarea*, but for the young seaman, it was a good learning experience.

The *Caesarea* was on a trip from England to New York carrying a load of arsenic. The captain had taken on new crewmembers who lacked the experience of even the young Phelax. On Christmas, the crew gathered for a cozy party in the warmth of the forecastle, but the party was interrupted by a vicious storm.

This was no ordinary storm: it was a killer gale. Almost immediately the foremast broke, falling overboard after crashing into the deck. The topmast shattered next in the gale-force winds, coming down with such force that it smashed through the deck and into the bunk area where Phelax slept.

The arsenic on the second deck was packed in dense barrels that took up little space but were very heavy. The next day, their shifting caused the deck to shatter as the barrels tumbled to the deck below, causing some spillage. The sudden and uneven shift of weight in the hold popped rivets in the hull of the *Caesarea*, sending water pouring in.

The crew went down and shifted the barrels by hand, not realizing the risk of the cargo. Many of the crew developed painful swelling from the arsenic poisoning, making the storm even more agonizing. As the water level belowdecks rose to several feet, the crew manned the pumps on the deck during the peak of the storm.

The pumping was grueling work, but it was better than sinking. When the crew slacked off, the captain ordered grog brought out for them, a nasty brew but enough to give them energy. Soon they were weary from both the work and the drinking. The *Caesarea* was fighting for her very life, and it appeared to be a losing battle. When the crew's exhaustion rose and the pumping effort became sporadic, the captain pulled a harpoon and threatened to stab them.

On his way to take his turn at the pumps, Phelax was slammed forward when a wave broke over the side of the ship. One man had his skull crushed as he hit the deck; two of the crew were washed overboard; another was badly maimed with broken bones. Phelax landed near some timbers on the deck that came down and broke his leg.

The young count had never been in such pain before. The risks he faced were life threatening. It was simple enough; if the men didn't pump, they would die. The captain ordered the ship's carpenter to splint Phelax's leg and have him man the pumps. With a block and tackle, the carpenter straightened the shattered limb and braced it with spare pieces of lumber. It was crude and painful but they needed every hand to keep the ship afloat.

The *Caesarea* was dying. Even with his contribution to the pumps, it was only a matter of time. The captain gave the order to abandon ship and the crew dove into the water to fight their way to the lifeboats. The crew tossed Phelax overboard and recovered him later in the lifeboat.

The *Caesarea* did not sink but careened in the water like an injured whale. What food they had was stale and soaked in sea water. The storm raged on for four days as the tiny lifeboats were tossed about in the churning seas. As the storm subsided the survivors spotted a steamship and wearily waved for it to save them, but it kept going on.

The surviving crew was beyond miserable. Poisoned with arsenic, weary from the storm and the pumping, they were running out of fresh water and food. Two days passed before an Italian steamer spotted the survivors and rescued them.

Phelax was taken to a German hospital. They considered amputating his leg, but he convinced them not to. It took eight weeks for him to heal enough to finally be able to once again put to sea.

Little did Phelax realize that the experience aboard the *Caesarea* was preparing him for an ordeal of his own making when he would one day be a captain on his own.

When the young von Luckner lived as Phelex Lüdicke he maintained some contact with his parents—sending them an occasional letter or photo. But while he traveled around the world, he became a fading memory to his family. According to his own account, he came across a copy of the *Almanach de Gotha*—the Almanac of German Royalty—and found his name in it, listed as missing. He wanted to go home but knew his authoritative father would not accept his rough sailor-son. If Phelex was to become Felix, he was going to have to return home as an officer in the service of Germany.

In 1903 he enrolled in Lübeck Navigation College under his true name, dropping his formal title. It was a struggle for the boy because his formal education had stopped at ten years of age, but when he graduated he acquired a commission as a ship's mate on the Hamburg-Südamerikanische steamship *Petropolis*. This commission was as a steward, technically an officer, albeit in civilian service.

When the German Navy opened up its ranks to reserve officers Felix finally had his chance. He enlisted in 1905, went through basic training, and was enthusiastic about the prospect of returning home as an officer. Then, he was summoned to the office of Admiral Count Friedrich Baudissin. The admiral confronted the youth and asked about his relation to Heinrich Luckner. Felix replied honestly about his father. The admiral drilled him more, verifying his name—going so far as to tell him that Felix von Luckner was missing.

"Why did you not write to your parents?"

The question may have seemed out of place and personal, but the young officer replied quickly. "I want to go home an officer in the emperor's service. I didn't write because I did not want my parents to know I was a common sailor. I don't want them to know until I return home an officer."

After a short pause, the admiral responded with one short response. "I am your uncle Fritz."

As it turned out, Admiral Count Friedrich Baudissin was his uncle on his mother's side of the family. He understood what the young man was saying and respected his desire to keep his whereabouts private. At the same time he knew that if Felix was to have any chance of graduating, he was going to need help.

Admiral Baudissin had his daughter, Felix's cousin, provide him with tutoring in grammar and language skills. With her help, and most likely some aid from the admiral, Felix was admitted to Papenburg Nautical College where he graduated in 1907 with his master's certificate.

Technically he was allowed to wear an officer's uniform, allowing him to return home to his family. The reunion seemed to have quelled the earlier tensions between father and son. Felix once again entered royal circles and was something of a unique man: a royal who had lived as a commoner for most of his life.

He received note in the local newspaper in Hamburg for rescuing five people from drowning in separate incidents. Prince Henry of Prussia made a point of meeting this rogue count and introduced him to the kaiser. The German leader became quite fond of Felix—enthralled by his storytelling and tales of life on the high seas. The two men developed a tight bond, one that would both serve von Luckner and work against him.

When he was called up to active service in February 1912, he was already a junior grade lieutenant in the reserves. The kaiser personally intervened on the young officer's behalf, predating von Luckner's commission so the count would be qualified for promotions the same as men who had been in the service eight years longer. For many officers, this action was an affront and served as an irritation; a runaway boy was suddenly just as qualified for rank and position the same as they, with more years of service.

When living as Phelax Lüdicke he had come across the SMS *Panther*, a state-of-the-art German cruiser. He had been penniless and living on the streets for some time but hoped fellow Germans would befriend him. Some of the ship's crew were friendly to him, but the officers saw him as nothing more than a tramp and kicked him off the ship. Eventually he was befriended by some of the crewmembers, but the ill treatment by the officers was something he had never forgotten.

Years later von Luckner relayed the story to the kaiser in one of his many meetings with the German ruler. The kaiser felt that a certain amount of poetic justice would be served to appoint the young lieutenant to the *Panther*—and he did so in 1913. Assignment so rapidly to such a prestigious command, while other officers received assignments aboard destroyers or torpedo boats, could have only added to the resentment against him. His cruise to Africa allowed him a taste of the life he had abandoned for many years, taking part in safaris and hunting expeditions.

The kaiser was said to have personally endorsed his appointment to the command of the *Seeadler*. It seemed obvious to those in command at the Admiralty that he was taking advantage of his relationship with the kaiser even though there was no evidence of such activity on the count's part. Having an uncle who was both royalty and an admiral also tainted him in the eyes of others. While he may have been the most qualified officer of rank in the German Navy to command the *Seeadler*, there would always be those who claimed that he earned the post based not on experience but on his relationships.

In their eyes the kaiser had personally intervened to help guide the career of the young royal. By the time he was working hard to ensure that his ship was properly outfitted and equipped, a faction within the Admiralty was working against him. It was both a matter of rank and standing in the Royal Court.

Most of this resentment and opposition was silent and secretive—but present nonetheless. On November 6, 1916, his fellow officers reported his behavior in Kiel to the Admiralty. In one case, the captain of the U-boat *U-48* sent a detailed report of names that von Luckner was dropping at a restaurant. The report had been requested from the Admiralty.

Von Luckner had managed to step on a number of toes in his rise to command the ship. His rapid rise to his rank and position, at the age of thirty-five, was unique in the annals of the German Navy and raised the ire of the middle class officers who had worked their way up the chain of command. Simply put, jealousy was working against him. While not direct sabotage, it was a form of subtle undermining that his crew was forced to suffer.

In the end, shrewd acts by cunning men and even something as simple as oil would twist fate against him.

5

THE RUSE

December 25, 1916

By Christmas Eve, the crew found themselves praying not for a successful cruise but for a change of wind. Late that evening, the gale-force winds began to run south. The late *Pass of Balmaha* had proven once again to be a lucky ship for the Germans. In the reduced sunlight of the shortened polar day, the *Seeadler* began to make a run toward the space between Iceland and the Faeroe Islands.

Von Luckner ordered the ship's auxiliary engine turned on. This was the true test of Krause's engineering skills. The engine came to life when needed. It helped keep the ship under control and heading south with the winds, but the exhaust was either plugged with ice or never well designed to begin with (after all, the windjammer was never intended to have engines installed). The ventilation shaft was low on the deck, coming up between the two sets of motorboat launches, and it would easily clog with salt spray in a rough storm. Regardless of the reason, diesel fumes filled several cabins on the ship, but it was a good sign. The captain would not run the engine unless he felt the risk from the Royal Navy was diminished.

It was not a quick thaw by any means. December near Iceland is never a warm experience; but after a half-day sailing south in high winds, von Luckner's men could begin the hard work of chipping the ice with axes and picks off of the deck and gear without the concern of refreezing. His Norwegian crew needed some help and the captain, believing he had skirted the blockade, allowed some of the hands below deck to come out and help.

Besides, it was Christmas.

The ship was about 185 miles south of Iceland. Even without the hard work of Carpenter Dreyer, the ship looked as if it had gone through a hurricane. The crew was exhausted, but they were alive.

The captain would have authorized a small party to celebrate their luck when a message came from one of the lookouts.

"Steamer ahoy!"

The British cruiser put a launch in the choppy seas and began to load a boarding party to inspect the *Seeadler* when Captain von Luckner realized he had a problem. On the stern of the cruiser was the name *Highland Scot*, but like the *Seeadler*, she was playing her own game of deception. The *Highland Scot* was actually the *Avenger*. Despite the problems with the auxiliary engines, they had been running to get the windjammer south to warmer waters and the ship reeked belowdecks with the stench of diesel fumes.

Normally such an aroma would not be a problem. But if you were trying to pose as a simple Norwegian merchant windjammer, it is hard to explain the presence of a very expensive and rare diesel engine. Windjammers simply didn't have auxiliary engines and the diesel was relatively new technology—and a German invention at that.

There was no way to air out the lower decks in time. So von Luckner went a different direction. He grabbed several of the deck hands. "Stuff a rug in the chimney of the kerosene stove and turn up the wicks of the oil lamps as high as you can." The crew didn't question his orders and leapt into action. The captain turned his attention back to the cruiser.

The *Avenger* was an auxiliary cruiser. This class of ships were merchant vessels impressed into service by the Royal Navy at the start of the war. At 15,000 tons she now mounted menacing deck guns and a belt of armor at the waterline running up. Her guns were huge, nearly eight inches, and were trained directly on the *Seeadler*. From the foredeck, von Luckner could make out the bridge of the *Avenger* and the fellow captain and officers staring back.

Von Luckner went to his quarters for a moment as the British launch made its way toward his ship. A friend of his had given him a bottle of Napoleon Brandy before his journey. He took the bottle and opened it, taking several deep warm gulps to settle his nerves. Napoleon had fought the British as well; perhaps he had one more fight left in him. He took a cud of tobacco and stuffed it into the corner of his mouth. It would be perfectly normal for a Norwegian captain to be chewing tobacco. Besides, his very slight German accent would be muffled at most.

With some satisfaction, he noticed the air in his cabin reeked of kerosene. That was good. The diesel fumes had been overpowered with the stench from the lamps and the stove. As a final touch, he turned on the gramophone to play "It's a Long Way to Tipperary."

The launch pulled alongside *Seeadler's* lee companionway. It carried two officers and sixteen sailors, all heavily armed. With the guns trained on him from the *Avenger* and such a heavily armed boarding party, Captain von Luckner wondered if the Royal Navy had been tipped off to the *Seeadler's* mission.

Despite the months of training, his mock Norwegian crew seemed agape at the British boarding party and a Royal Navy cruiser with guns trained on them. The brandy had stiffened von Luckner in his role of Captain Knudson. "Take a line, by Joe. Don't just stand there like wooden men." He tossed in a handful of curse-words in Norwegian as a reminder for them to remain in character. The crew of the *Seeadler* came to life and helped the British boarders climb up on deck.

Lieutenant Holland was the senior officer leading the boarding party and von Luckner shook his hand as he came on deck. The British officer's manners were not lost on the Norwegian merchantman, as he wished him a merry Christmas.

Von Luckner replied in broken English, typical of a Norwegian captain of his years. "Merry Christmas, Mister Officer. But if you want to see the kind of Christmas we have had, come along down to my cabin."

"A bit of a nasty blow this past week, eh what! From the look of your deck you've had more than your share of it. We went in behind the islands and waited for her to blow over."

Von Luckner nodded and mulled over the tobacco plug in his mouth. As the rest of the boarding party climbed on deck, Lieutenant Holland continued. "I must see your papers, Captain." Von Luckner led him down to his cabin where the gramophone was still playing the strained notes of "Tipperary." Seated in a rocking chair, her large feet concealed under a rug, with her knitting on her lap, was the captain's wife. Her jaw was wrapped and she held a handkerchief in front of her powdered nose to hold off the smell of kerosene in the room. Holland was followed by the other officer who had come on board.

"What a smell!"

Von Luckner nodded. "Excuse me, Mister Officer, but my stove is out of order. I could not know that you gentlemen would be giving me a visit today."

The British officers were more than polite. "Oh never mind, Captain, that's all right." Lieutenant Holland glanced over and noticed the captain's wife for the first time and bowed slightly. "Oh, excuse me."

"That is my wife, Mister Officer. She has been having a bad go with the toothache."

"Sorry, madam, to intrude like this, but we must do our duty," Holland replied.

Josefeena replied back in a muffled high tone of voice. "All right."

Holland scanned the cabin and saw evidence of water damage and wet clothing hung out to dry, complete with name tags reading "Knudson." There were signs of recent repairs from storm damage.

The Royal Navy lieutenant turned his attention to the task at hand, inspecting the papers and log of the *Hero*. Lieutenant Holland did not forget his duty despite the presence of Josefeena Knudson. "By Joe, Captain, you haven't much cabin left, have you? You *have* been through some rough weather!"

Von Luckner agreed, never dropping his guise. "I wouldn't mind the rest, Mister Officer, but look at my papers. They are soaked too."

"I can understand that, after the weather you've had."

"Yes, Mister Officer," von Luckner replied. Sensing an opportunity that his disguise was working, he boldly continued playing off of the officer's good manners. "It's all right for you to see them in this condition because you saw the storm yourself, but if later I meet some of your comrades who didn't hit the blow that we had, they might not take my word for it. That's what's worrying me."

"Oh, don't worry, Captain. I'll give you a memorandum explaining the condition of your papers. You are lucky to have saved your ship." The papers, bills of lading, shipping papers, all forged, were pulled together for the Royal Navy officer. Most were still soaked from the tossing of sea water in the quarters days before. Lieutenant Holland took out his own notebook and made careful notes from what he was able to read. The paperwork included German-made forgeries allegedly coming from the British Consul in Copenhagen telling Lieutenant Holland what he needed to know: the Empire knew about the cargo of lumber the ship carried which was due for use by the British government in Australia.

Minutes passed as Holland took notes. Finally he turned to Captain von Luckner. "These papers are all right, Captain." Lieutenant Holland called for one of the yeomen who came aboard the ship and had him draft a memo for his signature, stating the papers of the *Hero* had been inspected and were in good order, despite their condition.

Two things happened at once. Ship's mate Lüdemann, posing as one of the Norwegian crew, came in with the soaked ship's log that von Luckner had dunked in water days ago. At the same time, von Luckner lost control of the tobacco plug in his mouth, accidentally swallowing it.

A swallowed plug of tobacco was not a pleasant experience. It burned and caused a victim to gasp and eventually throw up—which would be a relief. In the case of Captain von Luckner, that was simply not an option.

Von Luckner's ruse was suddenly tossed into disarray. His inexperience in chewing tobacco might tip off the British officer. He bent over coughing and half-gagging on the act, trying desperately to appear as if he were wheezing from a cold. Just speaking was going to be difficult as his stomach churned.

"Oh yes, the log," Holland exclaimed, flipping through the book while von Luckner tried to maintain some degree of composure.

"I wish I'd had that officer's camel hair cape and hood," he strained, hoping to draw some attention away from the stolen log. "It would have been fine to keep a fellow warm while up there north of the Circle."

Holland did not notice the straining that von Luckner was going through, or at least didn't seem to show interest. "For rain and spray,

too," he replied in fluent Norwegian, telling von Luckner he was not dealing with an ignorant sailor but someone savvy to the high seas. "How is this, Captain? You were laid up for three weeks and a half?"

This was the period of time when the *Hero* had been sitting outside of port, awaiting orders to sail while the *Wolf* and *Möwe* put to sea and the submarine *Deutschland* was coming in. Von Luckner had reached the limit of his capability to suppress the tobacco quib in his stomach and was feeling more ill by the moment. Mate Lüdemann, generally a quiet man by nature, jumped in to save his captain as he sensed something was wrong.

Lüdemann told Lieutenant Holland they were not laid up for anything out of the ordinary. They had been ordered by their owners to hold up because of rumors of raiding German cruisers operating in the waters near Norway.

This caught Holland's attention. What cruisers? Lüdemann kept playing his ruse. The *Möwe* and the auxiliary cruiser *Seeadler*. Ironically Lüdemann didn't know the *Möwe* had indeed put out from port on a new raid.

Captain von Luckner gained enough control of his stomach to speak up. He told Holland they had heard rumors of the two cruisers and sixteen German submarines that had put out to sea. The other Royal Navy officer on the boarding party joined them in the cabin at hearing these words.

"I think we'd better be going," the officer said nervously. Lieutenant Holland was quick to agree. He turned once more to von Luckner. "Your papers are all right, Captain. You'll have to wait here for an hour until you get a signal to proceed."

Von Luckner thanked them and started up the stairs with the British officers. They had not been on board long enough for more than a cursory inspection. None of the crew had been interviewed, and it seemed that the sudden potential threat of cruisers and enemy submarines was enough to motivate them to get back to their ship as quickly as possible.

Lieutenant Holland's crew began to board the motor launch to return to the *Avenger*. The motor launch drifted slightly toward the rear of the *Hero/Seeadler* and for a moment, von Luckner realized that if he looked down, Holland would easily be able to see the propeller of the auxiliary engine. While it was not incriminating, it might cause him to take a more detailed look at the ship. The engine was not mentioned in the stolen log and was bound to rouse suspicion.

He needed a distraction, if only for a few moments. Von Luckner tossed a rope down to the motor launch and called for the British sailors to grab the rope. The boarding party scrambled about and grabbed the rope, tossing it back up to von Luckner as their launch drifted past the stern and out of position to see the propeller.

Elsewhere on the *Hero/Seeadler*, the ship was alive with activity. Some of the crewmembers overhead Lieutenant Holland's warning to wait for an hour as he had left the ship. While Von Luckner was happy at the news, believing he had pulled off his ruse on the British, this crewman was depressed and passed the word below decks, "All is lost."

To the crewman, there was only one reason the British would be waiting an hour. They would check their copy of Lloyd's Registry and not find the windjammer *Hero* listed. They would use their wireless to contact the Admiralty to verify. There were no records of the sailing ship *Hero* anywhere with the Royal Navy. All of the work on the paperwork, the log, everything, would be wasted. They would either force the ship to surrender, or sink her.

Von Luckner had always told them in training that if that was the circumstance, they were to sink the *Seeadler* rather than let her fall into enemy hands. While the captain himself had not sent the word down, the crew followed their implied orders. Fuses were lit on the three bombs attached to the keel of the ship to blow her up.

The length of the fuses on the explosives were precut; once lit, they would burn for fifteen minutes. It was enough time for the crew to abandon ship.

Sailors have a unique perspective about luck. Many will tell you that luck plays an important part in any time they spend at sea. There are omens they avoid—like the killing of an albatross, which could bring bad luck. They believe just as passionately in symbols of good luck, and they keep these around.

The concept of luck, good and bad, plays an important role and many sailors are quick to tell you when they have challenged fate—when they have ignored luck and trusted their skills. Luck becomes something to be honored and revered, yet at the same time tempted, beaten, and challenged.

The *Pass of Balmaha* was seen as a lucky ship for the Germans—for it had delivered to them a handful of British prisoners. Von Luckner, raised on the high seas, embraced that symbolism for both himself and his men. None of the men knew until after the war that their captain kept a small parcel of luck in a secret compartment in his quarters. Tucked away and folded with reverence was the American flag that had been the *Pass's* flag under Captain Scott. Captain von Luckner felt the Stars and Stripes had luck tied to it: he was counting on that luck to get through the blockade.

Aboard the *Avenger*, the Royal Navy *was* checking out the story of the *Hero*. A check in their copy of Lloyd's Registry came up empty, which seemed suspicious but not entirely out of the ordinary. Ships' names were sometimes changed and not updated. The next logical step was to check with the Admiralty to determine if the windjammer was indeed safe.

Ships were identified in the British records by names and registry numbers. The wireless operator sent a message to the Admiralty in London. But on Christmas Day, their staffing was small. On holidays, extra duty for double-checking ships was handled out of Liverpool. The *Avenger* wired Liverpool with their request, sending both the name and the number. The number had been taken from the ship's log—the log of the former ship, *Maleta*. Lieutenant Holland had recorded it himself from the soaked pages, not realizing that the number did not relate to the *Hero*.

The Liverpool offices checked their records for the name of the ship and came up with nothing. They in turn followed procedure and contacted the Admiralty in London to double-check the name and number. With the small holiday staff, an inexperienced operator received the message and checked his records. The name *Hero* was not found, but the registry number was valid—just for another ship entirely. For all intents and purposes, this should have been a warning. Whatever information the *Avenger* had been provided was not accurate.

Rather than double-check the name and number again, or send a message to the owners of the ship in Norway to validate her identity, the wireless operator in London sent a message to Liverpool: "All right." In defense of the young operator, contacting Norway would have been a pointless move; the owner's offices would have doubtlessly been closed for Christmas as well.

Liverpool relayed the message to the *Avenger*. The *Hero* had checked out just fine as far as the British Admiralty was concerned.

Just as Lieutenant Holland and his boarding party left, von Luckner made his way back to his crew. He was quite happy, feeling that his subterfuge and Lüdemann's timely words had more than fooled the British. He went belowdecks to one of the secret hatches to pass on the word to his crew hidden below.

He called, "Open"—but he was greeted by rustling noises behind the hatch before it finally opened. The men below looked slightly more than worried. Von Luckner called down to find out what the problem was.

They had heard him say "open" and assumed that on top of setting the time bombs to blow the ship up, he wanted the flood valves opened too. Captain von Luckner was stunned. He had no idea the fuses had been lit and hundreds of gallons of water were now rushing into his ship. He called down to the men to cut the fuses and close the valves.

He found the crewmember who told the crew all was lost and asked him why he would pass that message to the men below. From where von Luckner sat, everything was going fine. The sailor told his captain he knew the British would be using their wireless to check out the *Hero*. An hour was enough time for them to learn the ship was not what she claimed to be.

His words stunned the captain. He hadn't considered that the Royal Navy might be doing that. Days of sailing in the storm, fighting to keep the *Seeadler* afloat, had worn the edges of his nerves and thinking. The sailors' fears were well founded. The British might just be doing what they suggested.

He returned to the chart room where ship's mate Lüdemann kept watch on the *Avenger*. A few minutes later, a flag signal came from the Royal Navy vessel: TMB. A check of the codebook came up with the word "planet." They must have read the signal wrong. They checked again: TXB. The 1916 codebook is a confusing set of words, flag symbols, and columns of letters; the two men thumbed through, looking for the right code word.

The *Avenger* suddenly poured on coal and began to move. Black smoke billowed up from her three funnels and she took on speed. She swung wide, then took a heading toward their ship. The 15,000-ton *Avenger* appeared as if her guns were aimed right at the windjammer. At the last minute she turned sharply. Von Luckner deciphered the flag signal on her stern: Happy Voyage. He ordered their own Norwegian flag to be dipped three times, to signal thank you to the Royal Navy. The *Avenger*, under full steam, continued onward and away.

Afterward they found the code: TXB meant Set Your Course.

For the first time since setting sail, von Luckner felt as if he could relax. As soon as the *Avenger* was out of sight, he ordered his crew up on deck. The time for the ruse to get through the blockade was no longer needed. Most of the Norwegian lumber on the deck was dumped overboard.

The wife of the powerful German industrialist Krupp had sent Christmas gifts for the crew. The gifts had been packed away in a hidden compartment back in November. Now that the immediate danger seemed behind them, it was a good time to dig them out. With the powerful gale and the threat of the blockade, there had not been time for the men to enjoy the presents or Christmas itself. Captain von Luckner allowed his men a few hours to enjoy their holiday a little late.

The name on the ship's stern was still *Hero*, but that would change during the cruise. For the crew and her captain, the ship only had one name from this point forward: *Seeadler*.

✠ ✠ ✠

The mistake regarding the query about the *Hero* was discovered several days later in the British Admiralty's office. The Royal Navy's intelligence system suddenly sprang to life. The sailing ship posing as the *Hero* had to be German—otherwise why conceal its identity? Where was it heading? Perhaps it was a merchant smuggling war supplies into Germany. The British were unwilling to embrace the idea that the vessel might be a surface raider.

Orders went out and scouting patrols searched the North Sea and the Northern Atlantic for a mysterious sailing ship. Between seven and fourteen cruisers combed the seas hoping to intercept the ship. Their orders were simple: Locate and capture the vessel, if possible. If not, sink her.

6

THE *SEA EAGLE* STRIKES

January 9, 1917

Captain Felix von Luckner walked the deck, hopeful that his offer of a handful of German marks and a bottle of champagne would pay off with his watchful crew. Each man kept his eyes glued to the horizon searching for a ship, knowing that the captain would give the bottle and money to the crew who spotted that first ship, their first victim.

Early in the morning, a call came from the lookout in the crow's nest: "Smoke on the port quarter!"

The distant black smoke could only mean that coal was burning—and the smoke from burning coal meant a ship, a potential victim, and possibly first blood for this raider. It also meant someone in the crew would be collecting the money and the precious bottle of champagne.

Within an hour the ship came into view. It was not a warship, which was the worst fear that Captain von Luckner had at the moment. The lookouts in the rigging and high up in the crow's nest could not see a name on the vessel, just a dull black painted hull. This was a common British ploy, so that German U-boats might hold their fire, unsure if they were facing an Allied or neutral ship. Neutral ships were avoided. The *real* targets were those ships of the enemy.

There was no sign of a wireless antenna either, which to von Luckner was a good sign. A wireless set on a target ship would be a problem. If they managed to send off a message before they were captured or sunk, the *Seeadler*'s position could be transmitted to the Royal Navy.

The flag stating her nationality was also missing. This was another trick from the British maritime book of tactics. Von Luckner's target ships were not neutral vessels but those of Great Britain and her Allies. There was something in the lines of the ship, her looks, the deliberate deception (almost matching their own) that told him he was facing a British merchant.

The captain of the *Seeadler* wanted the ship to come in close. He only had two main guns on board—both were mounted on the bow, one covering each side. The 4.2-inch naval guns would seem small mounted on a dreadnought; but on the old 'jammer, they seemed much larger. He still wanted his intended victim in close, both for the guns to be effective and to close the distance if the other vessel attempted a getaway. Chasing a steamer in a sailing ship, even one with an auxiliary engine, was difficult even under the best circumstances.

Windjammers and other sailing ships used naval chronometers to determine longitude. Older sailing ships, like the *Seeadler*, had functional chronometers—but they weren't always very accurate. It was customary for ships to ask for time checks with other vessels on the high seas. The *Seeadler*'s chronometer was very accurate, but there was no way for the mystery ship to know that.

The count ordered his signalman to hoist a signal flag relaying the message, Chronometer Time, Please. He saw through his binoculars the steamer signal back that they understood. The ship came closer and swung to the windward side of the *Seeadler*. The move was deliberate, allowing the sailing ship to heave-to so they could call over the time.

Captain von Luckner ordered his crew up with rifles, telling them to keep low and stay close to the rails so they couldn't be seen. Under his own heavy overcoat, he wore the uniform of a German Navy captain. His crew had trained for this moment, and now was the true test of their efforts.

Von Luckner called out, "Clear for action." A drumbeat sounded on the deck of the *Seeadler*. Lieutenant Karl Theodor Friedrich Kircheiß, the navigation and gunnery officer, had been waiting for those three words since they put to sea. On the bow of the vessel, his crew jumped up and pulled the tarps off of the 4.2-inch deck cannons. The forward railing concealed the guns; but these could be dropped quickly with a metallic clatter to the deck below, to act as gun shields. Cases of ammunition were hurried to the guns and pried open as the ship armed for battle. The captain dropped off his overcoat and watched as the Norwegian flag dropped down the mast and the German flag ran up.

Lieutenant Kircheiß and his gun crews had drilled long and hard for this role. Their orders were clear in this situation: target the first shot across the bow. At the order of the captain, Kircheiß gave the command to fire. For the first time in the war, the raider *Seeadler* fired a shot at the enemy.

Captain von Luckner stared as the shell cleared the bow of the freighter and slashed into the Atlantic in the distance. He waited for signs of action on his intended victim but saw none for a long minute. Then he saw a British flag run up the mast of the steamer. They made no attempt to break away and flee, but no sign of her putting up a fight. The German captain checked the time for his own ship's log: 1115. Von Luckner turned to Lieutenant Kircheiß's gunnery crew again.

"Fire again."

Once more a shot crossed the bow of the British merchant ship. This time the ship reacted by altering her course. For a moment, he thought the freighter was going to make an attempt to run. At the captain's order, Kircheiß ordered his gunnery crew to fire again, this time across the stern of the ship. He then had them place a shot over her smokestack as well.

The British ship suddenly heaved-to alongside the windjammer. Captain von Luckner ordered the *Seeadler* to drop sail and come to a stop as well. As von Luckner turned he was stunned to see that the merchant had lowered a small boat into the sea and was heading over with a small party toward his ship. It made no sense. As the firing ship, his crew would traditionally be the one to send a boarding party over to the captured vessel. He ordered his crew, complete with rifles, to go and escort the captain of the British ship to him.

The British captain was named Chewn. He was a portly, older man with a scraggly gray beard. Von Luckner introduced himself to the man warmly but the Britisher demanded to know why he had been fired upon. Von Luckner told him he wanted to talk first. He learned that the small merchant weighed in at 3,628 British registered tons (Brt) empty and was carrying 5,000 tons of coal from Cardiff bound for Buenos Aires. The name of the merchant ship was *Gladys Royale*, registered out of Sunderland. Her crew was twenty-six men total, many from different countries and nationalities.

Count von Luckner told the older captain he hated to sink any ship, but the *Gladys Royale* had to be sunk. Captain Chewn protested. He was a British vessel, but he was sailing to a neutral port and was not carrying military supplies—just coal. The irony was clear to von Luckner in later years. Most surface raiders prayed to find a coaling ship to resupply and extend their voyage. He had found one as his first victim, but it did him no good whatsoever.

There were other reasons Chewn didn't want to see the ship sunk. He owned his ship and had a wife and family to support. The loss of his ship would mean the loss of his livelihood and the means of supporting them.

"Do you believe, Captain Chewn, that under the same circumstances, a British naval officer would show any mercy to a German ship?"

Captain Chewn declined to respond.

There were other questions that von Luckner wanted answered. Why did the *Gladys Royale* act the way it did when a shot was fired across its bow? Captain Chewn explained that years ago it was common for ships to mark clock time by firing a blank mortar as a starting time. The ship marking time would fire their mortar in response. He assumed with the first shot that the *Seeadler* was simply following the old British sailing tradition. It was, after all, an old windjammer.

Captain Chewn's ship cook spotted the second round over the stern hit the water and Chewn assumed the sailing ship had spotted a U-boat in the water and was firing on her. He ordered his own freighter to move evasively in the water to dodge a possible torpedo attack.

When the third shot cleared his smokestack, he noticed the German flag on the mast and the deck gun aimed menacingly at his ship. Only then did he realize he was not facing a fellow merchantman, but a raider.

Having captured the *Gladys Royale*, von Luckner ordered her crew transferred to his ship and even allowed Captain Chewn to pack up some of his personal belongings. He then ordered Prize Officer Lieutenant Richard Pries, his officer in charge of boarding parties, to go aboard the vessel and take anything of use as quickly as possible and then send her to the bottom. Captain von Luckner would have wanted more time to strip more goods from the *Gladys Royale*, but he knew that the North Atlantic was heavily patrolled by the Royal Navy.

There are several ways to sink a captured vessel. On some ships, you can open the flood valves and scuttle the ship—but she has to be heavily loaded and have enough valves to flood the ship in the desired time. You can also fire at the ship, but this can take time, produces smoke and noise, and wastes precious cannon shells—something a raider at sea cannot resupply. The final method is to plant a bomb in the bowels of the ship and blow her up. This requires some skill with cutting fuse lengths and knowing where to plant the explosives.

Lieutenant Pries had been ordered to blow up the *Gladys Royale* after sunset so the smoke would not attract unwanted attention from the Royal Navy. He and his crew did a final inspection of the ship and transferred a final load of provisions from the captured prize ship. Pries and his crew crawled down into the hold and planted a bomb with a fifteen-minute fuse. They scampered to their launch and returned to the *Seeadler* in time to watch the *Gladys Royale*'s final moments. Members of the crew snapped several quick photographs of the end of the ship.

The British merchant quaked in the water for a moment, then started to slide down stern first. Ten minutes into her death throes, she was nothing more than a bow sticking out of the water. There was a deep rumble of another explosion from within the remains of the ship, most likely trapped air under the pressure of the sinking ship. With that sudden release the *Gladys Royale* slid into the North Atlantic.

Captain von Luckner and his crew watched the ship sink, taking photos of it as it disappeared. Then he ordered the mainsails up and the *Seeadler* set off in search of other prizes.

✠ ✠ ✠

Several months earlier Captain von Luckner had been brought before members of the Admiralty (Admiralstab) to receive his formal operational orders for his mission. The orders he received were short and straightforward enough for any officer to understand. He was to take the vessel out as a merchant raider. He and his crew were to avoid enemy warships at all costs and destroy as much merchant shipping as possible for the Allied powers.

Neutral ships were to be avoided. That was fine with the count. Neutral ships were full of people who might report him. And he was not going to sea to kill innocents, but to cripple the Allies' shipping. It was an easy order to follow.

Enemy merchant crews were to be captured whenever possible. It was not a requirement. Captain von Luckner wanted to avoid potential problems with his prisoners. He asked and received permission to compensate captured crewmen as they had been paid by their employers. His motivations were obvious: happy prisoners were less likely to cause problems.

His ship was not to fall into enemy hands. This was not as much an order but a standing tradition. Losing a ship in battle was bad enough; having it captured was dishonorable and humiliating.

The Admiralty had reviewed von Luckner's planned modifications of the *Seeadler* and her overall capabilities and had determined that she was not fit to engage steam-powered vessels. As such, her orders were clear and concise: the *Seeadler* was *only* to attack and capture other sailing vessels. Captain von Luckner was asked specifically if he understood those orders and he made clear to his superiors that he did.

7

GHOSTS OF THE PAST

January 9, 1917

Minutes after the *Seeadler*'s first victim, the *Gladys Royale*, slid into the sea, the lookouts in the crow's nest spotted lights from another ship passing nearby. Von Luckner ordered his men to keep the deck clear for action while he attempted to gain some idea of what he might be facing.

The ship appeared to be a passenger ship and was running with full sidelights along her deck. Portals were open and light played out. In times of peace, this was not uncommon. In times of war, ships attempted to hide who they were—to become as invisible as possible, both day and night. This ship was not doing that. She turned casually away from the *Seeadler* and continued on her voyage.

Chances were she was a neutral ship—being so bold as to run with full lights in a war zone. Von Luckner had orders to not sink neutral ships, but those orders were not necessary. Sinking a neutral vessel was an act of war. The captain of the *Seeadler* had only one other concern: had the ship seen the sinking of the *Gladys Royale*? If she did, she might have a wireless and might send a message out that a ship had just been sunk. He was concerned; but given the time of day, the risks were minimal.

The *Seeadler* made sail that night heading south and west. The captain of the *Gladys Royale*, Captain Chewn, was shown his semi-private quarters on the ship and saw to the disposition of his twenty-six crewmen. He was told that his men would be compensated for their time on the ship and would have freedom aboard the *Seeadler*—with only a few restrictions. They were to stay away from the ship's magazines, where the ammunition and explosives were kept. They were to not touch any weapons or navigation gear. The wireless and the helm were obviously off-limits as well.

If they caused problems for the *Seeadler* crew, they would be restrained belowdecks. This was not an idle threat; previous raiders had not given their captives much freedom at all. Most spent their time stuffed into the darkness of holds, only coming out to swelter in the hot sun. Chewn seemed to understand he was being treated well and agreed to cooperate.

At noon on January 10 the *Seeadler* was heading south and the lookouts spotted smoke in the distance. Like their first victim, this ship was not flying any colors at all—a sign that she was most likely British. The *Seeadler* was still flying her Norwegian flag at the time. The unknown ship was on a diagonal course, heading almost straight at the *Seeadler*.

Captain von Luckner ordered signal flags up, attempting a trick similar to the one that worked on the *Gladys Royale*. Rather than requesting a chronometer reading, his message was a typical one for a ship wanting to know the other's name and identity: What Ship? Her reply should have been her name or nationality.

She did not reply, but instead remained on course. The unknown vessel did not seem to have a wireless antenna or any visible armaments. Her course was almost a collision course with the *Seeadler*. At first von Luckner was not concerned. Maritime tradition called for sailing vessels to have the right-of-way in such circumstances, but it seemed as if this steamer was not going to observe that tradition. It appeared that the captain of the other ship was intent on ramming the *Seeadler*.

Von Luckner did not want to play a game of chicken. He had to jibe and pull sail at a range of 300 yards to veer out of the path of the steamer. As they came to this range the order went out: "Clear for action!" The Norwegian flag was pulled down and the German flag was run up to the masthead.

Lieutenant Kircheiß and his gunnery crew uncovered the twin deck guns and loaded them. The false deck rail rattled down so they could be brought to bear.

Von Luckner gave the command. "Fire! Let's see if that will make him change his mind." The 4.2-inch gun barked and sent a shell across the bow of the steamer, sending a column of white water blasting upward like a tornado into the air. She did not alter course, stubborn to the end. A moment later, the smoke rising out of the funnels of the steamer showed the ship pouring on more steam. Surrender seemed to be the furthest thing from that captain's mind.

The steamer turned into the wind and away from the *Seeadler*. It was a good tactical move. The captain of the steamer had to know that a sailing ship such as the *Seeadler* would not be able to pursue them into the wind, not for very long. What that captain didn't know was the SK L/40 cannons on the windjammer had a maximum accurate range of over 9,100 yards.

Von Luckner did not like his next decision, but he saw no other choice. He told Lieutenant Kircheiß to target the ship. He had to stop her before she got away.

Weeks earlier while the crew of the *Hero/Seeadler* was awaiting orders to go to sea, they were essentially sequestered aboard the ship. Anchored outside of Hamburg, the crew drilled daily, practicing their roles and their Norwegian. The gunnery crew drilled in target practice and rapid loading techniques. The other crewmembers drilled on sailing skills, but adopted their false Norwegian names in their tasks. Lieutenant Kling performed a fake roll call using their Norwegian names each day.

During the several weeks of waiting for the order to get underway, von Luckner got to know his crew. He then told his crew and officers of his intention to wage war without taking any lives, if at all possible. He did not want to kill. If raiders and U-boats sent innocents to their death, it would only fuel the Allied propaganda efforts against Germany. He hated the slur "Hun" when it was applied to him and his fellow countrymen. This cruise was going to be different.

The men deeply respected their new captain. He already had a good reputation, thanks to the media in Germany. But the concept of not taking lives seemed out of place given the turns of the Great War. The majority of the crew didn't question their captain's words, but a few had turned the matter into a private joke—wondering how long it would be before the *Seeadler* would be forced to kill or be killed.

✠ ✠ ✠

Mate Lüdemann was at the helm when the *Seeadler* opened fire on the unknown ship. One round went high, into the funnel of the ship. Several shells plowed into the unarmored hull of the steamer and exploded inside. One shell struck the rear deck and exploded, tossing jagged shards of varnished wood decking in every direction. On the deck of the steamer, crewmembers ran about chaotically as lifeboats and men hit the water in an attempt to get away from the damaged vessel.

The steamer stopped her propellers and came to a halt.

"I guess you find there are a few casualties over there," Lüdemann remarked sarcastically to von Luckner, making reference to his fighting a war without killing. Von Luckner did not reply, but the comments certainly added to his anger and frustration at dealing with the steamer. The ship had ignored maritime etiquette in yielding the right-of-way to his ship, had ignored his courteous signals, and had risked his crewmen's lives attempting to flee. Lifeboats were falling into the water filled with crew, but there was no sign of the captain. Von Luckner ordered his own launch over to the steamer to bring back the enemy captain. The message he sent to the steamer was blunt and to the point, "Captain, come aboard."

The captain boarded the *Seeadler*'s launch while his crew, on their own accord, began to abandon ship. The captain, an Englishman named Bannister, arrived aboard the *Seeadler* shaken and very irritated. Von Luckner greeted him, but it was far from a warm reception. Von Luckner only wanted to know one thing: were there any casualties on the ship?

"Not a man scratched by Joe, and the blighters scurried around like rabbits at a dog show. Look at them in the boats out there. They haven't got here yet, the beggars. Let me at the gun by Joe and I'll sink them!"

It was not the kind of response von Luckner expected. The captain assured him that such action was not necessary. Bannister seemed to relax, if only slightly. His ship was the British merchant steamer *Lundy Island*, on a course to Gibraltar and France. Unloaded she was 3,095 tons and bore British registry out of West Hartlepool. Her keel had been laid down in 1899. She was carrying sugar, a precious commodity in any of the wartime countries because of its scarcity. Almost all sugar had to be imported. For most Europeans, sugar had become a memory once war on the high seas commenced.

Captain von Luckner pressed as to why he had behaved as he had. Captain Bannister said that at the sign of the first shot, his crew had broken into a panic. He personally took the helm of the ship and from there, managed to get his crew calmed until the German shells punched through the hull. The *Lundy Island*'s rudder chain had been severed with the last rounds and he was no longer able to steer. He saw the signal for him to come aboard the *Seeadler*, but he couldn't. His crew's panic had taken all of their lifeboats.

The key question still remained: Why had he acted the way he did? Why ignore the signals?

The *Seeadler*'s ship's surgeon, a cigar-smoking older man named Doctor Pietsch, came up on deck to see if he could lend a hand with the injured. When Captain Bannister saw the doctor, the older surgeon walked over and heartily shook his hand. "Hello, Captain."

Captain Bannister replied, "Hello, Doctor."

The most successful of the German surface raiders was the *Möwe*, German for Seagull. Her life began as the merchant banana transport ship *Pungo* and like the *Pass of Balmaha*, she underwent extensive refit and modifications. Her first of two cruises began on December 26, 1915, leaving port disguised as the Swedish merchant ship *Segoland*.

The *Möwe* was a different kind of raider than the *Seeadler*. One of her primary missions was minelaying. She carried five hundred sea mines and planned on planting minefields to cripple British merchant shipping. She also would capture merchants at sea. She had a range of 8,700 miles with her modified coal storage and a cruising speed of twelve to fourteen knots. Her commanding officer, Korvettenkapitan Burggraf Graf Nikolaus zu Dohna-Schlodien, was the first merchant raider in the German Navy and would become the template for those who followed.

She was heavily armed, mounting four hidden 15-centimeter guns, a single 10.5-centimeter gun, and two torpedo tubes, one on each side of the ship. The larger 15-cm guns had been stripped from another battleship. The *Möwe* was a quick-change artist. She had false superstructures that could be put up in a matter of minutes. Smoke-stacks could be put up or taken down rapidly, and even the length of the ship could be faked.

Her cruise took several long months, during which time she was responsible for sinking thousands of tons of merchant ships and cargo and capturing hundreds of prisoners. She was remarkable in that she returned on March 3, sailing back through the British blockade and returning to Germany. Her captain and crew were hailed as heroes. Captain zu Dohna-Schlodien received the Pour Le Merite, the infamous blue cross and golden eagle medal known more informally as the Blue Max.

The *Möwe* became a media sensation for Germany. Going through the British blockade twice and being nothing more than a refitted merchant steamer seemed to be the kind of story people enjoyed hearing about. A posting on the ship was a distinction for sailors.

Unlike most raiders, she went to sea again on another successful raid—this one four weeks before the *Seeadler* left dock. Whereas the *Möwe* had been fortunate to return from her raid, other raiders had been sunk, scuttled, or their fates were unknown. She went out on her second cruise without her new gunnery officer, Felix von Luck-ner, who had been given his own command. She also had a new ship's surgeon. Her surgeon, Doctor Pietsch, had been recruited by von Luckner for his own ship. Captain Dohna-Schlodien was the victim of his own success; his officers were being taken away from him for other assignments, in this case to the *Seeadler*.

The role of a surgeon on a raider was important, and von Luckner had wanted someone with experience. If he stayed at sea for several years as planned, he needed a doctor who could deal with combat in-juries, scurvy, and any tropical diseases they might contract. Doctor Pietsch seemed to be the perfect candidate: he was the only surgeon in the navy with raiding experience, and he understood the complex psychology of sailors in such circumstances.

Doctor Pietsch was in his fifties. Most of the crew of the *Seeadler* were much younger, and his presence had to offer some comfort since he was a raiding veteran himself. He smoked cigars and Lieutenant Pries made sure his boarding parties secured supplies of these when they captured ships. He had learned from his time on the *Möwe* that your best friend was the person in charge of salvaging goods from other ships.

By the end of the war, the *Möwe* made her way back to port yet again, flaunting the British blockade once again. In her two cruises, she was responsible for the sinking of thirty-eight ships totaling over 174,905 tons—not including cargo. Of all the merchant raiders, she was the best known and the most feared.

Doctor Pietsch had met Captain Bannister before, on the *Möwe's* first cruise. Bannister was taken prisoner when his ship, the *Corbridge*, was captured and sunk. The two men became good friends during the captain's internment. When freed, he was granted a formal parole. The parole was a written document where he had agreed not to engage in further war activity. Paroles were a matter of honor and were taken seriously. If he were found in violation of his written word, he feared he could be hanged, so when faced with a ship firing at him, he did all that he could to get away.

Once Captain Bannister and Doctor Pietsch explained the circumstances of their background and his behavior, Captain von Luckner found himself much less angered. This was, after all, a captain who had taken the helm of his ship himself when his crew had failed him. He had risked a great deal, but it was understandable. Von Luckner arrived at a quick decision: Captain Bannister had *not* violated the terms of his parole in the transport of sugar. If the materials he transported were used in war, that would be different; but sugar was nothing more than a luxury item.

The lifeboats from the *Lundy Island* were gathered and the crew was introduced to the captives from the *Gladys Royale*. Captain Bannister was bunked with Captain Chewn and the two men seemed to get along quite well. There were over fifty prisoners aboard the *Seeadler*. There were no clashes between the prisoners and the German crew; rather, they established a daily routine of work duties.

Captain von Luckner met with Lieutenant Kircheiß and made the decision to avoid sending a boarding party aboard the *Lundy*

Island. This was most likely due to the fact that their shells had produced damage to the ship and there was no way to determine how bad that damage was belowdecks. Adding to that decision was the fact that seas were getting rougher and he didn't want to risk a boarding party on rough waters. Lieutenant Kircheiß was told to sink the ship as gunnery practice; after several well-placed shots at her waterline, the *Lundy Island* sunk.

That night, over beer, Captain von Luckner dined with ship's mate Lüdemann. The two of them agreed that the last two days had been productive, but pondered how to do more. Lüdemann's sarcastic solution was simple: "You need to find more ships faster."

Von Luckner proposed an idea. What if the reward of ten pounds sterling and a bottle of champagne was extended to the prisoners that they had captured thus far? Would the British merchant sailors actually help spot other ships for capture? Lüdemann said it might just work. After all, the prisoners would not be released until there was no space aboard the *Seeadler* for them. The only way they would run out of space was to capture more ships. Helping spot other ships at sea would, in essence, get them freed sooner. And the offer of money and alcohol was something that would appeal to the sailors, regardless of nationality.

There was little risk in making the offer to the prisoners. By the next day and from then on, the yardarms and rigging were crowded with prisoners using everything they could to spy the horizon. Some used binoculars, some used spyglasses, some even used their personal opera glasses.

8

January 21, 1917

The renowned French composer Charles-Francois Gounod was born on June 17, 1818 in Paris. His father was a painter and a highly regarded architect who died when Charles was still a child. His mother, a rather skilled pianist, raised both him and his brother Urbain to the best of her skills.

Charles proved to have his mother's ear for music. He attended the Lycee Saint-Louis at his mother's urging and proved to be a bright child. At the age of thirteen, his mother took him to Rossini's opera *Otello*, and he became enamored with the art form. A performance of Mozart's *Don Giovanni* later in the year only fueled his enthusiasm. For him, opera would dominate his compositions and his passion.

After he received his degree at Lycee, he went on to study music professionally, becoming an excellent master of composition. In 1839 he wrote *Fernand* and won the prestigious *Grand Prix de Rome*. He traveled to Rome and Germany to study. A devout Catholic, he studied the classical works, with emphasis on the works dealing with the struggle between good and evil.

One of the works he came to love was Göthe's *Faust*, so much so that he wrote his own operatic interpretation of the work, which many considered one of his best works. He died in Paris in 1893, highly regarded by his peers and countrymen. His operas were performed for many years throughout Europe, with *Faust* being a favorite among the people of Austria and Prussia.

Many attended the opera for entertainment. But to truly appreciate the music, one had to attend many times. Given the costs, people who became enthusiasts in opera tended to be the aristocracy.

For ten days after the destruction of the *Lundy Island*, the *Seeadler* continued its voyage south toward the equator. Captain von Luckner was hoping the ship traffic in the warmer southern waters would prove ripe for potential victims. For ten days the rigging of the ship was filled with British crewmen competing for space with the Germans, all hoping to spot the next ship.

Their course took them past the Canary Islands and out into the equatorial waters along the African coast, far enough away to avoid detection from neutral ships. The crew passed time listening on their wireless set to the state of affairs in the war and watching for signs of any ship they might overtake. For a while, some wondered if their captain had led them to the wrong hunting grounds.

At 0900 on January 21, a lookout spotted a sail in the distance and called out for alert. The prisoners were ordered belowdecks and the crew moved into position, keeping below the railing on the deck so they could not be seen. The Norwegian flag still fluttered in the warm breeze as the ship got closer.

It was a three-masted barque running with full sail. Von Luckner ordered signal flags run up his own mast with the message: What News of the War? For friendly ships on the high seas, this might be a chance to get close and exchange news and sundry goods such as foodstuffs or newspapers before returning to their travels. The barque closed in. When she was close enough to confirm the Norwegian flag, she ran up her own tricolor—the red, white, and blue of France. The crew of the fellow sailing ship came out on deck and stared at the larger windjammer.

Von Luckner ordered his ship to turn to close the distance between them. He then ordered Lieutenant Kircheiß to unmask the guns. The Norwegian flag was taken down quickly and the black German eagle was run up the mast. The gunnery crews lowered the deck railing that hid their guns and uncovered the weapons, aiming them at the French barque.

Captain von Luckner ordered a new signal be sent up: Heave-to.

The crew of the French vessel were stunned. They stared at the German flag and the menacing barrel of the cannon that was trained on them. For a moment they did nothing. Then, almost in humiliation, they dropped their sails.

The *Seeadler*'s boarding party dropped the motor launch in the water. Led by Lieutenant Pries they traveled over to the French ship and boarded her. Von Luckner ordered his own ship to turn and drop sail near the Frenchman. On the stern he could make out her faded name: the *Charles Gounod*.

The *Charles Gounod* was owned by the Société Nouvelle d'Armement, which meant that her primary role was to transport supplies for the French army. She weighed 2,199 tons and was registered out of Nantes. Her cargo was corn from Durban for the French war effort. Her crew was twenty-four men.

Her captain met with Lieutenant Pries and the rest of the *Seeadler*'s boarding party on deck. He informed the lieutenant that he wanted to meet the captain of the German vessel. The *Seeadler* boarding party agreed but moved quickly to secure the vessel and to scour it for anything that might be of use by the crew of their own ship. His cursory search paid off. The *Charles Gounod* had three hogs on board, which Pries ordered trussed up and loaded on the launch to take back to the *Seeadler*. He also found numerous cases of fine red wine, which he also ordered taken back to the ship. The lieutenant sent a launch with some of his captured goods and the captain of the French barque back to his own ship.

The captain of the *Charles Gounod* was a proud man with a thick black beard and a deep, rich voice. Von Luckner met with him and despite his best negotiations, realized that his ship was going to be sunk. Lieutenant Pries took the captain back to the ship to gather his personal effects while he commanded the transfer of the crew of the ship.

The French crew was different from the others the *Seeadler* had captured. They were not a mixed crew. The prisoners from the *Gladys Royale* and the *Lundy Island* were racially mixed, which was common on British vessels. Africans and Orientals hung in the rigging each day, hoping to secure the reward of ten pounds sterling and champagne.

The *Charles Gounod*'s crew was all French. Where the British employed men from other nationalities, French vessels tended to favor

French crews. Unlike the other crews, it was going to take several days for them to get used to their new role in the war.

The capture of the *Charles Gounod* proved to stir deep feelings in the *Seeadler's* captain. Von Luckner knew he would be sinking the sailing ship, but this was his first in the war. While it had been the core of his targets per the orders from the Admiralty, he did not relish the thought of sinking sailing ships. While the Frenchmen stood on his deck, hats in their hands, Lieutenant Pries planted three charges in the steel hold along the keel. The *Gounod* slid down by her bow. Von Luckner claimed that as the ship sank, he hummed one of the famous French composer's well known tunes—always one of his favorite operatic works. The entire operation from the time the French barque had been boarded to the time she sank was less than an hour.

Part of Lieutenant Pries's role in leading a boarding party was to secure the log of a captured ship. He presented this to Captain von Luckner and a quick check of the last few day's entries confirmed what the captain had suspected. The *Charles Gounod* had been in contact with several other ships in the previous few days, most of them French. The French captain had even noted where the ships had met, giving Von Luckner a good range to patrol. He finally had validation that these waters were rich with potential targets.

9

FORTUNES OF WAR

January 24–February 9, 1917

The *Seeadler* trolled the area for three days. There were other ships in the area, that much was known from the log from the *Charles Gounod*, so both the crew and their captives took to the rigging in search of not only a ship, but also the bounty for spotting one.

A three-masted schooner was sighted on January 24. This type of ship was favored by the Americans and the Canadians. The difference between them was that one was part of the British Commonwealth and was a legitimate target of war. At that time, America was still maintaining its cloak of neutrality in the war. That would change soon enough. In the meantime, this schooner was flying no flags at all, making her a completely unknown vessel.

International law allowed for neutral ships to be stopped on the high seas. They could be stopped and inspected to see if they were carrying contraband cargo. If they were, the ship and crew were subject to the same treatment von Luckner had provided his enemies—capture and sinking. If the cargo was not war material bound for an enemy port, the neutral ship could pass. Americans tended to chaff at this twist of the law—in fact, it was that same loophole that had turned the *Pass of Balmaha* into the *Seeadler*.

The first step was to determine what country she was from. Von Luckner ordered the Norwegian flag run up the mast. Usually this gesture would have sparked a similar response from the schooner. Instead, she did nothing. The ships would soon pass and the opportunity for the *Seeadler* to take action would be lost. The captain ordered the main-topsail backed to cut speed. He then ordered the flag dipped up and down three times as a gesture of salute between sailing ships.

On the bridge, von Luckner and the ever-sarcastic Lüdemann watched intently. The schooner did not return the gesture. Wary of a complete unknown, von Luckner assumed it was an American vessel. "Better leave the lubber alone," he commented. His reasoning was the risk of exposure. If it was an American with non-contraband cargo, it could report the *Seeadler*. Thus far the cruise of the ship had been covert. A report of her operations would bring the might of the Royal Navy down on her.

A call went up a moment later from the lookout. The ship was raising its flag—a British flag.

The *Seeadler* crew sprung to action. The Norwegian flag was quickly lowered and replaced with the German ensign. The orders went to the gun crew—fire a shot across the bow. Kircheiß swung one of the deck guns into play, placing a shot over the bow of the ship, sending a towering splash into the water. The schooner didn't stop; she attempted to make a break for it, hoping to outrun the sailing ship.

Von Luckner sent the order to the gun crews: one more shot over the bow. This time the schooner seemed to understand. They weren't getting away. Dropping sail, they hove-to.

It was Lüdemann who pointed out the obvious first, "Hey, there's a woman!" On the deck of the smaller schooner, the crew could make out a female running around wildly on the deck. Von Luckner only smiled and signaled to Lieutenant Pries to commence boarding operations. The lieutenant rounded up his prize party and took along one of the ship's dogs—Piperle. The dog had become a mainstay of boarding parties.

The female seen on deck was the new bride of the ship's captain, Kohler. He brought his wife along for their honeymoon, and it would be one of the most memorable that a merchant captain's wife could ever talk about. This was their first cruise together, and the events leading up to their capture caused an argument between them. When the *Seeadler* first signaled, the captain apparently made a gruff comment about the windjammer and not wanting to waste time with the old ship. When the *Seeadler* saluted by dipping her flag and the captain refused to raise his in return, the captain and his wife ended up fighting. The argument was cut short with the shots across her bow. Captain Kohler saw the first shot splash into the water and thought it was a whale, but the second shot convinced him that he was facing a real threat.

Pries brought them back aboard their new home. Their schooner was the *Perce*, a Canadian ship. Registered at 364 tons and carrying a load of dried fish, the three-masted ship was not much of a prize. Her small crew was transferred aboard the raider and the schooner was sunk with gunfire.

Having a woman aboard was going to add a new and challenging dynamic. The *Seeadler* had plenty of private quarters and the Kohlers were assigned one. Orders went out to the crew and the prisoners regarding appropriate treatment of their new prisoner. These were sailors after all. Mrs. Kohler proved to be a model prisoner. While the count warned his crew that they needed to treat her well, it was the sardonic Lüdemann who countered that he had treated a woman well once before—and she had run off with another man.

Richard Pries would prove to be something of a wildcard. Von Luckner's own account was that he knew him previously and recruited him personally for the cruise. That much is true. What made Pries different was that he was the only recorded member of the crew who was personally selected from scratch by von Luckner. The rest were preliminarily chosen by Lieutenant Kling and interviewed by von Luckner at a later date. There are no records of Luckner turning down any of his first officer's choices.

The selection for the crew of the *Seeadler* began in August of 1916. Lieutenant Kling had prepared a preliminary list of the crew that the *Pass of Balmaha* might require. His superiors, at that time, identified the need for a leader of the prize missions. They also made note at that time that Kling would be the first officer of the cruise, not the captain.

Lieutenant Pries apparently attended Lübeck Navigation College with von Luckner. At the time, the young count was still living under the assumed name of Phelax Lüdicke. The exact nature of their relationship was not fully known, but they seemed to have bonded as friends.

At six foot four, Pries was a big man. By the accounts of the prisoners of the *Seeadler*, he was arrogant—though the count described him as "gallant." He had the distinction of being the man chosen personally by the captain and placed forth in command of the ship. He was the only crewmember who had a personal relationship with Count von Luckner prior to the cruise. It is not out of the realm of possibility that this gave him a sense of overconfidence and power.

His role in the saga of the *Seeadler* would show that his arrogance was something that both the prisoners and the crew would have to cope with.

Several clear days passed as the *Seeadler* hovered near the equator looking for more prey. On February 3, her next opportunity presented itself in the distance as a four-masted brig. Through his telescope, von Luckner could see that the ship was not just in pristine condition: she was painted fancifully. Her portals were decorated as if they were gunports—the kind of style favored by the French.

Swinging in by the stern of the ship, the count was considering lowering sails and using the engine to overtake the ship. They could make out her name, the *Antonin*. When she spotted the freshly raised German flag, the brig turned away and made a break for freedom.

The *Seeadler's* engines refused to cooperate and with a strong wind picking up, the count ordered full sails and set off in pursuit of the *Antonin*. The *Seeadler* was an American-built windjammer and capable of fast speeds in a strong wind. While the *Antonin* had a head start, the *Seeadler* began to catch up after several miles. It was a classic race between sailing ships.

A squall blew up and the *Antonin* sailed for it. Sailing ships are difficult to handle in storms and risk losing their masts; in keeping with those concerns, the captain of the French brig lowered her royals and upper gallants. He still had plenty of canvas to keep his distance from his pursuer—assuming the *Seeadler* would reduce sail as well. Count Luckner, however, had other ideas.

As the gale broke, he ordered that none of his own canvas be pulled. The *Seeadler* had already sailed through a gale in breaking the blockade, and the crew knew the feel of the ship in a heavy storm. With full sails, she bore down on the *Antonin*. Dark purple clouds loomed behind the white canvas of the ship as it swept toward its target. On the stern of the French ship, the captain stood with a camera, snapping a picture of the ship overtaking him. The *Seeadler* was so close that Count Luckner commented to his helmsman Lüdemann, "We must capture that snapshot for our collection of photographs—if we have to take a trip to Davy Jones doing it."

Firing the cannon at a moving target, in a storm, while roaring at full-sail, was a potentially dangerous proposition. The captain called for one of the machine guns to be mounted on the bow of the ship. With the wind howling and the ship listing in the gale, Kircheiß's gunner loaded the machine gun and received orders of where to target their fire.

By 1917 the machine gun had changed the nature of warfare on land. It was a weapon of fear. The sound of machine gun fire was a disturbing sound for merchant sailors. The sputtering rat-tat sound of the weapon could mean quick deaths. As if to emphasize the point, the shots hit through lower sails and rigging, ripping some of the canvas. Given the strong winds, even small bullet holes ripped into larger damage. The message from the German raider was clear—surrender or die. As the *Seeadler* settled in next to her, the French captain cursed out his frustrations long and loud.

The boarding party from the *Seeadler* climbed aboard the *Antonin* and began what had become a routine. They checked for the location of the captain, crew, and the ship's log. They searched for stores and took what the Germans needed. They gave the crew time to pack their personal belongings, under their watchful eyes, and then took them to the *Seeadler*.

Lieutenant Pries discovered that the *Antonin* was loaded with 3,071 tons of nitrate and 50 tons of salted hides. The ship was bound for France from Iquigue, Chile. The surly French captain, named La Coq, was dazed. Lieutenant Pries asked the captain if he wanted to bring any personal belongings, but the Frenchman said no. He went over with only the clothing he wore and the slippers on his feet.

Pries made a point of recovering the camera from the ship and ferried Captain La Coq over to the *Seeadler* to talk with Captain von Luckner, whose interrogation was light at best. The count asked what ships they had recently seen, and Captain La Coq responded they had seen none. Pries verified this in the ship's log.

Something wasn't right. This man was saving nothing from his personal life—and that struck von Luckner as suspicious. The count made sure his new captive understood; the *Antonin* was going to be sunk. La Coq responded that if he had to lose his ship, he didn't want to save anything.

Didn't he want to save anything?

"No, let everything go down with the ship."

Von Luckner had been at sea most of his life and had met the stubbornest sea salts, but the stubbornness of this Frenchman seemed out of character. Turning to Lieutenant Pries, he ordered him to return to Captain La Coq's cabin and pack for him. La Coq said that was not necessary, but the count insisted. As a point of courtesy, of course.

Pries took the launch back over to the *Antonin*, the chop from the passing gale making the trip less than smooth. His prize crew was still there, setting bombs in the hold of the ship along the keel and checking the cargo to make sure they were not leaving anything behind. Pries went to the captain's cabin to pack for him—and there he discovered the reason the Frenchman had not wanted his possessions.

Returning with a bag of clothing and personal effects, Lieutenant Pries also brought a page from the ship's log of the *Antonin*. Captain La Coq had carefully torn the last page out of his ship's log and hid it down in his cabin, which explained why he did not want to go there under the watchful eyes of the prize crew.

Lieutenant Pries handed Captain von Luckner the removed page. They had met a cruiser a few days ago.

The words had to have shaken the *Seeadler* captain deeply. He ordered that the French crewmen be questioned and interrogated. Captain La Coq offered nothing but stern defiance. He had hoped to keep the cruiser a secret so the British warship would discover the raider that had just overtaken him. Before the *Seeadler*'s prize crew came aboard, he had asked his crew to say nothing of the cruiser.

Now, facing an armed and irate German crew, the French crewmembers provided the details missing from the log. The cruiser had searched the *Antonin* a few days ago. The patrol route took the cruiser south of the current position of the two sailing ships, and the cruiser patrolled the route of ships coming from the Pacific and heading north into the Atlantic and searched every ship it met. The *Seeadler* was headed right into their patrol route.

Captain La Coq was indignant and did not offer an honorable apology for the deception. Von Luckner felt that once the truth had been discovered, such an apology was necessary. Captain von Luckner was angered with La Coq's attitude but restrained his temper. The *Seeadler* band, which had assembled to play as they did at most of the captures, was dismissed without playing any tune. The usual joyous mood had faded quickly. Von Luckner was frustrated with the French captain and hoped he had seen the last of such behavior from his new prisoner.

He had not. In fact, Captain La Coq would prove to be a thorn in his side for weeks to come.

I O

LIFE AT SEA

February 1917

After the capture of the *Antonin*, shipboard life aboard the raider changed. The French crew's deception disturbed the *Seeadler's* captain. The atmosphere aboard the raider was relaxed, but tightened up after the capture of the *Antonin*—with restricted hours for the prisoners and other measures. He had anticipated that some of the prisoners would work against him, but Captain La Coq's ploy had almost worked.

The ship patrolled a smaller area within the shipping lane, roughly a rectangle in shape. The intent was simply to avoid heading south toward the British cruiser. The other reason was more mercenary: the pickings along the equator in terms of shipping seemed quite good, so there was no reason to move on.

The crew manned three-day shifts. Sundays tended to be light-duty days; when crewmembers weren't on watch, most spent their downtime writing letters to loved ones—in the hope that one day the ship would reach a port where the letters could be mailed.

The changes to the ship itself were subtle. The hull got a touch-up of black paint. The name on her stern, HERO, was painted bright white so it could be seen against the dark background from a long distance. Von Luckner also refined some of the elements of her disguise as a neutral Norwegian.

The time it took to take the Norwegian flag down and pull the German flag up, as required by maritime law, seemed too long. The captain and his crew had experience capturing ships by now, and they knew timing and speed were everything to a raider during an encounter. In order to improve on their timing and still adhere to the terms of internationally recognized law, the count ordered that the Norwegian flag be painted on the hull of the ship. The flag was not small and measured almost ten feet long. Next to it, in letters measuring several feet each, the word "Norge" was painted to further declare their neutrality.

In order to cover the painted flags right before battle, thick strips of canvas were attached to the top of the deck railing that were long enough to reach the water and cover the word and the flag. These were kept rolled up on the deck.

Von Luckner could order the canvas to be dropped, covering the neutrality symbols for Norway, and at the same time run the German ensign up. It would only save a few minutes, but those minutes might be the key to bringing a potential victim in closer.

The marines kept up their target skills by drilling with weapons on the deck. Lieutenant Kircheiß drilled his gun crews while at the same time the marines would emerge with Mauser rifles and at least one machine gun at the ready. The crew's time was occupied during the long days with pistol and rifle drills, complete to stripping and reassembly. When the *Seeadler* encountered an enemy merchant cruiser armed with a gun, these men had the task of shooting at the gun crew. Captain von Luckner did not want to kill if he didn't have to. If the gunners could shoot to keep the gun crew suppressed, they were to do so. If they had to shoot to kill, then so be it.

The officers of the *Seeadler* had little time to relax and spent some of their time planning future captures. They would be going up against ships such as steamers that were faster and able to flee. How would they handle that situation? How could they suppress a ship with a wireless? How could a ship be lured in for quick capture? The officers spent time working through various scenarios: plotting, planning, and building props that would help them in battle.

Given the abnormally large number of men aboard the *Seeadler*, von Luckner did not want sickness to incapacitate his crew. Doctor Pietsch inspected each new prisoner brought on board. Once they came on deck, the doctor would set up a line and check each for illness. The prisoners found to be sick were quarantined and treated until they were better. The doctor and other officers understood that operating a long time away from any friendly port meant that one of their greatest enemies was illness.

When the boarding parties went aboard ships, they searched for more than water and food. They recovered spare lifeboats and life preservers. Most of these were stored belowdecks on the *Seeadler*. If the ship sank, the prisoners had some chance at survival.

Some of the other changes were more subtle. In keeping with international maritime law, the crew could not fight while wearing civilian clothing. To do so would technically mark them as pirates. They would show up on deck wearing civilian clothing, and as the flag ran up they would change their clothes. A shot could not be fired until the crewmen on the deck were changed. In time, the crew made some compromises—such as wearing their pristine white German naval uniforms under their civilian clothes. It was hot near the equator, but this made their transformation from Norwegians to German sailors much faster.

The number of prisoners now on the *Seeadler* brought about more changes for the German crew. Each night, two guards were posted at 2000 hours over the prisoners—and that number grew as the number of prisoners increased. They were not there to prevent an uprising so much as to give warning to the rest of the crew. It was a restrained reminder to the captives that they were on a warship on a dangerous mission.

There were parts of the ship that were simply banned. The poop deck and helm compass were off-limits without an invitation from Captain von Luckner. The engine compartment and forward holds were also prohibited. This was made clear to every prisoner.

"My magazines are in the forward half of the boat. I do not want you to know where they are exactly placed. After you are released you might reveal the secret. Then one of these merry days, if some cruiser takes a shot at me, and if the location of my magazines is known, they'll aim right at that spot. A shell there and up in the air we go." Von Luckner met with each captain and crew when they came aboard the ship and secured their promise, on their word of honor: that they would stay away from off-limits areas and would not make notes or sketches of the ship.

With such large gatherings of men, especially sailors, certain problems were to be expected. Such was the case with alcohol. When captains were captured their private stock of liquor was theirs to keep and use as they saw fit. Von Luckner followed the standard British practice of selling alcohol to his prisoner crewmembers. While he was paying them their going rates, they were essentially limited to the amount of spirits they could purchase and consume. He rationed the amount of alcohol given to his own German crew. With the mixture of nationalities on the ship, this measure prevented wild drunken brawls. It also ensured that no one under the influence might gather up the courage they might not normally have and attempt to take over the ship.

As more people were taken prisoner, cooking became a much larger task. Captain von Luckner insisted that his crew and the prisoners receive the same food. While he proclaimed this openly, the meals the German crews ate were off of a somewhat better menu. The captured cooks were used to help feed the large number of men, and this added to the variety: one night a Chinese cook made dinner, followed by a French cook the next night, followed by an Indian.

The captain walked the deck every day, followed closely by Schnäuzchen, his favorite dog. He almost always wore his uniform and had his pipe in his mouth. The fact that von Luckner mingled with the crew, regardless of rank, stood out among some of the French prisoners. He did not ignore the men and prisoners who were ordinary seamen; he seemed to seek them out, swapping stories and making them feel a part of his crew.

The German crew developed their own sense of identity. They called themselves "die Seeadlers," or the Sea Eagles. It was a mark of pride. Most got to know the prisoners not as captives but as fellow sailors. At night, when the guards were posted, the prisoners would play a gramophone and listen to music. On some nights, they came up on deck at the captain's invitation and the ship's band would play.

In later years, some would characterize the *Seeadler* a party boat more than a ship of war.

While not discussed in the war diary or specifically in his own writings, Count von Luckner employed a rather extensive counterintelligence operation aboard the *Seeadler*. His crew intermingled with the prisoners daily and he made sure they spread disinformation each and every chance they could.

For example, the prisoners told several different versions of how the *Seeadler* had sailed through the blockade. In later years, some would claim it was the *Avenger* that stopped the ship; others would claim it was the *Highland Laddie* or *Highland Scot* (which, ironically, was one of the notations in *Seeadler*'s war diary); others would drop different names of ships that the crew of the *Seeadler* had told them during their time. Some prisoners were told when the ship left Germany, she was accompanied by several U-boats. In one case, an officer revealed that they had sailed out of port with the *Möwe*, a raider name that instilled fear among merchant captains. (Actually, the *Möwe* had sailed only a few days before the *Seeadler*.) Most never compared their stories, and those who did never bothered to confront the Germans to get to the truth. This allowed misinformation to spread among the prisoners.

Where was the *Seeadler* heading? Some prisoners were told she was going to lay mines off the coast of Australia. Others were told she was going to the southern tip of Africa, around the Cape of Good Hope. Others were told she was going to continue raiding in the central Atlantic. If the prisoners ever got a chance to talk, their stories would send the enemy in many different directions at once.

Other deceptions were spread personally by the captain. When he brought captured crews aboard, he would lay out the rules of the ship. The prisoners were to be paid their normal wages. He could hold them locked away; but as long as they behaved, they could roam the ship. No one was allowed to sketch or document anything of the interior or armaments of the vessel.

These instructions began with the capture of the *Gladys Royale*, and Captain von Luckner added some over time. One that he became fond of telling was that he had a way of dealing with any prisoner uprisings on the ship: poison gas would fill the lower decks. "I only need to press a button to asphyxiate all of you in two minutes." While false, the word spread. Most of the prisoners had seen some of the hidden compartments on the ship where weapons were stored, leading them to believe there was indeed the possibility of poison gas belowdecks. With gas warfare being used on the continent, and with the horrors it implied, this was a good way to keep potential uprisings in check.

There were other elements of the *Seeadler* that von Luckner enjoyed bragging about. He had metal canisters on the deck that were painted with the word "smoke" on them. They were empty, but the prisoners became convinced these were designed to create a smoke-screen—even though they appeared to be ad hoc additions to the ship.

Then there was the threat of torpedoes.

The main armaments of the ship were two forward deck-mounted guns, located behind the false deck railing that could be lowered instantly at Kircheiß's orders. Von Luckner covertly told several of the captured captains that he also had two torpedo tubes. The word of these weapon systems spread, and soon it was known by all that *Seeadler* was a sailing torpedo ship—even though that was the furthest thing from the truth.

And although the *Seeadler* carried a total of six machine guns, six grew to sixteen in the rumor mill of the ship. The stories were easy enough to plant—and they could apparently grow all on their own.

The *Seeadler* had to cope with other threats at night. Ships would black out all their running and ship lights and become virtually invisible in the darkness. The odds were long they would collide with a ship. But it was a possibility in this heavily used shipping lane, so at night the *Seeadler* would run to the northeast on a parallel course with other merchant ships to reduce the risk of collision. During the day, the *Seeadler* would then cut southwest.

Precautions took a number of forms. The crew of the *Seeadler* took many of photographs of their cruise—not just of the crew, but of their victims, too. People might have interpreted this as ego on the part of her captain; in reality, von Luckner was protecting himself and his crew. As a raider, the *Seeadler* operated at the fringes of maritime law and there was a fine line between outright piracy and raiding. If von Luckner and his ship were captured, the British press would attempt to exploit their activity for propaganda purposes. Having a photographic record of the ships and the relaxed and joyful atmosphere on board would serve as an excellent rebuttal to any charges that might one day be leveled against von Luckner.

Lieutenant Kling had overseen a great deal of the work in changing the *Pass of Balmaha* into the *Seeadler*. When Count von Luckner took command, much of the heavy lifting was already underway or completed. There were some aspects that he oversaw—primarily the installation of the ship's main armaments and arrangement of the quarters for officers, prisoners, and prisoner captains. Most of this work was done at the Tecklenborg shipyard at Gestenmünde. Von Luckner and Kling took unusual interest in this aspect of the ship's refit because they shared the same view of how they would treat their prisoners. The other raiders treated their prisoners like prisoners: they locked them up and brought them out for some respite in the sunshine—but for the most part, they were traditional prisoners. Captain von Luckner wanted his prisoners to be free but respectful of his authority.

The addition of private cabins to the deck plans of the forecastle was an attempt to treat captured captains with some degree of respect. The captain had bigger plans. He knew, based on his experience on the high seas, that the secret of maintaining order from the captured crews was to start at the top—the captains.

By February, von Luckner had initiated daily meetings of "the Captain's Club." Von Luckner dined with them at least once a day to discuss their concerns, either for themselves or their crew. The count was able to bond with the merchant captains, for he had lived in their world a good portion of his life. They traded stories, chatted about sailing matters, and discussed news intercepted on the wireless to pass onto their crews.

Many of the crew of the *Seeadler* saw the Captain's Club as an elitist organization and their captain's folly. Captain von Luckner was much wiser. This club helped him indoctrinate newly captured crews to life aboard the raider. Feeding word from the outside world to their crew gave the captains some degree of authority aboard ship. They held a small amount of power, the power of communication—

and that was a legitimate source of authority because it was backed by von Luckner.

On February 9, 1917, the *Seeadler* spotted another ship during the mid-day. She was a steel-hulled ship with three masts, smaller than the raider and loaded with cargo. Her lines were distinctively English but her flag was Italian, making her fair game. She surrendered with a single shot over the bow.

The ship was the *Buenos Aires* and when Lieutenant Pries boarded her, he found the ship to be a filthy mess. The pudgy captain, Antonio Barbieri, seemed to be setting a less-than-stellar example—overweight, unshaven, and lacking in the area of clean clothing. The ship's port of call was Napoli and her hold was full of saltpeter from Chile, destined for munitions factories. The 1,811 ton ship was checked for usable food and cargo that, along with her crew, were transferred to the *Seeadler* while the ship's band played a gleeful rendition of the "Marseillaise."

Her captain came aboard, disheveled and carrying an umbrella. Von Luckner was unsure if he should break out laughing or not. The newest member of the Captain's Club seemed to be quite happy with his new lot in life—and his fresh, new quarters on the *Seeadler* were much better than the squalor he had left behind.

Lieutenant Pries planted bombs on her keel and sent the *Buenos Aires* to the bottom. It was the sixth vessel the raider had sunk since breaking through the British blockade.

I I

THE PINMORE

February 18–February 19, 1917

On the 18th of February the *Seeadler* crew sighted their first ship since the sinking of the *Buenos Aires* nine days ago. From the distance, the ship was seen to be flying the Stars and Stripes, marking her as a neutral. As tempting as it was to stop and search her for possible contraband, von Luckner steered clear. As a rule, American sailors were very willing to share information with vessels they encountered. If the ship wasn't carrying military cargo, von Luckner would have to let them go—knowing almost certainly they would spread the news about the *Seeadler*.

Von Luckner didn't feel like pressing his luck, not since he stumbled into such fertile hunting grounds. He decided to let this unknown go on her way.

The ship was the U.S. schooner *Orleans* heading for Africa. Her captain noted the sighting of a Norwegian windjammer. Over time that story would grow into ravenous boarding parties, sightings of torpedo tubes, and the usual exaggerations of sailors at ports of call.

The next morning the sailors hanging on the rigging caught sight of a four-masted, square-rigged barque. Once again the charade that had worked so well for the *Seeadler* crew took form. Crewmembers draped clothing over their uniforms and the raider assumed the guise of a Norwegian windjammer.

As they swung to close in on the ship, the other captain did not seem interested in allowing them to get too close. She turned to catch the wind and ran up full sails to get away. Captain von Luckner ordered up his full sails as well and set the *Seeadler* off in chase. With a stiff breeze, the race between the ships was fairly even. Making the chase even more tantalizing was the fact that they spotted a Union Jack flying from her mast, marking her as a perfect target.

The chase was likely to take hours and there was no way to be sure the sailing ship did not have a wireless set. She might be leading the *Seeadler* right into a trap—and matters needed to be settled quickly. Captain von Luckner called down into the bowels of the ship for the ship's engineer, Krause, to fire up the auxiliary engine. The diesel was tricky to start but the recent overhaul after the incident with the *Antonin* had left it in fairly good running order. When it was working well, the startup time for the engine was four minutes. When facing a potentially hostile ship, four minutes seemed like an hour. It eventually kicked in, belching black smoke from the low exhaust pipe on the deck. The *Seeadler* suddenly got the speed she needed; as they gained on the fleeing ship, the captain gave the order to clear the decks for action. The crew revealed their uniforms, dropped the canvas over the Norwegian flag on the side of the hull, and ran the German flag up the mast. Ammunition was uncrated and the guns were readied for action.

As they gained on the ship, her lines and shape seemed disturbingly familiar to Captain von Luckner. The ship was one he had seen before, and it took a moment for his mind to place the image.

"Signal her and ask for her name," he bellowed as the gap closed and the British merchant realized she was not going to be able to outrun the raider.

Flag signals flashed between the ships. The signal came back—and when he saw it, he felt a chill of remembrance. There was a reason why he didn't recognize the ship outright on sight. He had rarely seen her from a distance. Most of his time on the *Pinmore* had been spent on her deck.

After successfully running away from home and sailing to Australia aboard the *Niobe*, Phelax Lüdicke took on a number of odd jobs to get by. He got homesick after the horrible conditions on the *Niobe*, but he wanted to return home as an officer. There was an army recruiting in the Australian ports with pristine uniforms, bands, everything that caught the attention of a young man. Speaking with them, he revealed that he was a young count from Germany who had run away from home. They told him that given his background, they would help him become an officer, in the Salvation Army.

He got some of his early public speaking experience from the Salvation Army. He was touted as the young German royal who had come to the army for his future. His talks brought in people and were a public relations coup for the army. He made a meager living by selling copies of *War Cry* but eventually realized this was not an army his father would respect. The army members helped him get a job at a local lighthouse, polishing the massive lenses.

Problems arose at the lighthouse when he became a little too friendly with the lighthouse keeper's daughter. Von Luckner/Lüdicke claimed it was nothing more than an innocent kiss, but the lighthouse keeper didn't care and chased off the young man. He got work hunting kangaroos in the outback and working with a guide in the fields.

He was spotted by a local fight promoter, who saw the large muscular sailor as a potential boxer. The young count was trained in a local boxing school and made a living from his boxing career, albeit a short one.

He took to the sea again on the *Golden Shore*, a four-masted schooner, and got a chance to see more of the Pacific. He eventually found himself in Seattle, scrounging on the docks and shore to make a living. Working his way north, he eventually got to Vancouver and got a job as a mate on a four-masted English ship docked there, the *Pinmore*.

The ship would sail from Vancouver around Cape Horn and on to Liverpool. She was carrying rations for 180 days and fresh water for at least that long. The voyage was estimated to take well over two hundred days but it was not uncommon for a merchant to barter and trade with other ships along the way for the extra food and supplies they might need.

The pay of a thousand marks was great for a young sailor, but it was clear the voyage would take the better part of a year. For the young Phelax, it would be the longest voyage of his life under sail.

The voyage of the *Pinmore* was going to be one of the greatest tests of Phelax's survival skills. Sea water seeped into the ship's fresh water storage, spoiling much of the fresh water supply. Sailing ships on the high seas for extended periods of time usually gather additional water from rainstorms, but on this voyage the *Pinmore* did not pass through storms of any significance.

The long trek around Cape Horn became more unpleasant as the captain ordered the crew to half-rations in an attempt to stretch out their food supply. Usually on such a voyage, several other ships would be encountered to trade with. Not on this journey. The *Pinmore* was seemingly a ship alone at sea.

Forced to survive on brackish water and fresh fruit and vegetables, the crew became sick with scurvy and beriberi. The scurvy came from a lack of vitamin C, resulting in severe joint pain and black and blue marks on the skin. A victim's hair can fall out and their gums can swell and bleed to the point where eating is painful due to loose teeth.

Beriberi leaves its victims with tingling or pain in their hands and feet. The extremities can develop paralysis. While scurvy showed up more externally, the damage from beriberi was much worse because it was harder to see on the outside of the victim. Untreated, it could easily lead to brain damage and death.

While scurvy and beriberi wracked the crew, others were plagued with a variety of other health issues. Some of the crew became bloated and others had symptoms of dysentery, most likely from the spoiled water supply. As a result, normal tasks on the ship were simply not done. The ship became a foul-smelling vessel of sickness, slow starvation, dehydration, and death.

Phelax's legs swelled up so badly that he could no longer climb the rigging and could barely walk the deck. As the crew ran out of food and water, they were able to run up their storm sails so that the ship could hopefully make it on its own to the coast.

By the time a tug pulled alongside of the ship to guide her into port, the crew was all but crippled. Those crewmembers who were able to cried out to the tug crew for water, since they had suffered so badly from dehydration. In total, six members of the crew died on the *Pinmore*'s 280-day voyage to England.

The survivors were paid for their service, but it was hardly worth the ordeal they had gone through. Phelax was taken off of the *Pinmore* only to spend two weeks in a hospital.

Seeing the vessel again stirred bad memories of the longest voyage in the count's career. Now the ship was under his guns. As he pulled alongside, he ordered Lieutenant Pries to prepare his prize crew. Under the command of James Mullen, a gentle, older captain, the *Pinmore* weighed in at 2,431 gross registered tons (GRT). She was loaded with grain bound for England.

Captain von Luckner greeted Captain Mullen and his crew, finding himself scanning the faces and eyes of the crew that he had just captured—looking for some familiar old friend. None were there. The *Pinmore* was the same ship, but the crew were strangers to him. Captain Mullen was a seasoned sailor and greeted his captor warmly.

"Well Captain, our hard luck is your good luck," he said to Von Luckner.

Von Luckner was torn with old feelings. "Lucky? Do you call this lucky?"

Captain Mullen didn't understand, nor did the crew of the *Seeadler*. Von Luckner felt the pain of being forced, by orders, to sink a piece of his own past. Pries oversaw the transfer of supplies and other goods and asked for permission to plant the bombs and send the ship to the bottom.

Captain von Luckner had him hold. He ordered the motor launch to take him back to the *Pinmore*. The count went on board alone to walk the decks of the ship that had nearly killed him in his youth. He went to the forecastle where he had bunked down. It was the same, but oddly different. His crew was unsure of how to react—their captain said nothing to them at the time about his motivations. There was something about this ship that was different from the other vessels they had sunk.

On the stern of the ship, von Luckner went to the rail where he had been assigned watch at the compass. There, a lifetime before, he had carved his name: Phelax Lüdicke. The wooden railing had been weathered with age and the elements and coated in countless coats of naval varnish, but he could still make out the faint letters of his name. Without a crew to tend her, the wheel tossed slightly, the rigging creaked and groaned with the rocking of the waves. The ghosts of the past and that long painful voyage existed only in his memories.

He could have spared the *Pinmore*—left her adrift. Phelax Lüdicke would have. Felix von Luckner could not. He boarded the motor launch and returned to the *Seeadler*. He gave the orders to Lieutenant Pries to complete the job.

The count retired belowdecks to his quarters. It was the only time on the cruise of the *Seeadler* he did not stay on the deck to ensure that the captured enemy ship was finished. This was one sinking he didn't want to witness. From his quarters, he could hear the band on the deck strike up "God Save the Queen," in honor of their new prisoners. In the distance he could hear the low moaning rumble and growl of the explosive charges going off below the decks of the *Pinmore*.

12

THE FRENCH BETRAYAL

February 25–March 4, 1917

The sinking of the *Pinmore*, despite its nostalgia, did not alter the routine aboard the raider. On February 25, a week later, the lookouts in the rigging spotted a four-masted sailing ship. She seemed unimpressed by the *Seeadler* as she made her way east to match her course. The ship made no move to run, yet no attempt to communicate. Captain von Luckner sensed a challenge and swung the raider to block her path. He ordered the signal flag run to ask the ship to identify herself.

The ship refused to signal back and continued on her path. The signal was sent again; again, she did nothing except ignore the *Seeadler*.

Von Luckner followed what had become routine for his men. They covered the Norwegian flag on the hull and the sailors on deck dropped their extra layer of clothing to reveal their pristine white uniforms of the German Navy. The German flag was run up the mast.

The signal flags ordering the sailing ship to surrender were run up. She continued to ignore the message. Lieutenant Kircheiß and his crew swung into action, loading the cannon. At a command from von Luckner, they fired a shot over the bow of the unknown ship.

No response. This ship was nothing if not stubborn.

Captain von Luckner ordered another salvo fired over her bow. The blast in the water was impossible to ignore, a column of salt water rising as the shell exploded under the surface. A flag emerged, running up her mast. As the flag went up, the *Seeadler*'s captain felt an ill feeling. The flag was Danish—a neutral country. He ordered the *Seeadler* to swing alongside and commanded Pries to form a boarding party to check the cargo of this neutral vessel.

Von Luckner had good reason to be nervous. If she was a neutral ship carrying neutral cargo, there was a risk she could tell others about the *Seeadler*—how she looked, how she posed as a Norwegian, even how many crew were seen. He had done so well to avoid this unfortunate confrontation up to this point; but now the *Seeadler's* disguise and technique was at risk.

Lieutenant Pries and a small party boarded the ship. She was the *Viking* and her log held up that she was indeed of Danish registry; a ten-year-old ship built by Burnmeister & Wain. Pries inspected her cargo hold and verified her bills of lading. If the cargo was war materials bound for an enemy port, her Danish flag would not save her.

The cargo was not contraband, but corn being shipped from Buenos Aires to Copenhagen. As if to validate the matter of her neutrality, her captain carried papers from the German Consul in Buenos Aires asking German ships to give the *Viking* due consideration.

Pries consulted with von Luckner and there was little that could be said or done. The captain did not want her to flee; but at the same time, there was nothing he could do. The *Viking* did not have a wireless, so she could not tell anyone about the *Seeadler* until they came aboard her or she made port. That would buy him several days and upwards of a month, if she made the rest of her voyage without encounter. Von Luckner bade the *Viking* good luck and withdrew his prize crew.

Now it was only a matter of time for the British and French to learn of his raids. And when they did, the full force of their navies would come to hunt him and his men down.

The morale on the *Seeadler* didn't suffer from the encounter, and von Luckner did his best outside of his circle of officers to not let the crew—and especially the prisoners—realize the depth of their potential problem with the chance meeting.

He was approached at one point by Mrs. Kohler, the only female on board. Von Luckner had made a point to talk to her often, to make sure she was being taken care of and not facing any problems on the ship. She jokingly confided in him that she was lonely. "Count, I wish there were a woman aboard I could talk to. Why don't you catch one?"

His reply was, "Madam, I'll do my best." Little did he realize that on February 26, that opportunity would present itself.

The weather that day was misty and rainy with heavy clouds. In the early morning, it seemed to be clearing to the west and the lookouts spotted a barque casually sailing along. Captain von Luckner ordered the *Seeadler* readied for action and ordered the ship turned to the west to intercept her by coming up alongside. She flew a British flag, meaning that they would not have to worry about the problem they had faced with the *Viking* the day before.

During the fifteen minute pursuit, he was surprised to see a white-clad figure on the deck in a dress. It appeared that he would be able to fulfill his promise to Captain Kohler's wife much sooner than expected.

He spoke with Lüdemann and quickly came up with a good way to lure this ship in once they came alongside. It was a trick worthy of Lüdemann's sense of humor. They brought the prisoners up on deck. The Chinese stood in one group; a group of West Indians took their position along the deck rail, alongside the captured merchantmen from Africa, then the captured British and French crews. The prisoners lined the deck of the *Seeadler* and made a colorful display of her success to date. In an effort to ease the tensions even more, the gramophone played "It's a Long Way to Tipperary." The crew of the raider milled in and around the prisoners on deck, still wearing their civilian overcoats. On the British ship, the crew came out as well, feeling quite safe.

The captain of the British barque, seeing the menagerie of men on the deck, called over to the windjammer at his side. "Hello, collecting volunteers?"

Von Luckner leaned over the railing. "Volunteers? Oh yes!" he yelled back. The prisoners and crew on the deck of the *Seeadler* chuckled at the response.

"Any news of the war?" the fellow captain queried. His crew and wife all listened intently, hoping for an update.

"Much news of the war," von Luckner called back with a smirk. "I will signal it." All eyes went to the mast to see the signal flags.

Three brilliantly colored flags went up and went taut in the breeze. CID, meaning Heave-to or I Will Open Fire.

The captain of the barque began to flip through his codebook, attempting to make sense out of the white flag with the blue trim and the red-banded flag on a yellow background, or perhaps the blue flag with the yellow ribbons on the top and bottom. This was not your typical friendly signal, after all. Von Luckner sent the word to his crew. They dropped their overcoats and civilian garb, returning to their German uniforms. The German flag ran up the mast. The railing in front of the cannon slammed down on its hinges, exposing the deck gun on that side. Lieutenant Kircheiß pivoted the weapon to bear on the barque, in case there was any sign of resistance. Given the ruse, none was expected.

It was not known if the captain of the merchant ship found the CID code or spotted the German flag first. It didn't matter. They had been tricked and tricked good. General commotion broke out on the barque as crewmen abandoned their posts at the sight of the cannon aimed at them at nearly point blank range. It took the captain of the smaller ship a few minutes to regain control of the situation.

The ship was the *British Yeoman*. The captain, Campbell Neilson, had sailed the ship out of Canada but it was registered as an American ship with a San Francisco port of registry. At 1,953 gross registered tons, she was built in the previous century, in 1880, but had been well taken care of. Because the *Yeoman* had flown the British flag she could not claim neutrality. Ironically, this was the same technicality that had handed the *Pass of Balmaha* to the Germans.

The members of the Captain's Club mustered on the gangway to greet the new members of the crew, somewhat delighted at having taken part in the latest capture—albeit in a cameo role on the deck. Mrs. Kohler asked Captain von Luckner if he could find some flowers. The count located some artificial flowers and had them dosed with perfume. When Jessie Neilson, the wife of the *British Yeoman*'s captain came aboard, she was greeted with cheers from the prisoners and crew and a bouquet.

Lieutenant Pries took over a prize crew and raided the hold of the ship for goods and supplies they could use aboard the *Seeadler*. Some of the supplies were unique: they were animals. The *Yeoman* had live pigs on board, and these were transferred to the *Seeadler* as future meals. The captured ship also had a small coop of chickens that were destined for the raiders' dinner table. Also brought aboard were the pets of the crew, a rabbit and a pigeon. The *Seeadler*'s dog Piperle adopted the other pets almost immediately, protecting them from the cantankerous Schnäuzchen. Once the barnyard menagerie was transferred, bombs were placed on her hull and fuses were set. In just a short period of time, the *British Yeoman* slipped beneath the waves.

While Captain Neilson and his wife were settled into private quarters and formally introduced to the Captain's Club, Captain von Luckner met with his officers and planned for some more elaborate ruses. He had rather enjoyed the variation to their normal capture procedure and planned for several other alternatives.

That night, the watch spotted a flash of light astern of the ship. Since most ships traveling during the war were blacked out, the flash was a signal that some ship was behind the raider. Von Luckner ordered his own ship to alter course. When the sun came up, he made sure the rigging was full of lookouts—to spot whatever they had seen the night before.

The ship was spotted quickly. It was a four-masted barque flying the French flag. When she spotted the *Seeadler* she actually closed with the ship, apparently thinking her to be a friendly vessel. Von Luckner ordered his men to show their true colors, running up the German flag, unmasking the cannon, and changing to their uniforms. Von Luckner had the signal flags sent up: Stop, We Have Important News.

The French captain was stunned. His thoughts of running were dashed at the sight of the Kriegsmarine ensign billowing in the wind. Even worse was the 4.2-inch cannon that seemed anxious to fire at him and his ship. He quickly dropped sail and ordered his ship to heave-to. There was no hope for escape.

The ship was named *La Rochefoucauld*. Owned by the Societe Nouvelle d'Armement, she was registered in Nantes. At 2,200 gross registered tons, she was loaded with saltpeter for the armaments industry.

La Rochefoucauld was commanded by Captain Malbert. He was so shocked at the early morning capture that when he boarded the *Seeadler*, he was still wearing his carpet slippers. Greeted by the other captains, he had thought the *Seeadler* was possibly a British submarine tender. Only when he saw the gun aimed at him did he realize the fate that awaited him.

La Rochefoucauld's crew was transferred to the raider while Lieutenant Pries checked the ship's log, her paperwork, and her hold to see if there was anything out of the ordinary. Once cleared, Pries planted charges in the hold of the French vessel and lit the fuses. In just a few minutes, the barque was sent to the bottom.

The sheer number of prisoners on the *Seeadler* was becoming a problem with over two hundred on board after the capture of the *La Rochefoucauld*. The German crew was outnumbered nearly four to one, but so far order was maintained. Some of the formality found on most military ships was somewhat relaxed on the *Seeadler*, however. She was not like other ships operating on the seas—and even unlike other raiders.

At times, Captain von Luckner ran his ship more like a rowdy hotel than a strict military ship. There was a time for strict military discipline, and that was when the ship was seizing another vessel. The prisoners knew that their lot was thrown in with their German captors. If a British cruiser attacked the *Seeadler*, they would suffer just as much, if not more, than the Germans who commanded the ship.

The usual quiet of the ship was shattered one night with the sound of a gunshot. It had come from the captain's saloon where Captain von Luckner and some of his officers had gathered for a nightcap. The sound of the shot spurred the members of the Captain's Club and other prisoners to rush in and see what had happened.

They found Lieutenant Pries holding up a watch bob, its chain shattered. Pries had a stunned look on his face. In the far wall of the saloon was a bullet hole. Von Luckner held a small pistol. The Germans were laughing loudly at some inside joke.

When pressed for what had happened, the officers claimed that after a drink, Lieutenant Pries had gotten into a debate with the captain about his ability to shoot his pistol. As if to goad von Luckner more, he held up his pocket watch and challenged his commanding officer, "You couldn't even hit my watch."

According to the officers present, Captain von Luckner drew the pistol and fired one shot, shattering the watch square-on. The debate was over. It also confirmed for the prisoners who witnessed the event that the normal military rules aboard the *Seeadler* would never be the norm.

Only one man consistently challenged Captain von Luckner: Captain La Coq of the French ship *Antonin*. He was a proud man and defiant to the wishes of his German captor. He was a member of the Captain's Club, but it was obvious that he did not enjoy himself as most of the other prisoners did.

When he had been captured, he had attempted to deceive the captain of the *Seeadler* by hiding the fact that British heavy cruisers were operating in the area. He had bitterly accepted being a prisoner of the Germans, and he made it clear from his attitude that he did not willingly accept his fate. He saw the other captains as disloyal to their countries. La Coq was a merchant captain like his peers, but in his heart he was a French patriot.

The French captain drew attention to himself by not associating with his peers. Instead he chose to wander the ship alone, or only spend time with his former crew. His suspicious behavior reached a peak when Captain Mullen of the *Pinmore* finally confronted La Coq. Their discussion quickly erupted into a physical confrontation—one that drew the attention of the German officers and Captain von Luckner.

Captain Mullen had seen Captain La Coq walking through the ship apparently making notes about the ship's design. Such behavior was not only forbidden, but the captains had each individually sworn on their honor that they would not make notes or sketches of the *Seeadler*. There were areas of the ship that had been declared forbidden: the forward holds and the poop deck. There were reasons for this security. If someone could pinpoint the *Seeadler's* magazine where her ammunition was stored, an enemy ship would only have to fire one well-aimed shot to destroy the windjammer.

Captain La Coq had violated his word of honor. More importantly, he had snuck into the forward holds and was in possession of sketches showing exactly where the munitions were stored.

The actions of La Coq were something that von Luckner should have expected. His prisoners were civilians and were not bound by the same rules as prisoners of war. Von Luckner was pressing a gentleman's promise on them and he placed more weight on that than apparently La Coq did.

There are few times when anyone on the ship recorded the captain of the *Seeadler* losing his temper—but all accounts agree on this one instance. He bellowed with his deep booming voice at the Frenchman. He pointed out that Captain La Coq could be shot as a spy for his actions and sent a chilling note in the air among the gathered crowd.

He drove home the ultimate punishment. "When I release my prisoners and send them off to some port, there will be one Frenchman who will remain behind, and that Frenchman will be you. You will continue to cruise with us. You know where my magazines are and I cannot trust any promise that you now give me!"

The sentence was one that seemed to shatter Captain La Coq. Von Luckner gathered up the notes that the French captain had made and stormed away. La Coq's actions had cost him dearly and he knew there would be no appeal with the *Seeadler*'s captain or crew.

What Captain von Luckner did not know was that Captain La Coq was not the only member of his Captain's Club who had violated his word of honor. Captain Neilson of the *British Yeoman* had in his pocket his own set of sketches, standing only a few feet away as La Coq was dressed down. Other captains had their own form of notes and diagrams as well. If and when they were freed, the Royal Navy would have everything they needed to destroy the *Seeadler*, if they ever got the chance.

From the start of the war the German Navy was plagued by intelligence problems. The British seemed to know their movements before they left port. The theory as to why was twofold: either the docks were covered with British agents, or the commercial fishing fleet had been infiltrated with spies with wireless sets.

Giving the *Seeadler* the false name of *Walter* was part of a countermeasure to the British intelligence network. Not only was security tight around the "training ship," but false rumors were spread about the ship among the dock workers. The use of a sailing ship for training was not out of the ordinary during the period. The German Navy had used a schooner, the *Niobe* (coincidentally the same name as Luckner's first ship), for many years leading up to the war.

When the *Seeadler* left dock, no transmission or inquires back to or from Germany had been made about the ship. It was as if the vessel had never existed. The ship's orders were vague and left to Captain von Luckner's discretion. While the *Seeadler* had a powerful wireless set, strict orders were in place not to use it for transmissions. Once she left port, the ship was alone. Neither her enemies nor her homeland would know where she was or if she was succeeding in her mission. There were other reasons for this. Two other raiders had put to sea at the same time as von Luckner's ship—though none of the raider captains were aware of the others.

That wasn't to say that the rumor mill in the ports and docks before departure hadn't done their job. Word about the German raiders *Wolf* and *Möwe's* pending raids were known to at least three members of the crew—validating that sailors were more than willing to share secrets.

The *Seeadler* had managed to sail through the blockade and, despite being stopped, had managed to skirt the Royal Navy. But by the end of February there were signs of unusual activity in the Atlantic. British and French merchant ships were not making port; some were long overdue. Other ships at sea found debris as would be the case with a surprise torpedo attack from a U-boat. Suspicions rose in the Royal Navy that there might be a merchant raider operating in the shipping lanes. But without confirmation, these suspicions would remain nothing more than speculation.

The German Navy was also operating in the dark, just as their British counterparts were. From the time the *Seeadler* set sail, the Germans had no verification that any of their raiders had been successful in slipping past the blockade—beyond the fact that the British had not crowed about it in the press. Clippings from London newspapers with queries about ships that were late to port were placed in the German Admiralty's files as officers in intelligence tried to piece together whether any of their raiders were operating successfully.

There was one thing that they did believe: as no news surfaced about captured raiders in the North Sea, it seemed their various ruses had worked. They believed it was the work on the docks that had prevented their British counterparts from learning about the *Seeadler* and the other raiders. The truth would not surface until the end of the war—that the British had cracked the wireless codes used by the German Navy. Most of the subterfuge on the docks and in the bogus naming of the ship had been pointless. The fact that the ship and the Navy itself had not sent any messages out via wireless on the ship and its mission is what kept the Royal Navy in the dark.

The covert nature of the raiding mission would continue until someone, anyone, could confirm that German raiders were operating in the Atlantic.

I 3

THE BATTLE WITH

THE *HORNGARTH*

March 5–March 12, 1917

The night of March 5 was clear with a bright moon. Captain von Luckner had the ship's band come up on deck and play for the crew and the prisoners. Most enjoyed the warm evening and the chance to relax. Suddenly, the crow's nest called out that they saw something in the distance, a ship. The prisoners were immediately sent below and the crew of the raider snapped to action, donning their civilian attire.

The ship was clearly visible in the distance against the moonlight: a four-masted sailing ship with the lines of a French-built schooner. Captain von Luckner ordered the *Seeadler* swung to port so that she would move to the dark side of the horizon. This would allow her to remain almost invisible to the other ship, while keeping the other ship in clear light. Carefully, he closed the distance with the other ship, convinced it was an enemy.

Studying the ship for a moment, he opted to try a different tactic with this vessel. He ordered the signalman to send a light signal to the other ship.

The message was aimed at getting their attention and was intentionally vague: Stop Immediately—German Cruiser.

The other ship acknowledged receiving the signal. Then he and the crew heard a sound in the water they had not expected. A boat was being lowered and there was the splashing of oars in the water as a launch drew nearer. In the dark, the *Seeadler* crew could make out a small rowboat approaching their ship.

A voice called from the side of their raider, asking in French for permission to come aboard. At this point von Luckner was unsure of what to make of the situation, but he opted to play along with the ruse. Reaching down, he helped the captain on board. The man identified himself as Captain Charrier of the *Dupleix*.

"What a relief—instead of a Boche cruiser, I find you are an old windjammer like ourselves. Why the joke? Your signal fooled us completely. I suppose you want to tell us something about the war?" This was revealing for von Luckner. It meant that the ship did not have a wireless on board. If she did, she would have the current news of the war. Still playing the role of the merchant sea captain, von Luckner smiled.

"Come aboard. We have lots of news."

Captain Charrier quickly surveyed the deck of the *Seeadler* but could see nothing amiss. "I am a Frenchman," he said politely.

"Fine. How is France doing?" von Luckner queried.

The proud Captain Charrier was quick to respond. "Ah France, she is victorious or will be very soon. *Ravi de vous voir!*" (Delighted to see you.)

Von Luckner offered the fellow captain a drink, captured wine. Charrier was appreciative, slapping his host on the back and thanking him.

"Captain, you are a terrible fellow to have fooled me like that. But now I feel as though a stone has dropped from my heart."

There was little that von Luckner could say at this point. He offered to take his guest down to the saloon and Charrier was quick to agree. They walked down through the bowels of the *Seeadler* where pictures hung on the walls; pictures that were not friendly in the eyes of a Frenchman. Portraits of the kaiser, Hindenburg, von Tirpitz, and a large German naval flag adorned the walls. It took a moment for the image to sink in with Captain Charrier. Finally he turned to his host.

"*Des allemands!*" (Germans)

Von Luckner grinned broadly. "Yes, we are Germans."

"Then we are lost?"

"Yes, you are."

The captain of the *Dupleix* was clearly depressed and shaken.

"Well, Captain, you are not the only one to lose a ship during the war," von Luckner consoled. When von Luckner pressed him, Charrier said that he felt foolish. He had recently been in the port of Valparaiso with several other French vessels. The other captains had told him that before he set sail, he should contact his ship's owners and check with them as to the best course to take. Captain Charrier had ignored their advice and had simply taken off. Now he would have some explaining to do to the owners of the ship, the Société Anonyme des Armateurs Nantais.

Von Luckner asked him which captains he had spoken to in Valparaiso. Simple enough, the *Antonin* and *La Rochefoucauld*. Why? Captain von Luckner signaled to one of his officers who left the saloon. A few minutes later he returned with two men, the captains of the *Antonin* and *La Rochefoucauld*.

"*Eh, tout la France!*" (All of France)

The comrades greeted each other and helped ease some of the embarrassment that Captain Charrier had felt. They too had fallen to the ruse the *Seeadler* had played on them.

The *Dupleix* had been built in 1900 by Ateliers et Chantiers de la Lorie of Saint Nazaire and registered at 2,206 gross registered tons (grt). Lieutenant Pries organized his prize crew and went to the ship to inform the crew that they were now prisoners. The ship had been carrying a load of saltpeter. With their now usual efficiency, the prize crew stripped the ship of anything of value, placed explosives in her hold, and set them off—sending the *Dupleix* to her grave.

Sailors are a superstitious lot. They place a great deal of weight on traditions, even those that seem to lack any logic. Sailing across the equator is one such tradition.

The first time a sailor crossed the equator he was put through a series of hazing rituals. The ship would fly under the flag of King Neptune—usually a hand-painted sheet that had been converted to a flag. One of the crewmen would dress up as Neptune, another would usually put on a dress and become Neptune's wife, Amphitrite.

After a round or two of drinking, the neophytes who had never crossed the equator would be subjected to a number of different rites. None of these were standardized, but all were aimed at initiating the sailors on their first voyage across the mythical line. One of the common highlights of this venture was lathering up the sailor with coal tar and soap and shaving him bald.

The *Seeadler* was not immune to the tradition. Nearly thirty of her crew and many of the prisoners had never sailed across the equator. Schmidt was able to avoid slipping into a dress on this occasion, the role of Amphitrite going to the ship's steward, Smitty. Assisted by the two captain's wives, he made a wig of yarn and a dress to fulfill the role.

Captain von Luckner had ordered a canvas tank and tube to be made on the deck for the formal ceremonies. The young seamen were brought forward and lathered up, then shaven clean by one of the husky crewmembers. They were then tossed into the canvas tank and forced to squirm their way through the long canvas tube— harassed and cajoled the entire time by both the German crew and the prisoners. At the far end, they were greeted with a high pressure hose to clean them off and add to their humiliation. This was indeed a bond that brought all of them together, regardless of nationality.

One of the young prisoners, an English boy, tried to avoid the entire event. He scampered into the rigging. The crewmembers followed him. Just as they were about to catch him, he shot over to a stay and got away. The crew followed. Each time they were about to catch him, the youth managed to dodge their grips, determined to avoid the ritual. In the end, he won out.

After a few hours of this ritual, the *Seeadler* once again got underway. Now she was in the South Atlantic sailing under the Southern Cross at night. Soon, she would face one of her greatest challenges.

In 1914 two great opposing navies equipped themselves with dreadnoughts: the Royal Navy and the German Navy. One had centuries of tradition behind it, along with the attendant pride, prestige, and obligations. The German Navy, on the other hand, was the newcomer. This force was not built on a long history, but it was out to make history.

Up until the spring of 1916, the navies had engaged in several battles but none were large scale engagements. The toughness of the dreadnoughts were demonstrated many times as the battle cruisers, battleships, and heavy cruisers slugged it out in places such as Dogger Bank. But none of the battles were conclusive. There was an apprehension on both sides to commit everything they had in the North Sea to an all-out fight.

That wasn't to say that the Royal Navy's Grand Fleet didn't want to fight. Their admirals had visions of another Trafalgar, where the Royal Navy could once again, in one titanic clash, smash an opposing navy.

Their chance arrived at the end of May 1916. Admiral Reinhardt von Scheer had taken over the German High Seas Fleet and was willing to risk an all out engagement with the vaunted Royal Navy. Sending out a fleet of ships to the Danish coast, he wanted to use them as bait to lure out the Grand Fleet. Then he would sweep in with his other ships.

Admirals Beatty and Jellicoe of the Royal Navy were more than willing to respond. On May 31, 1916, the fleets engaged in a slugfest between giant ships that was later called the Battle of Jutland. Opening shots in the fight were at a range of over fifteen kilometers—unprecedented until the Great War. The German battle cruiser SMS *Von Der Tann* sank after five massive hits. The HMS *Indefatigable* sank with over a thousand crewmen aboard. The HMS *Queen Mary*'s magazine exploded and she went down in less than two minutes' time.

The fleets sent tons of explosive shell into the air every minute of the battle. A single shell could weigh over 850 pounds, some topping off at much more. Naval gun crews would fire, to see if their shots were long or short of the target. The turret officer would adjust the shot and fire again. Once shots had gone over and short of the intended target, their range could be determined. Then salvo after deadly salvo could be poured on the ship—each volley hitting the intended target.

The shots most dreaded were termed plunging shots. These rounds would arc in and punch through the superstructure and deck, ignoring the armored belts at the waterline. Deep in the hull, the huge shells would explode, ripping the bowels of the ship apart.

One of the most dangerous places to be was in the turret of the ships. The ship's massive guns were fed from magazines. Here, the powder, cordite, and shells were moved through the ship like a small rail line. They would be lifted by elevators to the turrets far above and loaded into the cannon. A hit to a turret, if the shell penetrated, would most likely detonate hundreds of pounds of powder instantly—vaporizing the turret crew in a millisecond. The fire would then burn down the elevator shaft, feeding on any powder being hoisted at the time. It would then follow the tunnels through the ship in a white-hot searing flash of death, burning until it found the mother lode—the powder magazines. When these ignited, tons of explosive powder burst upward and outward. A battleship whose magazine exploded could measure its life in seconds.

At the Battle of Dogger Bank earlier in the war, the crew of the SMS *Seydlitz* learned this all too well. She had been hit in one of her turrets. It exploded and burned down, moving to the next turret. That turret then exploded upward and outward. The fast action of a handful of crewmen managed to slam shut a fire trap and cut the lightning-fast wall of flame from reaching the magazine. From that time on, the Germans improved their fire doors so they could attempt to contain such explosions. Still, the risks were real and both navies suffered from catastrophic magazine explosions.

At the Battle of Jutland in May 1916, the German fleet showed the illustrious Royal Navy that it could and would tangle with them head on. The fleets slammed into each other, then recoiled—like two boxers fighting in a prize match. British Admiral Jellicoe was convinced that the Germans were attempting to lure him into a trap with their U-boats. German Admiral Scheer ordered Admiral Hipper and his fleet to turn into the British.

The fleets collided several times, each time breaking off. The German dreadnought SMS *Lutzow* sank and the battle cruisers *Seydlitz* and *Derfflinger* were badly damaged in the fighting. Eventually, Admiral Jellicoe ordered the Grand Fleet to withdraw from the area. Both the Germans and the British were able to claim some degree of victory from the fight; though this was not another Trafalgar. The German Fleet had proven itself in battle, taking the lives of over 6,100 Royal Navy sailors and sinking some of the pride of the fleet. The British had a numerical superiority and had inflicted significant losses on the German Navy—but not enough for them to claim a victory that Nelson would have expected.

The SMS *Kronprinz* was one of the ships involved in the Battle of Jutland. During the fighting, it had fired 144 shots from its twelve-inch cannons, raining tons of explosive metal down on the Royal Navy. From the *Kronprinz*, officers watched as ships like the *Pommern* sank at the hands of the British.

Shells exploded so close to the *Kronprinz* that the ship shook in the water. Somehow she managed to avoid being hit during the fight. The turret crews worked in the dimly lit darkness, hauling up bags of powder, loading the massive guns, and firing. The air was stifling, choking, filled with the stench of cordite that imparted a tangy feeling in the back of the crews' mouths. Despite being in the cold North Sea, the turret was like a furnace when it fired. They stuffed huge wads of cotton into their ears to help protect them when the cannons fired, though it was not much help at all against the deafening roar.

Each shot that missed the *Kronprinz* created a gigantic funnel of water that rose into the air, marking where the enemy shell had missed. Each missed shot meant that somewhere, miles away, aboard a British warship, a turret officer was attempting to straddle the *Kronprinz* with a salvo. A missed shot allowed for that vital correction to trajectory that could spell death.

And each minute they were in battle, the turret crew knew they were at risk of instant death. One shell slamming into their turret would obliterate them: there wouldn't be enough left of them to even think of recovering.

Felix von Luckner was one of the officers in charge of the turret designated "Dora." He watched the fight through a pair of binoculars. For him, it was a test of nerves and courage. The fires of the Battle of Jutland would temper him, train him for fighting his own battles later in the war.

The morning of March 11, 1917 found the *Seeadler* heading south and west with light breezes. A lookout spotted a plume of smoke on the horizon from a steamship that was painted flat black. It had been a while since the raider had tangled with a steamship, but when he saw the Union Jack blowing in the wind, Captain von Luckner knew that he would have to attempt to take her.

Problems were readily apparently at the onset. Von Luckner needed to get her close and intimidate her into a quick surrender. If she bolted and got up enough steam, she would be able to outpace the windjammer, even with her auxiliary engine. He had to get the ship in close. He summoned his officers. They had put together several plans for such an encounter: now was their chance to try them. Von Luckner would attempt to lure the ship in with one of their established ploys. But if that didn't work, they might have to resort to other measures.

From a long distance, still flying the flag of neutral Norway, he ordered the signalmen to run up the flags for a time check: Chronometer Time Please. The message was not even acknowledged by the black steamship. She simply kept on her present course.

The *Seeadler*'s captain hoped the tactic would work, but it hadn't. The plan he wanted to use to lure the ship in closer was to fake a shipboard fire. He was counting on the fact that the British captain might be too stubborn to give the time, but too chivalrous to let a sailing ship on the high seas burn.

He and the crew had worked out the mechanics of the ruse in their idle time. The galley would fire up the smudge pots mounted on the deck. This would bellow a thick black cloud of smoke through the funnel to the deck, covering the deck in a black haze. These smoke-making devices had been attached after the ship had cleared the blockade. They were commonplace in naval warfare and usually used to create smokescreens that other ships could hide behind. In this case, they could be used to attract attention. Additional ingredients were added to the smoke mixture to create a twisting white-burning flame to add to the black columns of smoke. He ordered the crew to fire off two emergency flares as well, adding to the drama of the situation.

If that wasn't enough to get the attention of the steamer's captain, von Luckner called for Schmidt to slip into his Josefeena disguise. Running around the deck, along the rail, Josefeena would help solidify the illusion that this was nothing more than a commercial wind-jammer in distress.

But something changed as von Luckner got a better view of the steamer. He saw two things that disturbed him. First, a wooden shack had been added to the deck of the steamship. It had a looped aerial on top of it: a wireless. The addition of the shack was not out of the norm. When ships added a bulky wireless set, they would add a place to keep it, usually right on the deck.

The second thing he saw was even more unsettling. The steamship was armed. On her foredeck was a cannon—a five-inch deck gun that was larger than his own armaments. The British government had seen fit to arm this merchant in the event of a raider attack.

Seeing the gun and the wireless, he knew he was going to have to intimidate this vessel more than any other. He ordered the majority of his crew to arm themselves with Mauser rifles and the machine gun. They were instructed to keep low, below the rail, unless he needed them. They crawled on the deck into position, well out of view of the steamer.

His crew had created a sound cannon—a section of duct work that was made to look like a cannon. Packed with a small explosive charge, this "boom cannon" did not do any damage; but when it triggered, it created a loud explosion. This was pulled into position below the rail for when he needed it.

There was one other weapon he might need. He armed three crew with megaphones. He arranged a signal with them and gave specific orders as to what they were to do when he signaled them. Each man took to the rigging in each of the *Seeadler*'s masts, their eyes fixed on the helm. His plan was one of pure intimidation, if all else failed.

Returning to the helm, Captain von Luckner stood with the sarcastic Lüdemann. The conversation was quick and to the point.

"Look at that wireless, Lüdemann. And that five-inch gun."

Lüdemann was not intimidated at all. "Knock the wireless over and let's have it out with the gun."

It was time to lure in the prize. He adjusted his merchant seaman's overcoat that covered his naval uniform and waited a moment longer. Then, he triggered the bait.

Thick rolls of black smoke billowed out of the galley funnel and across the deck of the windjammer. Several of the false Norwegian crewmen ran about the deck, apparently in a panic. Joining them, in a bright white dress, Schmidt was dressed as the captain's wife. The magnesium was ignited in the pan a few minutes later, adding to the confusion on deck. First one emergency flare, then another shot up in the morning air. All along the rail, laying and crouched low, German sailors made sure their rifles were loaded and ready.

In the lower decks, the prisoners silently hoped the steamer would somehow get away.

The black steamer swung toward the *Seeadler*. The ploy was working. The captain of the steamship came on the deck with a megaphone in hand and bellowed across at the confused *Seeadler*.

"What in the hell is the matter with you?" a British voice demanded.

The time had come. Captain von Luckner called out to his crew. "Clear the deck for action!" The Norwegian flag on the hull was covered with tarp. A German flag went up the mast. The men posing as civilians on deck stripped off their civilian attire and stood, wearing the brilliant white of the German Navy.

Perhaps the most stunning image was that of the large-footed Schmidt, pulling the dress down over his narrow frame and tossing his wig off, revealing a lean German sailor.

At von Luckner's signal the mock cannon was brought to the rail and ignited. The tube erupted with a large bellow of sound that shook the air between the two vessels. For a moment, it seemed to stun everyone on the steamer's deck, except her grizzled captain. He refused to give his ground. Still holding the megaphone, he called out to his engine room for full steam. He then bellowed the words that showed his resolve.

"Clear for action!"

He intended to slug it out with the windjammer.

The forward railing dropped near the *Seeadler*'s 4.2-inch gun. Von Luckner called out to Lieutenant Kircheiß and his crew to target the wireless shack first. He was worried that the steamship might transmit their position and plight and bring the might of the Royal Navy down on his ship. The gun slowly and methodically targeted the small wooden shack, then fired.

The wireless shack on the black ship exploded in thousands of splinters. The wireless mast dropped in the blast. The steamer would not be sending any messages, but she was far from out of the fight. The ship started to swing away and the captain called out for his gun crew.

Captain von Luckner took no chances. He signaled the crewmen huddled below the rail. They rose at once to their captain's beckon. His orders were clear: Keep the steamer's gun crew from reaching their weapon. The threat that the 5-inch cannon posed was deadly real. They began to pour fire at the enemy ship, including several short bursts from the machine gun, rattling the metallic superstructure. The metallic pings and twangs of ricochets reverberated in the air.

Using his own hand-held megaphone, von Luckner called over to his fellow captain. "Lay to or I will sink you!"

The captain of the British ship was not intimidated in the least. His voice carried back to the *Seeadler* loud and clear.

"Gun crew to their posts. You scalawags, gun crew to your posts I say."

But the staccato of rifle fire kept the men pinned down some distance from the 5-inch cannon. None of them was willing to risk a burst of machine gun fire to reach the exposed cannon.

The ship refused to surrender. The standoff continued, with Lüdemann at the helm of the *Seeadler*, concentrating on keeping the raider close to the steamship. Von Luckner signaled the gun crew and ordered them to fire again at the enemy ship. The shot punched through the deck of the ship and exploded deeply within the hold. White steam rose up, indicating that either a boiler or a steam pipe had been hit in the blast.

Still, the steamship captain urged his gun crew to rush to their weapon. With one well-placed shot on his part he could end the stalemate with the destruction of the thin-hulled windjammer.

Von Luckner knew that time was running out. He looked up to his masts and made eye contact with the men he had positioned there. Once he was sure they were watching him, he gave the signal.

In unison, the three men in the masts with the megaphones all yelled out in clear English.

"Torpedoes clear!"

Torpedoes. One of the most menacing weapons to emerge in the First World War, these weapons had a reputation with ship's masters. One hit meant hundreds of pounds of guncotton, explosions, and almost instant death and sinking. They were legitimate weapons of war—but at the same time, the mention of them made them a weapon of terror.

"For God's sake," screamed the steamship captain. "Not torpedoes!" A white flag broke out, then another, then a shirt, then a handkerchief. Suddenly anything white at all that could be waved was in the air.

It appeared for a moment that the matter was over with, but the steamship suddenly broke into a long turn as if she were making a break to get away. The drastic change of course confused von Luckner. Perhaps the ship was going to make a run for it after all. He ordered the gun crew to fire another shot into the black ship. They complied with a shell that plowed into the deck under a lifeboat, blasting the small craft into thousands of shards. Four of the ship's crew were struck and wounded in the blast and a hole was left gaping on the deck where the lifeboat had been.

The steamer continued her arc and turn—and it was then that von Luckner realized the ship was not making a break for freedom. She was out of control. She cut her steam and slowed and the *Seeadler* pulled up alongside, watching as her crew still waved their ad hoc flags of surrender. Lieutenant Pries and his prize crew were ordered to take one of the launches and head over.

The launch reached the ship and von Luckner watched his crew board. They were there only a few minutes when Pries came back. He wasn't alone. He brought with him the captain of the other ship, and something else—the limp form of a young boy covered in blood.

The boy was carried on board and the situation looked grim. He had been in the wireless shack when the *Seeadler* had opened fire on it. His face was torn from shrapnel—either from the shell or the exploding shack itself. The boy's eyes were both badly damaged; even if he lived, his eyesight was going to be questionable. The back of his head was a soaked mass of hair and blood.

The captain, Ivor Stainthorp, quickly introduced himself to von Luckner. He told him the boy was Richard Douglas Page.

Von Luckner acted quickly. He called for Doctor Pietsch. He examined the boy and said he needed to work on him, immediately. They carried the young Mr. Page down to the saloon. There the dinner table was wiped clean for surgery. The boy was laid out and Doctor Pietsch began the arduous task of attempting to save his life.

Captain von Luckner called down Captain Neilson of the *British Yeoman*. He wanted Neilson and Captain Stainthorp present during the operation with him, to ensure that he was doing everything he could to save the boy's life. Captain Stainthorp told his captor that Richard Page was only sixteen years old.

On deck, First Officer Kling and Lieutenant Pries completed the necessary prisoner transfer from the ship. The steamer was the *Horngarth*. Built in 1911 she weighed in at 3,609 gross registered tons and was owned by Horngarth Steam Ship Company out of Britain. They learned she was a well-outfitted vessel, with a wide complement of musical instruments, including a Steinway piano that was carefully winched aboard the *Seeadler*.

Per her official bills of lading, the *Horngarth* carried tons of grain and corn. That was the official story. In her hold also held cargo that was even more precious for the sailors: 2,300 cases of Veuve Clicquot champagne and 500 cases of cognac. Ample amounts of the cargo, as much as practical, were transferred over to the *Seeadler*. The arrival of such a booty should have been reason for happiness, but that was not the disposition of the crew or the prisoners. The injured young boy had soured any thoughts of celebration.

There was no celebration with this capture, no band playing. Gone was the humor that had been tied to so many of the other captures. In all of her cruise, the crew had never taken a life. Now a young boy was near death because of their handiwork. Captain von Luckner had made it clear that he wanted to fight the war honorably, that he didn't want to be responsible for taking the life of another.

The *Horngarth*'s seacocks were opened and a bomb was placed in her hull. She slid to her watery grave that night. Captain Stainthorp and von Luckner talked while they watched over the young boy. Stainthorp learned the truth, that the *Seeadler* didn't have any torpedoes. The fake fire on the deck was simply a ploy to lure him in.

At 0200 on March 12, Richard Page's battle for life ended. Doctor Pietsch and the captains had been with him through the night.

At 1100 on March 12, the crew and prisoners were assembled on the poop deck of the *Seeadler* for a solemn ceremony. The body of Richard Douglas Page was on a small table, draped in a Union Jack flag. The crew of the *Seeadler*, in full white uniforms, stood rigidly at attention on one side of the body. Their hats were removed in tribute to a fallen sailor. On the other side stood a much larger gathering—the prisoners captured by the raider. The body lay between them. At the foot of the body was a small table covered in white cloth. It had two candles on it and a Bible. The flag flying on the ship was not the Norwegian flag; the German naval flag flew, lowered ceremoniously to half-mast.

Von Luckner was shaken by the death. "In life this boy was my enemy. In death he is a brother," he said to those who were gathered on the deck.

He recited the Lord's Prayer, joined by the crew, in German. Giving a nod to his men, an honor guard moved forward. They lifted the boy's body and carried it to the rail. The count spoke a few words softly in German, and those words have been lost to all time.

The boy was lowered into the sea. The ship's band sounded taps. The two captain's wives aboard the *Seeadler* could no longer hold back and burst into tears.

14

March 13–April 1, 1917

The *Seeadler* had become a crowded place. With 207 prisoners and several pigs, dogs, and chickens, it was nearing its capacity. Just provisioning this many prisoners, plus the crew, was beginning to turn into a logistical nightmare. Eating had to be done in shifts, given the numbers of people involved. It was becoming more and more necessary for the raider to capture new ships for food and water.

Other raiders put a prize crew on a captured ship, and that prize crew would sail the ship to a neutral port to discharge the prisoners. The *Seeadler* had problems with this tactic, however. Her crew was very small, and even for a short time, Captain von Luckner could not do with a portion of his crew gone—for days if not longer. This meant the raider had to come up with another solution for its burgeoning prisoner population.

After the capture of the *Horngarth*, von Luckner ordered the ship to steer to the south. The hunting grounds near the equator had proven profitable. But he knew that staying in the same area presented some risks if word of his ship got out. The Danish ship *Viking* would soon make port; when she did, the Royal Navy would know the vicinity of his recent raiding and how to identify his vessel. Best not to stay in that area but move further south.

On March 21, the lookouts spotted sails in the distance. The ship had four masts and was flying the French flag. Turning back to the tactics that had worked so well for him, von Luckner ordered the *Seeadler* to intercept the ship. When he got close to the vessel, he covered the Norwegian flag on the hull and ran the German ensign up. Once more, the deck railing slammed down to reveal the 4.2-inch gun, trained on the French ship. The crew had suddenly turned into German sailors. Their range closed to 2,000 yards and the men were only visible from telescopes.

As if to emphasize the point, signal flags ran up with a message: Stop or I Shall Fire. The ship dropped its flag in submission and dropped its sails.

The ship was the *Cambronne*, a fairly large barque weighing in at 1,863 gross registered tons. Her destination was Rio. This time the captain gave Lieutenant Pries and the prize crew different instructions. They were to inspect the ship for use by the *Seeadler's* prisoners. Nothing was to be said to anyone until von Luckner got a report.

The captain of the *Cambronne* came back with Pries. The lieutenant indicated that the ship had ample space aboard for the prisoners and could sustain the water and food they would need. The French captain pressed von Luckner as to what was going to become of his ship. He seemed quite convinced that the raider was going to sink her.

"No, we're not going to sink your ship. She will go right on to port. She will take our prisoners."

For the first time, a captain brought aboard the deck of the *Seeadler* was relieved. That relief was short-lived, however. Captain von Luckner made it clear that he would not be captaining his own vessel back to Rio. It would be a captain of his own choosing. There was protest, but von Luckner had his own reasons. This new captain was an unknown quantity to him. He wanted someone else, someone from this Captain's Club who he could trust.

The Danish ship *Viking* made port in Copenhagen. She had an interesting story to tell—the story of a German raider operating in the Atlantic and posing as a Norwegian ship. This was no ordinary merchant. She was a windjammer, but one with two large naval cannon hidden on her bow. They even had a name: the *Hero*.

The word spread through the docks and eventually the British consul met with the captain of the *Viking*. Their information was a month old, but the *Viking* did have the location where she had been boarded and inspected north of the equator. There was no reason to think the raider was not still in the same area. With U-boats operating in the ocean it was also entirely possible that ships late to port had met a similar fate.

The British Admiralty checked its records of a ship called *Hero*. Slowly and methodically, they pieced the information together and realized they had been duped the previous Christmas. But now the Royal Navy would have a chance to seek its revenge, by posting warnings for merchant ships with wireless sets and in ports all along the Atlantic.

Taking the captain of the *Cambronne* with him, von Luckner went to meet with the members of the Captain's Club, to discuss his plans for releasing them and their prisoners. Lines became drawn along nationalities. The *Cambronne* was a French-registered ship. The French captains insisted that it be captained by a Frenchman. As a raider that struck at many nationalities, the argument was lost on von Luckner.

There was one captain he trusted more than the others: James Mullen of the *Pinmore*. Mullen had honored his agreement to the letter with von Luckner regarding security. He had turned Captain La Coq in for making plans of the *Seeadler*, and von Luckner knew he could trust Mullen once they were cast aside.

Von Luckner made it clear to the captains of his "club" that they were to be trusted on their word not to reveal anything regarding the *Seeadler*. The *Cambronne* was to proceed to port directly, without engaging in contact with other ships in the Atlantic. The captains all agreed. Captain Mullen was singled out for further promise. If the *Cambronne* came across a ship with a wireless, they were not to contact them. Von Luckner was quite frank with Mullen. He wanted time.

Both men knew that as soon as the *Cambronne* made port, the secret of the *Seeadler* would be out. The Royal Navy would come after them with everything they had, as would the French. Their disguise as a Norwegian windjammer that had worked so successfully would be almost worthless.

Every day that the *Cambronne* was at sea was another day the *Seeadler* could get further away. He didn't tell Mullen where he was headed, but he made it clear that he was going to put some distance between the trade route he had been raiding. Von Luckner ordered his carpenter Gustav "Chips" Dreyer to join the prize crew aboard the *Cambronne* with orders to saw off the upper masts of the ship. She could still make sail, albeit slowly.

The *Cambronne* was carrying eighty tons of saltpeter. A crew of prisoners working with the French crew of the *Cambronne* hoisted out the munitions material and dumped it into the ocean.

There was another point that von Luckner pressed. The ship was to be captained by a British captain, and she was entitled to fly the Union Jack. The French captains again launched a protest, but von Luckner did not waver on this point. It was a minor issue, but it was clear that Captain von Luckner was taking one well-placed shot at the Frenchmen before they left. He had his reasons for distrusting the French—and they could be summed up in the name La Coq.

This was a subject the members of the Captain's Club still pressed with von Luckner. Von Luckner was the most agitated. When La Coq had come on board, he tried to hide the fact that there were British cruisers in the area. He had violated their agreement and mapped the lower decks the *Seeadler*. In von Luckner's eyes, he was a man who could not be trusted.

The members of the Captain's Club argued differently. The risks, they pointed out, were minimal at best. Even if La Coq spoke to authorities about what he knew, the chances of that information being of practical use to a warship would be limited. After all, if the *Seeadler* should face a warship, wouldn't the odds of survival be slim anyway?

After considerable debate he relented. There would be stern conditions though. Captain La Coq would have to sign a document to promise he would not reveal what he knew about the *Seeadler*. If he did, von Luckner assured the Captain's Club members that he would release the document and it would be enough to paint La Coq as a spy. The cantankerous French captain was relieved that he would be leaving with the other prisoners and agreed to sign anything.

All of the members of the Captain's Club had to agree that for the duration of the war they would not haul war matériel or assist those fighting the Germans. It was a word of honor that all of them agreed to. Their only real risk was if the *Seeadler* got away, if their promise was made public, and if they got caught again by the Germans. It was an easy promise for them to make.

Provisions were transferred to the *Cambronne* while Chips went about sawing the masts. The trip to Rio would take approximately ten days. Von Luckner made sure that there were thirty days' worth of food and water, if rationed. The prisoners were informed that they would be departing and they should gather their belongings. The captured sailors came up onto the deck of the *Seeadler* and were paid their wages while aboard the raider in German marks and British pounds. A typical payment was 150 marks; a handful of the men refused to take their pay, out of honor. The payment had the overall effect of raising morale among the prisoners: they were commercial seamen heading to port with cash in their pockets.

The *Seeadler* hosted a final dinner with everyone aboard the ship. Using champagne from the *Horngarth*, the captives made a toast to the *Seeadler* and her crew; the Germans toasted their prisoners and wished them a safe voyage. The motor launches made several trips to shuttle the prisoners and their belongings over to the *Cambronne*. Most of the *Seeadler* crew were on the deck, saying their goodbyes, passing on letters to be mailed back home to let their loved ones know they were alive and well. One crewmember who was not on the deck was their wireless operator. His job was a monotonous one. He did not send messages but listened to them day-in and day-out.

A flurry of messages came across the wireless set about the *Hero*. The wireless operator, nicknamed "Sparks," furiously noted the messages. There were references to the *Viking*, and to a raider. He called for the captain and relayed the information.

The word was out.

Von Luckner did not panic but insisted that the process of transferring the prisoners be sped up. Once the prisoners were all transferred, both crews lined the deck and waved to each other. The *Cambronne*'s crew, now free, gave three cheers to the *Seeadler* crew.

The *Seeadler* sailed west while the *Cambronne* sailed east. Von Luckner waited until he could no longer see the prisoner's ship. Then, he turned due south. It was time to make a break for Cape Horn and the Pacific. Now that the Allies had transmitted warnings far and wide, the Atlantic would no longer be a safe place.

✠ ✠ ✠

Captain Mullen was as good as his word. The *Cambronne* reached Rio on March 30, 1917. It was a shocking sight, a barque loaded with over three hundred souls. Once they arrived in port, a flurry of interviews began. The French and British consuls sent interviewers to meet with the captains and crews and their story unfolded—albeit slowly, given the sheer number of interrogations. The neutral Americans questioned the former prisoners as well, but they mostly relied on information from the French and British.

Their story corroborated that of the *Viking* with more exacting details. The outside world knew the raider's true name, *Seeadler*, for the first time. The intelligence about her armaments, hopelessly distorted by the misinformation campaign that the German crew had waged, were known, right down to the torpedoes that didn't exist. The stories from the prisoners and the captains were contradictory, complicated by the wide range of languages and nationalities involved. Von Luckner and his crew couldn't have hoped for anything better.

Telegrams arrived at Atlantic ports warning about a raiding windjammer posing as a Norwegian merchant. Wireless messages went out, mostly to newspapers, about the sensational story that was unfolding. The Germans had the audacity to sneak through the British blockade of the North Sea with an armed sailing ship. And whereas a successful German U-boat mission might sink a single ship each time out, the *Seeadler* was responsible for eleven sinkings in four months.

The London *Times* and the *Washington Times* printed the story within two days of their arrival. When ships arrived in ports all along the Atlantic, they heard of the mysterious raider. Some of these ships added to the muddled intelligence picture. The U.S. Navy Intelligence Files in the U.S. National Archives indicate that the U.S. Navy thought it would be difficult to track the *Seeadler*. Ships that picked up the warnings from wireless or from other ships told sordid stories of being boarded by a mysterious windjammer armed with four cannon and multiple torpedo tubes. The stories in the archive files have the *Seeadler* placed on the coast of Africa and the coast of South America within a day of each sighting. One story from a ship named

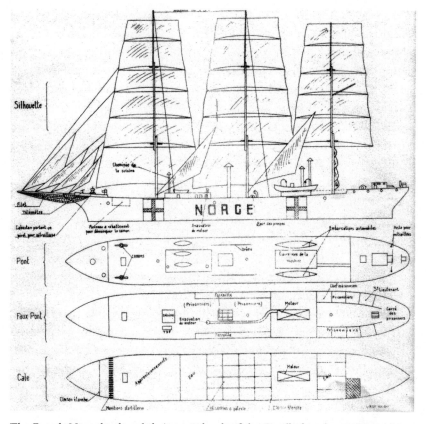

The French Navy developed their own sketch of the *Seeadler* based on prisoner interviews. *Source: U.S. National Archives.*

the *Orleans* went so far as to name members of the *Seeadler*'s boarding parties by name. It had become a matter of celebrity to have been part of the *Seeadler*'s cruise. This particular story was provided in such detail that the American Navy sent out warnings to merchant ships, complete with the erroneous details as to the torpedo tubes the ship was allegedly fitted with on her hull.

If the neutral Americans' intelligence reports were confusing, the same could be assumed of the British and French governments. The

French Navy received word that the steamer *Medina* had been followed by "an enemy sailing ship" that was automatically assumed to be the *Seeadler*, when in reality it was most likely nothing more than an innocent merchant. The French shared their intelligence interview information with the Americans and the British, but there was no coordinated effort to attempt to locate and capture the raider.

The Royal Navy seemed to have the best understanding of the ship and where it was heading. They knew that Captain von Luckner would have to make a break for new waters once the *Cambronne* made port, and that he had only two choices. The first was to navigate the difficult waters around Cape Horn and move into the Pacific. The other was to go around Africa and into the Indian Ocean.

The German Admiralstab often referred to the Indian Ocean as "a British lake"—due to the extensive Royal Navy presence, the lack of friendly or neutral ports, and the numerous English colonies along the coast. It would be rich hunting grounds, but the chances of surviving for any period of time were limited for a ship like the *Seeadler*.

The only alternative was Cape Horn. It was a dangerous trip, even for a raider equipped with an auxiliary engine. But it would also take the ship into the safer waters of the Pacific where it could still terrorize British interests.

When everything was considered, the Royal Navy understood von Luckner. The prisoners had last seen the raider sailing west, but the intelligence experts knew they were dealing with a captain who used deception to his advantage. They knew he would risk sailing around Cape Horn. Yes he had a lead on them—but by a few days at best.

The Royal Navy mobilized. The *Lancaster* and *Otranto* were at San Nicolas, Peru. The *Avoea* was in British Columbia, too far away to do much more than cover the patrol routes of the other ships. The *Orbita* was at Mejillones. On April 1, 1917 the British admiralty transmitted wireless messages with specific orders for the *Lancaster*, *Otranto*, and *Orbita* to move south, patrol Cape Horn, and intercept the *Seeadler*.

Another government got its first confirmation about the presence of a windjamming raider in the Atlantic—Germany. Since she had set sail before Christmas, the German Admiralty was as much in the dark as the Royal Navy about the *Seeadler*. From records in the Admiral-stab, it is obvious that the arrival of the *Cambronne* launched a series of telegraph and wireless messages seeking information about their ship. Embassies and consulates were contacted and asked to check with port facilities to see what information could be obtained. Agents in London and Copenhagen clipped newspaper articles on the ship and sent them back to Germany for review. Oddly enough, the German Navy seemed more in the dark about their raider than its enemies.

Articles ran in a variety of newspapers in Germany regarding the *Seeadler*. For the families of the crew, this was the first time they had received news about the ship. Her successes had to have resonated well with worried loved ones. More importantly, the Admiralty played up the exploits of the daring captain and crew, crafting them

RAIDER.

Rough Sketch made by a Master of a captured Ship.

A circular prepared by the U.S. Navy to warn ship's captains to be on the lookout for the *Seeadler*.

into a propaganda coup. There was something to be said about the daring and audacity of taking a sailing ship up against the might of the Royal Navy, and it was a story that buoyed hopes for a German victory.

There were differences between the two navies, British and German, in regard to the *Seeadler*. The Royal Navy mobilized its assets and moved to block the raider. But there was nothing that the German Navy could do but wait and monitor its foe to see what the British would learn about their own ship.

15

April 2–April 11, 1917

In 1914, nearly three years before the *Seeadler*'s cruise, Germany's Vice Admiral Count Maximilian von Spee was a man with a massive problem. When the first sparks began to presage the Great War, he was in command of a squadron of ships located in the Pacific. His ships were isolated, half a world away from the rest of the German Navy. The reach of the German empire was not like that of the British. The coaling stations, vital for keeping a fleet mobile, simply didn't exist for von Spee's tiny fleet. The British naval presence in the Pacific and Indian Oceans was substantial, with ports to repair, rearm, and recoal. What he had was a tiny foothold on the Yellow Sea, a lone German colony. Admiral von Spee's ships were huddled in Tsingtao harbor, if war broke out. If the Japanese joined the war against Germany, the small colony port was almost certain to fall quickly.

Von Spee knew that his men's long-term survival depended on getting back to the rest of the German fleet. At the same time, he was deeply compelled to wreak as much havoc as he could on the British when hostilities erupted.

His first action was to set sail across the Pacific on an extended cruise. On this trip, he detached the cruiser *Emden* to head to the Indian Ocean as a threat to the British Navy and commercial shipping there. The *Emden*'s cruise and her crew's story of survival became the stuff of legend in the young German Navy. With the formal breakout of the war, he was in the middle of the Pacific, commanding a squadron of ships that included the *Scharnhorst* and *Gneisenau* and a handful of light cruisers and support vessels.

The declaration of war put Admiral von Spee in a difficult position. His standing orders were to engage the enemy fleet, but he was operating in the isolated waters of the Pacific. He was best suited to threaten commercial shipping, though the composition of his squadron was not geared for commercial raiding operations. Worse yet, some of the ports he went to for supplies turned him away—fearing repercussions if his ships were spotted in port by the British.

He hoped to make it to Chile. Neutral Chile would be a place where he could find some respite. As he approached the South American coast near Coronel, he came across a squadron of the British Navy. He did not hesitate to engage them, pummeling the vessels at long range. The *Otranto*, a commercial ship turned into an armed merchant cruiser with hastily mounted deck cannons, was among them. The battle was fast and furious, and when it was done, the German ships prevailed. A handful of ships, including the *Otranto*, managed to escape, but most were badly damaged or sunk. Word of von Spee's victory spread and he became one of the first popular heroes of the German Navy.

His ships had traveled across the Pacific and managed to avoid problems with their engines, the heat, the lack of supplies, and dry-dock. They engaged the enemy and were victorious. Realistically, however, the British forces he faced were not the epitome of the Royal Navy but the second-string.

Moving down the coast, he swung around Cape Horn and into the South Atlantic. On December 7, 1914 Admiral von Spee intended to strike at the small British outpost in the Falkland Islands. He did not know that the British Navy had made port there. Von Spee hoped to arrive at Port Stanley, shell the wireless outpost there, and depart. It was to be a short raid. Von Spee had even arranged to send a party to the islands for a picnic.

At 0200 the *Scharnhorst* arrived to a dark and cloud-shrouded island with no idea that a British squadron lay on the other side of the tiny bump in the water. At 0530 they could make out what appeared to be columns of smoke rising into the air. The Admiral assumed that the locals were burning off their coal reserves rather than let them fall into the Germans' hands. In reality, it was the fleet firing up its engines for battle.

A small party of British sailors on the island helped align and co-ordinate the first salvo from the British ship *Canopus*. Columns of water shot 150 feet into the air alongside the *Gneisenau*. Through the early morning light, Admiral von Spee could make out the ships he was facing. It must have been a disturbing realization—that the odds were against him. The British ships, like the *Canopus* and *Invincible*, could fire 12-inch rounds weighing 850 pounds. The *Scharnhorst* and *Gneisenau*, the best ships of his squadron, mounted only 8.2-inch guns with 275-pound shells that seemed puny next to those of the British. They also had significantly greater range on him. This would allow the Royal Navy to do what he had done at Coronel, to close with him and fire at ranges where he could not return fire.

Von Spee was no fool. He turned away and broke for the open sea. The British commander, Vice Admiral Frederick Sturdee, realized what was happening and ordered his flagship, the *Invincible*, to pursue the Germans. The flag signal sent up made it clear to the British that the blemish of Coronel was to be erased and gave the order for a general chase to the squadron.

The Germans hoped that a weather front might roll in, enabling them to escape. But as the morning fog burned off, they realized that their hopes were lost. As the British closed with the fleeing Germans, at 13,000 yards, they were able to acquire the *Leipzig* at the rear of the German line. She was straddled and the *Invincible* poured shots into the ship, turning her deck into scrap metal.

Admiral von Spee had one more trick he could try: survival. He ordered his squadron to split up into two forces. What he didn't know is that the British had already anticipated this maneuver and had plans for dealing with it. They too split their forces, sending their auxiliary cruisers after the light cruisers while the heavier ships dealt with the *Scharnhorst* and *Gneisenau*.

The chase went on for another two-and-a-half hours. In the middle of the pursuit, a three-masted sailing ship appeared, running with full canvas. She was flying the Norwegian flag and cut between the two fleets. For a moment, all of the sailors drank in this relic of another age—then they resumed their fighting.

The *Gneisenau* accepted battle with the British and was pummeled at long ranges, but she still hung in the fight. Von Spee's ship, the *Scharnhorst*, was hit by over forty shells. Her deck and superstructure were a shambles of twisted metal, yet von Spee would not allow his flag to be taken down. There was a standing order in the German Navy to not allow their ships to be taken. At 1617 hours, the ship slid into the icy cold waters of the South Atlantic, taking Admiral von Spee with her.

Aboard the *Gneisenau*, Captain Maerker decided at 1740 to honor the orders of the Admiralstab. Her captain ordered the ship scuttled. At 1800, the last battle cruiser of the Asia Pacific Squadron slid into the sea. While the hunting of the light cruisers took a little longer, with the sinking of the *Gneisenau*, what became known as the Battle of the Falkland Islands came to a chilly end.

Admiral von Spee was a hero in the eyes of the officers and men of the German Navy. He had not shirked from battle. The odds were against him. But rather than cower, he dared to take the fight to the British. He died in the end, but his death was seen as glorious. The relatively young German Navy needed heroes and von Spee was among the first.

Just over two years later, the *Seeadler* was pouring on every bit of sail she could and heading south toward the Falklands. The ship had several days' headway while the *Cambronne* made her way to Rio—but they knew that lead would be diminished. Not long after the former prisoners arrived in port, the wireless messages warning ships about the German raider went out. For the crew of the *Seeadler*, it had to be a sobering moment as they realized that the risks for them were as great as when they ran the blockade.

Captain von Luckner took action. First, he ordered that the name of the ship be changed. He chose *Irma*, the name of his fiancé—a name that had been rejected earlier in the cruise. Also gone were the Norwegian flag and the word "Norge" along the sides of the ship. A full physical description of the *Seeadler* would be given by her former prisoners and then sent out—and the captain wanted to alter his ship and hopefully confuse his foes.

Rounding Cape Horn was not going to be an easy task—and now that word of their escapades was out, a sense of urgency must have overcome the crew. The engine crew had little to do when the engine was not in use during the run south. Von Luckner came up with a task to keep them busy and asked them to create a traditional German Iron Cross using a piece of scrap steel. When the ship passed the Falklands, von Luckner intended to honor the German dead there.

The weather fought the *Seeadler* as well. The storm season made travel tricky and treacherous as the ship sailed south, forcing constant changes to the sails and the course to make the passage difficult. Each mile south took them into colder climates and grayer skies. On April 4 the winds changed direction, forcing the ship to head east by northeast, costing them precious miles and time. The next day it changed again, and once more the *Seeadler* was able to head south toward the Cape.

The crew belowdecks was given tasks to keep their minds off the risks they were facing. Von Luckner had them take the life preservers and spare lifeboats captured during her raid, strip off the paint from the previous ships, and repaint them with the ship's true name, *Seeadler*. The reason was simple: von Luckner planned a ruse at some point. If he had the chance, he planned to jettison the spare gear. With any luck, the British might think that the *Seeadler* had been sunk or abandoned. For now, they were held at the ready.

First Officer Kling was given the task of plotting a route so the *Seeadler* would pass close to where the Battle for the Falklands Islands took place. The ship reached that location on April 11. For a few minutes, von Luckner paid tribute to the men who lost their lives in the battle. He ordered the crew onto the deck for a ceremony to honor their fallen comrades.

"Glorious fallen comrades, we bring you a message from home. Your comrades have kept their promise to your commander. On sea and on land they are fighting for the Fatherland. We of the *Seeadler* salute you and solemnly swear that we, too, will endeavor to live and die as gloriously as you. We too are hunted on the sea, even as you were. So perhaps it will not be long before we join you down there in Davy Jones's Locker. If we do, our one hope is that we will be able to fight our last fight as gallantly as you."

The mechanics brought out the steel cross they had created during their flight. Von Luckner led the crew in a short prayer and ordered the cross dropped into the water. After a few moments of solemn silence, the crew returned to their duties.

Ahead lay the perils of Cape Horn and the deadly intentions of the Royal Navy.

A photo of Count Felix von Luckner, circa 1930, from his file at the Office of Strategic Services.

U.S. National Archives.

"Old Peter," Count von Luckner's mentor, who helped him take to the sea at the age of thirteen.

Reprinted by permission from The Sea Devil *by Lowell Thomas.*

A photo of von Luckner from the time between his participation in the Battle of Jutland and his commission as captain of the *Seeadler*.

Author's private collection.

The *Pass of Balmaha* shortly after her internment by the German Navy, still laden with cotton.

Reprinted by permission from The Sea Devil *by Lowell Thomas.*

The *Seedler,* officially known as the *Hero* for security reasons, fully loaded with provisions.
Archives of the Deutsches Schiffahrtsmuseum, Bremerhaven, Germany.

The German Navy often took photos of the crew before a ship left port, and released this previously unpublished photo as a postcard in 1918.
Author's private collection.

The *Pass of Balmaha* during her refit and conversion into the *Seeadler.* The false name *Hero* can be made out on the stern. Since she rides high in the water, she was evidently not yet provisioned.
Archives of the Deutsches Schiffahrtsmuseum, Bremerhaven Germany.

The fake Norwegian sailors of the *Hero* pose on the deck.
Reprinted by permission from The Sea Devil *by Lowell Thomas.*

A promotional card of the *Seeadler* under full sail. Von Luckner gave these out at his tours and lectures after the war, often autographing them as in this case.
Author's private collection.

The *Seeadler*'s full complement in dress whites prior to her mission.
Archives New Zealand/ Te Rua Mahara o Te Kāwantanga.

The *Seeadler* crew in everyday German naval uniforms standing on the *Hero*'s false cargo of Norwegian lumber.
From Unter Graf Luckner als Obermatrose *by Heinrich Hins.*

Captain von Luckner and crewmember Hugo Schmidt dressed as the Norwegian Captain's wife "Josefeena."
Reprinted by permission from The Sea Devil *by Lowell Thomas.*

Hugo Schmidt as "Josefeena" in a previously unpublished photograph.
National Archives of the United Kingdom.

These two photographs, taken from the *Seeadler*, show the *Gladys Royale* as she was captured and as she was sunk.

Reprinted by permission from The Sea Devil *by Lowell Thomas.*

The French ship *Antonin*.
Reprinted by permission from The Sea Devil *by Lowell Thomas.*

The *Charles Gounod* sinks by the bow, as seen from the *Seeadler*.
Reprinted by permission from The Sea Devil *by Lowell Thomas.*

An archive file photo of the *British Yeoman* prior to her capture by the *Seeadler*.
Reprinted by permission of the Mariner's Museum, Newport News, Virginia.

The *Seeadler*'s band, posing with champagne pillaged from the
Horngarth. This is the only known photograph of the interior of
the *Seeadler*, presumably the forecastle.
Author's private collection.

The cargo ship *Buenos Aires*, captured and sunk by the *Seeadler*.
Reprinted by permission of the Mariner's Museum, Newport News, Virginia.

Seeadler crew and prisoners celebrate passage of the equator with King Neptune. Lieutenant Richard Pries, in uniform, stands on the right with a pith helmet.
From Unter Graf Luckner als Obermatrose *by Heinrich Hins.*

A photograph taken by the *Seeadler* crew and recovered from Mopelia island, most likely the French ship *La Rochefoucauld*.
Archives New Zealand / Te Rua Mahara o Te Kāwantanga.

The American merchant ship *Manilla* as it was captured under gunpoint by the raider.
Archives New Zealand / Te Rua Mahara o Te Kāwantanga.

The *Seeadler* anchored at Mopelia island before the disaster.
Archives New Zealand / Te Rua Mahara o Te Kāwantanga.

Hull cleaning operations at Mopelia just prior to the wrecking on the reef.

Archives New Zealand/Te Rua Mahara o Te Kāwantanga.

The horrific damage to the *Seeadler* in a photo taken on a mission by the U.S. Governor of Samoa to confirm that the German raider was indeed destroyed.

U.S. National Archives.

A photo of the port gun from the U.S. Governor's mission. The railing that concealed the gun has burned away.

U.S. National Archives.

This image shows the damage from the fire on the *Seeadler* and deliberate sabotage of the starboard gun. The breech is badly damaged and there are signs of damage on the barrel of the weapon itself.

U.S. National Archives.

The crew of the *Seeadler* poses with the locals on Mopelia after the departure of Captain von Luckner.

Archives New Zealand / Te Rua Mahara o Te Kāwantanga.

"Seeadlerdorf" from the lagoon at Mopelia island where the castaways made their home.

Archives New Zealand / Te Rua Mahara o Te Kāwantanga Wellington Office.

The *Kronprinzessin Cecilie* on trial runs in the lagoon at Mopelia before her departure across the Pacific.

Archives New Zealand / Te Rua Mahara o Te Kāwantanga.

Captain von Luckner (middle) and the rest of the crew of the *Kronprinzessin Cecilie* after being captured the first time.

Archives New Zealand/Te Rua Mahara o Te Kāwantanga.

The motor launch *Pearl* used by Count von Luckner and a handful of prisoners to escape from their New Zealand prison camp.

Reprinted by permission from The Sea Devil *by Lowell Thomas.*

After capture, the count was transferred from the *Moa* to the *Iris*.

Royal New Zealand Navy Museum, Devonport.

Adventure's end. Aboard the *Moa*, Count von Luckner was searched at bayonet point.

Royal New Zealand Navy Museum, Devonport.

The *Moa,* moored alongside the *Iris,* returns to Auckland with her infamous prisoners.

Royal New Zealand Navy Museum, Devonport.

Alfred Kling, former first officer of the *Seeadler,* after the Great War in promotional material to advertise a cruise ship also called the *Seeadler.*

Author's private collection.

Kapitän Alfred Kling
Kapitän des Polarschiffes „Deutschland" während der großen Südpolfahrt 1911/13 Begründer und einer der Kommandanten des „Seeadler"-Unternehmens im Weltkriege, übernimmt die Führung der vier Fahrten auf dem modernen Seeadler

The count aboard the yacht *Maria* two weeks before his first U.S. tour in 1926.

Author's private collection.

The count shortly after his celebrated return to Germany.

Archives of the Deutsches Schiffahrtsmuseum, Bremerhaven, Germany.

Shortly after the evacuation of Halle, General Terry Allen and members of the 104th Division pose with von Luckner, evidently relieved by his role in saving Halle, and in saving American and German lives.

U.S. National Archives.

16

THE ROYAL NAVY'S TRAP

April 12–May 1, 1917

Cape Horn is the southernmost tip of land of South America and
the dividing point between the Atlantic and Pacific oceans. Discovered in 1616 by Dutch Captain Willem Schouten of Hoorn, Holland, it is an icon for sailors; a threshold, a rite of passage. The Horn,
as it is called, is a volcanic rock formation, bleak, wind-beaten, storm
battered. South of this tip of land is Antarctica, though the sea north
of that land mass is full of icebergs, making chances of reaching the
polar continent risky at best.

The Andes Mountains run north and south along the western
edge of South America. The prevailing winds hit the mountain range
and seek out the path of least resistance—south to Cape Horn. Likewise, the currents of the Pacific funnel through Cape Horn to reach
the Atlantic.

The combination of current and wind make Cape Horn a churning area of storms, raging white-capped waves, high winds, and ice-
cold seas that can kill a man in a matter of minutes. Every bit of ill
weather is channeled to this place and a ship attempting to pass from
the Atlantic to the Pacific fights ever-changing, gale-force winds
that—more often than not—are blowing west to east, making passage
difficult at best. Churning gray-capped waves sixty feet high are not
uncommon. Sailors refer to the region south of the 40th latitude as
the Roaring Forties.

Rounding the Horn is an especially difficult rite for sailing vessels
as they tack to the south and north, whittling away at the currents
and the winds and making way slowly against the headwinds. A ship
is often forced to swing back in hopes of finding a better wind. Cutting too close to the north risks smashing into the cape itself. Sailing
south risks the peril of icebergs or becoming trapped in ice floes, depending on the season.

Even steamships found Cape Horn's erratic weather and constant storms treacherous. Their primary advantage is that they were not governed by the wind and had some degree of control over their course.

The *Seeadler* and the Royal Navy converged on Cape Horn in mid- to late April 1917. It would be a test of the elements, their sailing skills, and the luck of both sides.

Captain von Luckner's conversation with his helmsman summed up what he knew he faced. "You are the fellow who likes yacht racing. By Joe, it's to be a race now—a race to see who gets to the Horn first."

The ever-pessimistic and sarcastic Lüdemann did not offer his captain any solace. "And then, even if we do get to the Cape before any cruisers that may be sent down from the north, they may have a cruiser or two nosing around at the Pacific end of the Straits. Unless we round the Horn before those chaps reach Rio, the jig may be up."

What both men didn't know was just how determined the Royal Navy was to make sure the *Seeadler* did not slip out of their grasp. On April 5, the disposition of the search zone at Cape Horn had been sent to the ships that were to ambush the German raider. The *Otranto* and *Orbita*, along with the collier *Finisterre*, were to patrol north and south from Cape Horn. With both cruisers moving north and south, spread apart in terms of distance, it would be quite difficult for anyone to even contemplate getting past the Royal Navy.

The *Otranto* reached the patrol area first. Alone, she headed south and by April 13 was a half-day north of Darwin Bay, Antartica. The *Orbita* had not yet reached the Magellan Straits, leaving something of a gap in the patrol line. At the same time, the *Seeadler* was a half-day away from Staten Island, the last discernible land mass before the turn would have to be made to run the Horn.

Lüdemann was not far off in his thinking. The Royal Navy's ship *Lancaster* was steaming down the coast but was still a long way from the patrol area. Depending on when the *Seeadler* made her run at the Horn, she might be poised to join in the ambush, or to sweep into the Pacific in pursuit. By April 13, the *Lancaster* was between Valparaiso and Coquimbo. If she cut straight south at full steam, she could almost ensure that the windjamming raider would not escape.

The *Otranto* was an auxiliary cruiser; in essence, she was a commercial ship that had been armed and manned by the British Navy. The *Otranto* was part of a fleet of ships that had run mail on the Orient mail line. She weighed in at 12,000 tons and could go eighteen knots. In many respects, this steamer was a merchant kin to the *Seeadler*, a commercial ship that had been pressed into active military service.

Her war service had been one more of honorable luck than skill. At the Battle of Colonel against Admiral Count von Spee, she was one of the two ships that had escaped. She had fled the battle zone, not out of fear, but pure logic. Her short-ranged guns, limited speed, and lack of armor made her more of a target than a tool of war, and as such she was relegated to the role of acting as additional eyes to the British patrol line—nothing more. Her fate lay elsewhere.

Some ships seem to be in the wrong place at the wrong time. Such was the fate of the *Otranto*. By October of 1918 she was performing a new role in the war, that of an armed troop transport. On the approach to England carrying U.S. soldiers on their way to the war, she collided with the liner *Kashmir* in bad weather. Badly damaged, she drifted ashore near Scotland at Islay Island. The crash and her demise would eventually cost the lives of nearly three hundred Americans and a hundred of her own crew as they desperately attempted to get to shore in the rough seas.

But in April of 1917, her future was unknown as she sought a sailing ship disguised as a Norwegian.

There is an old military maxim, "No plan survives contact with the enemy." Such was the case of the mission of the *Orbita*. By April 14, the *Orbita* was moving at fourteen knots and was near Cape Horn. With the *Otranto* to the south, her original orders were to patrol near the coastline. This would leave very little chance for the *Seeadler* to pass Cape Horn undetected.

The Royal Navy plan ran into a snag, one that could have come from only three possibilities. Either the captain of the *Orbita* decided to ignore his orders, the orders never arrived, or the senior officer changed the order on his own prerogative. Regardless, the cruiser's patrol route altered. The *Orbita* sailed around Cape Horn on April 15 and headed for the Straits between Staten Island and the mainland. Rather than running south and augmenting the patrol route of the *Otranto*, the *Orbita* went off on a proverbial snipe hunt.

For seasoned sailors who knew sailing ships, this patrol station made no sense. It was too confined, too close to shore for von Luckner to have chosen it as the course for his raider. At best it was a bad guess on the part of the person who issued the order and demonstrated an ignorance of sailing ships and the conditions around Cape Horn. Moreover, it demonstrated that the Royal Navy had lost its understanding of fighting in the age of sail. That era had come to an end.

Captain von Luckner was having problems of his own. The winds of the Horn were being as uncooperative as he had come to expect. Rather than being lucky enough to catch a rare east-to-west breeze, he was facing strong headwinds. This forced him to head south. He assumed that if he took this course, there was less of a chance that the British would patrol in the Antarctic waters. The winds were of gale intensity and he was forced to only put up minimal sails. The *Seeadler* used its auxiliary engine to keep the ship on course, but the going was slow and tedious as she tacked southward, creeping slowly to the west.

On April 16, the *Seeadler* had technically tacked her way across the meridian of Cape Horn, but she was still in harm's way. The *Otranto* had arrived at Orange Bay and the *Orbita* had turned around and was still hugging the coastline. The *Otranto* wasted no time heading south into a gale. Each ship wanted to be the one to outfox the *Seeadler*.

By mid-afternoon on the 17th, the watch spotted the outline of a ship to the east of their position. It was heading south as they plowed painfully north and slightly west. In the raging storm, it was difficult to make out the form, but from what the officers of the *Seeadler* saw, it could only be one thing—the British auxiliary cruiser. Still limping and fighting the wind, the captain ordered the raider hard over, taking cover in the storm and massive waves. Their only hope was that the ship had not spotted them—but the odds of that were slim. A sailing ship running with white sails, even in a storm, was hard to miss. The only thing that would preserve them was pure luck.

And apparently that was what they had. The official Royal Navy records of the war indicate that there was no way the two ships were this close. But in reality, they passed only a few miles apart.

By April 18, the *Seeadler* was making her way south by southwest when the lookouts spotted an iceberg in the distance. It was large and—as with most icebergs—what was seen on the surface of the ocean was only a fraction of the real threat. The ship began a turn to the north but the currents and winds brought the ship and the iceberg even closer together.

Just when von Luckner thought that he would pass the ice without incident, the *Seeadler* shuddered. The windjammer moaned as the ship scraped up against an outcropping of the iceberg. The crew dashed belowdecks and found water coming into some of the holds. Captain von Luckner ordered the pumps manned and the men took shifts in the frigid water, pumping it clear while the carpenters waded into the icy waters and attempted to patch the damage. Matters were made worse given that the storm raging above was dumping in more water than the leak itself—filling the lower decks with seeping ice water.

The water coming into the ship was freezing cold and the work belowdecks had to be mentally and physically numbing. The *Seeadler* had her motor launches and plenty of lifeboats, but a sailor could not expect to last in the choppy waters for more than a few minutes before hypothermia took his life. To abandon ship was a death sentence. To use the wireless to signal for help would bring the Royal Navy and the humiliation of capture. For the crew in those dark holds, the only alternative was to work hard to patch the damage.

It took hours as the carpenters, mechanics, and pumpers did their work. The survival of the raider depended on the actions of everyone to pitch in. Slowly, painfully, they repaired the damage and pumped the water coming in from the storm. Captain von Luckner himself took a shift at the pumps. The *Seeadler* was slowly making her way north and slinking to the west. Her crew was near exhaustion, but they were still alive.

By April 19 the *Seeadler* was fully repaired and had pumped her water clear. Captain von Luckner ordered that the spare lifeboats and preservers be brought up onto the deck. Now bearing the name *Seeadler* as a result of their efforts during the run south, von Luckner now intended to use them for his final ruse. Every so often the crew lowered a boat or tossed a life preserver overboard in the hope that the Royal Navy would find the debris and assume that the *Seeadler* had sunk. If they had no prey, they would break off their search.

April 19 proved to be a special day for the Germans, though they did not know it at the time. They had sailed past the Royal Navy's trap. Having sailed so far south, and with the *Orbita* not following a patrol route that would have been practical, the *Seeadler* was safe—from the British cruisers.

The ship sailed northward to warmer and calmer waters in the Pacific Ocean. Four days later they picked up a wireless message. One of the *Seeadler* lifeboats had been found by a coastal patrol craft near Cape Horn. During the next few days observers spotted three more empty lifeboats along the shores of South America.

The Germans used merchant raiders to strike at the economy of Great Britain and her Allies. Lloyd's of London, the venerable insurer, set commercial rates for companies to insure their cargos and vessels. If word got out that raiders or submarines were sinking ships, the rates went up. When that happened, some companies would keep their ships in port, for increased insurance rates made voyages unprofitable.

Raiders also struck fear into the hearts of merchant sailors. If there was even rumor of an enemy raider, captains would often elect to keep their ships in port. Naval officers had no choice in such matters. But civilian merchant captains would not risk the ship and their crew. This was more than a business for them: it was home, it was their very lives.

The *Seeadler* was not a rumor. The former prisoners began to enjoy their fifteen minutes of fame, giving interviews that stirred public interest. While such stories sold newspapers, they also served to raise Lloyd's insurance rates and caused many ships along the Atlantic trade routes to hold up in port.

As much as Captain von Luckner had waged a misinformation war with his former prisoners, the Royal Navy was not above a few tricks of their own. On May 1, a message came over the wireless and was picked up by the *Seeadler* crew . . . much to their amusement.

"*Seeadler* gone down with flags flying. Commander and part of crew taken prisoners and on their way to Montevideo."

Imagine the surprise of the crew of the *Seeadler* to hear that they had been sunk. The intent was clear, the Royal Navy was attempting to quell the fear that the raider had slipped through their trap. At the same time, with the lifeboats and life preservers washing up on shore, and no additional sightings of the windjammer, they may have assumed that she had gone down. While there was bound to be entertainment from such a report, there must also have been some concern. If the crew's families in Germany heard this news, they might think their loved ones were dead or captured.

Von Luckner decided to turn the tables on the British. He contacted his wireless operator, Seaman Walter Renz, who went by the name Adolph, as well as the nickname Sparks. To play back the trick to the Royal Navy, von Luckner sent several broken messages warning of submarines: "SOS . . . SOS . . . German sub." Within a few days, Sparks picked up wireless messages warning that German subs were operating along the Pacific coast. The threat of the *Seeadler* that had been dulled by the Royal Navy's message was rekindled with a new fear.

As the ship made its way to warmer climates, it prepared for a risky leg of its journey and a new enemy threat. America had entered the war. It would offer new targets and new dangers.

✠ ✠ ✠

What the crew of the *Seeadler* did not know was that the Royal Navy had not been entirely fooled by their lifeboat ruse. They knew the raider was a difficult customer to apprehend. On the assumption that the *Seeadler* had not sunk, the Admiralty sent the cruiser *Avoca* on April 28 to depart from Esquimalt on a course to the Galapagos Islands. Regardless of the messages they sent to calm the merchant ships, the Royal Navy had not given up their hunt for the *Seeadler*.

17

YANKS

May 2–July 9, 1917

Tensions between the United States and Germany had been growing steadily since the beginning of the Great War. While America was formally neutral at the start of the war, merchants made money by selling goods to both sides. The British blockade of Germany eventually led to more contraband material being sold to the United Kingdom.

Matters were made worse in 1915 when a German U-boat sank the passenger liner *Lusitania*, killing 1,201 passengers, including 128 Americans. Even this was not enough to provoke the United States to enter the war. The United States did call on Germany to halt unrestricted submarine warfare, however. Rather than a German U-boat simply firing a torpedo at a ship and sinking it, the sub was to surface, signal the target, confirm the identity of the ship, allow the ship to evacuate, then torpedo the vessel. This was restricted submarine warfare and the German Navy chafed under such rules.

The reality was that the Royal Navy had its own surface raiders in the guise of Q-ships and also offered a bounty to a crew for sinking a U-boat, usually accomplished by ramming the submarine. Restricted submarine warfare ruined the submarines' advantage, the element of surprise. In attempting to identify a ship, they usually found themselves targets of ramming attacks. While the rules seemed civilized, they were oftentimes deadly for the U-boat crews. Eventually the German Admiralty won out—and once again the submarines began unrestricted warfare.

Even this reversal was not enough to prod the United States into war. What it took was the infamous Zimmerman telegram. Germany was allegedly goading Mexico into attacking America in exchange for regaining lost territory, including Texas. When the Americans learned of the secret plan, there was no choice but for them to declare war on Germany, which they did on April 6, 1917.

The crew of the *Seeadler* would have received word of America's intentions by wireless during their run south around Cape Horn. The only references to it appear in their war diary after the run was completed, which implies that Captain von Luckner may have withheld the information until the ship was clear of the British trap. The impact on morale had to be minimal; most Germans were of the conviction that the Americans would eventually enter the war. There was also a prevalent belief that the United States could not muster a significant military force and transport it to Europe in time to be of much use.

This political decision had other implications for the crew. It meant that the formerly neutral American ports would be off-limits to the ship—though taking advantage of them was never really part of von Luckner's plans. It also meant that the U.S. Navy would now be a threat to the *Seeadler*, though its presence in the Pacific was thin. Overall, the crew eventually became depressed and embittered by the declaration of war.

From a more opportunistic perspective, it also meant that American merchant ships were now viable targets for the raider.

As they ran to the northwest, the *Seeadler* found little of interest. The wireless picked up messages from the British cruiser *Kent*, which was in the vicinity but too distant to be a real threat.

At the same time, there were no opportunities for raiding because they encountered no ships for several days. The *Seeadler* made her way south of the Galapagos Islands. Near Robinson Crusoe Island (Más á Tierra), the ship began a more westerly track, south of Hawaii. While the weather became much warmer, von Luckner had not yet succeeded in coming across an active shipping lane where he could ply his craft.

On June 14, at around 1600, the *Seeadler* spotted the *A. B. Johnson*, a four-masted American schooner bound out of Tacoma taking a load of lumber to Newcastle, Australia. She was registered at 529 gross registered tons and was relatively young—only seventeen years old. The wind was light but thanks to her auxiliary engine, the German raider was able to close rapidly on the American ship.

The American ship was running without her flag up, but when she sighted the approaching ship—seemingly a fellow merchant—the order was given to run up the Stars and Stripes. At 2,400 yards, Lieutenant Kircheiß fired a round across her bow. The shot was almost a hit, exploding some twelve feet from the ship with such force that the ship's master running the flag up was knocked flat to the deck. The blast also doused the helmsman at the wheel in a wash of salt water. The sight of the German battle standard in the light breeze and the close proximity of the shot across the bow was enough to convince the captain of the ship to surrender.

Lieutenant Pries led the boarding party, accompanied aboard by Doctor Pietsch. As they had before, they ordered the small crew to gather their belongings and to prepare to take their own lifeboats over to the *Seeadler*. The ship's log and papers were confiscated as well. The first boat that was lowered caught on the edge of the schooner's hull and tipped, spilling the men and their gear into the water.

The captain of the ship was Andrew Peterson, who came aboard with his wife, Gladys. Initially this was not a problem; the *Seeadler* crew had dealt with women prisoners before. However, Peterson met quickly with Captain von Luckner and asked that he show some degree of discretion by not mentioning his wife in the records. As it turns out, Gladys was not Gladys Peterson, but Gladys Taylor. The last thing that Captain Peterson wanted was for his *real* wife to read about Gladys in the newspaper once the raid of the *Seeadler* came to an end. Nor did he want the crew to know of his infidelity, mostly because of the way they might treat the young woman. Von Luckner demurred, at least until his accounts were published in the 1920s. Even then, he never printed the name of the American captain. The official records list seven crew members and one captain of the *A. B. Johnson*; Gladys Taylor is listed as an American stowaway.

After the evacuation and formalities, Pries placed explosive charges in the bottom of the *A. B. Johnson* and sank her. For the first time since March, the *Seeadler* was carrying prisoners, although this time they were Americans.

Four days later, late in the afternoon on June 18, the lookout on the *Seeadler* spotted another sailing ship in the distance. She had come up from behind the schooner and was closing slowly, thanks to a light breeze and the fact that *Seeadler* was running with full sails and could put up more canvas than the smaller schooner. The ship was not flying any flag, but Captain von Luckner felt that boarding her was a good idea. At this point he had little to risk with boarding a neutral ship. In the middle of the Pacific, he felt safe from the hands of his old menace, the Royal Navy.

It was the *R. C. Slade*, a four-masted schooner registered out of San Francisco. She had been plying the Pacific trade routes, heading back to her homeport after sailing from Sydney with a load of copra. Her captain was a wily man, Haldor Smith. When he saw the ship slowly closing behind him, he climbed the mast and took a look for himself. It was out of place for another sailing ship to close without some sort of signal, but Smith was not in a communicating mood himself. He had been warned when he left Sydney that there were German raiders operating where he was heading, but such warnings had been up since the start of the war—and the Pacific was a long way from the docks of Hamburg. The mysterious ship shadowing him was closing slowly and he did not perceive her to be much of a threat. Climbing down the mast, he went to his cabin and started dinner. It was 1700 and he figured he had plenty of time before the distant ship would pose any real danger—if it was indeed a raider.

When First Mate Baer came down a short time later, he claimed he had seen a shell explode two miles ahead. A shot across the bow. Captain Smith came up on deck and surveyed the ocean, praying for some option to present itself to him. The mysterious ship was still closing and the seas were clear. He had been hoping for a rain squall or bad weather, so he could break away and possibly hide. Without that, his only hope was to outrun the firing ship, pray for a sudden storm, or hope that nightfall came and he could escape in the dark.

As the sun dropped, the ship behind him got closer and fired again, sending a column of water spraying up into the air. This shot was a miss, but much closer. The shots came every seven minutes, and each one crept closer and closer to the *R. C. Slade*. Her hull was made of wood, which was tough—but hardly a match for the firepower he was facing. One hit from an exploding shell would take her down in a matter of minutes. The ninth shell splashed just under the ship's stern and exploded there. There was no doubt, the next round was going to sink the schooner. Captain Smith ordered the American flag to identify themselves, then struck their colors. The *R. C. Slade* dropped her sails and hove-to.

Night was beginning to fall as the *Seeadler* pulled alongside the ship. Lieutenant Pries went with his prize crew of ten men, also carrying Doctor Pietsch. When they came aboard the crew was ordered to depart the ship immediately. With nightfall coming up quickly, attempting to transfer between the ships would be risky. They would be allowed back aboard the next morning to pick up their personal gear. Doctor Pietsch did a quick inspection of the small crew as they left to make sure they were fit. Only one member of the crew was not allowed to depart to the *Seeadler*, ship's cook Takemoto, the sole Japanese member of the crew. He was kept on board to cook meals for the prize crew.

Von Luckner greeted the prisoners and Lieutenant Kling gave them the now-traditional orientation to the ship and her rules once they got settled in. Captain Smith and Captain Peterson both knew each other, which added a little tension when Captain Smith discovered that the "wife" his friend had brought with him was not the woman he knew to be Peterson's wife. For von Luckner, this only provided amusement.

The two ships remained close throughout the night as the prize crew spent their first night ever on a captured ship. The next morning the crew of the *R. C. Slade* went back to their ship to gather their personal belongings. Once the prisoners had returned, von Luckner gave the order to sink the *R. C. Slade* by gunfire. Several of the 4.2-inch shells were fired into the wooden vessel but she seemed to weather the fire well, water logging the ship but not totally sinking her. The shots continued as the gunnery crews attempted to finish the task of sinking the vessel. The copra that it carried as cargo was highly combustible and burst into flames. Within minutes the *R. C.*

Slade was a roaring inferno on the seas, but only for a short time. The damage from the shells caused the ship to slip into the sea, hissing as the burning hull and deck hit the water. It had taken thirty-eight shells to finally send the *R. C. Slade* to her demise.

Von Luckner attempted to rebuild his former Captain's Club with the American captains, who were initially wary of his overtures. The American captains were different from the sailors he had captured in the Atlantic. What was similar was the mix of prisoners: Americans, Japanese, French, British, Swedes, Norwegians, Finns, and Russians were on board. The German crew of the raider was cordial, but with America's entry to the war, there was some bitterness. The American turn from neutrality to a state of war was a frustrating turn of events for the *Seeadler* crew. The state of war meant there was one more enemy navy that would be searching for them. The crew had been at sea for a long time, under constant stress, and some of their comments to the Americans about the U.S. entry into the war reflected some of that pent-up anger.

The *Seeadler* also faced a growing problem with its fresh water supply. The extended duration of the voyage and the heat had begun to turn the stale water green as microorganisms multiplied in it. The crew was forced to rig sails to catch rain water, which could be used to supplement their own spoiling water; but given the number of crew and prisoners, the ship would soon need to find a more reliable and stable supply of fresh water.

Aboard the ship other issues surfaced in the form of crew morale. The *Seeadler* had been at sea for half a year without making port and the crew was beginning to show signs of frustration and fatigue. In the Atlantic, they could occasionally take a short swim to relax, but in the middle of the Pacific, sharks constantly followed the raider. The crew, bored and tired, began to play games with the dangerous fish—catching two of them, tying their tails together, and releasing them to watch the struggle. At one point they even tossed a grenade wrapped in bacon to the sharks to watch one of them explode. The long months of sailing from the frigid polar regions to soaring heat of the equator, the escape from the Royal Navy, and the tension of being far from home on hostile seas were all starting to wear away at the morale and spirits of the German crew.

The 731-ton American schooner *Manilla* was a typical merchant sailing vessel. Built in Oregon in 1899, she was a four-masted, wood-hulled ship that was doing what she could to make a living for her owner, Comyn Carr of San Francisco. In the summer of 1917 the ship had left Puget Sound with a cargo of timber heading for Sydney. Needing a cargo to take back, they went to Newcastle, Australia, and were loaded with a shipment of coal that would bring a good price at Honolulu. There were warnings in port about the possibility that raiders were operating in the Pacific, but the *Manilla's* captain, Fred Ernest Southard, chose to ignore those. Such warnings were commonplace in her ports of call: the *Manilla* had been making such runs for years with no difficulties.

By July 8, 1917 the *Manilla* had been out of port thirty-five days and was about 450 miles southeast of Honolulu when low, gray, rain-laden clouds appeared and squalls broke out. Captain Southard saw a ship looming astern of his own vessel, another sailing ship emerging from the gray weather. Almost immediately he heard a sharp crack and a shell exploded just over the stern of the *Manilla*. He stared at the approaching ship and could make out the German flag. A voice, yelled from a megaphone, boomed over the waves to him.

"Are you the master of this schooner?"

"Yes."

"This is the auxiliary cruiser *Seeadler*. Your ship is captured."

"Well, I can see that sticking out a mile. But as I cannot do anything about it, you're welcome to her. What I want to know is—are you going to give my crew a chance to get out of her?"

The voice, that of Lieutenant Kling, replied quickly. "Why certainly. We're not pirates and you won't need to walk the plank just yet. I'll send a launch over and we'll try and board you if the sea will give us a chance, so stand by to take up her line." He paused for a moment, then added. "*We'll* sink your ship after taking you out of her." The message was clear—don't attempt to scuttle your own vessel.

Captain Southard had only learned of America's entry into the war less than a month before. He ordered his ship to heave-to and ordered his men to prepare their lifeboats. The voice on the megaphone called out to him again as the windjammer pulled alongside of his own ship. "Never mind getting into your boats. I'll send men to take yours off."

A motorized launch with an officer and eight armed men came over from the *Seeadler*. They moved with precision and efficiency. Lieutenant Pries and Doctor Pietsch went straight to the captain's cabin to inspect the alcohol supply. When Captain Southard (referred to by his crew as "the Old Man") came over to them, the doctor informed him that his good alcohol was contraband and the doctor suggested finishing it off. From the looks of it, the good doctor already had a head-start. The captain and some of the crew joined them in a final drink and grabbed their gear for departure. Within thirty minutes, the eight personnel from the *Manilla* were aboard the launch and on their way to the German vessel.

Captain von Luckner greeted the crew of the *Manilla* as they came aboard. His prize crew went to work on the *Manilla*, taking foodstuffs and other supplies that they might need while von Luckner oriented the new prisoners to his ship. The only oddity that they discovered was the crew's pet and mascot—an opossum, which was transferred over to the raider. Von Luckner introduced Captain Southard to the two other American captains. Captain Smith, in a quirk of humor, presented the *Manilla* captain with a dozen artificial roses. Prize Officer Pries informed von Luckner that the holds were full of coal—of no use aboard the *Seeadler*. After five hours of searching and removal, the time had come for the prize crew to set their charges and abandon the schooner.

Captain Southard suddenly grew panicked. "Holy mackerel, I've forgotten my best set of teeth." Laughing, Lieutenant Kling replied, "Well, Captain, better send for them for you're going to be our guest for some time and probably will need them."

Charges were placed fore and aft and Captain Southard was invited onto the bridge to witness his ship's sinking. The charges went off a few minutes later, sending a fiery flash bursting through the wooden deck. As the ship slowly settled down, von Luckner noticed that the prize crew had forgotten to remove the American flag from the mast. The ship's band did their best at playing the "Star Spangled Banner" in tribute to the new prisoners, but the ship seemed to slow its descent and the flag hung defiantly out of the water.

Von Luckner rarely displayed his temper so openly. He called the prize crew forward and verbally disciplined them for the breach of etiquette. The removal of a ship's flag was done to avoid humiliating a prisoner captain; it was also given to the captain, as a memento of his former command. It was an honorable tradition and a breach of etiquette that the count deeply regretted.

Life aboard the *Seeadler* settled quickly into a routine for the American prisoners and their German captors. Captain von Luckner would pass information to the prisoners from the wireless on a daily basis—carefully editing and spinning the news he let them hear. Just as he had done in the Atlantic, he was doing what he could to wage a war of disinformation. Several of the prisoners reported that von Luckner had passed news to them regarding American defeats in Europe, even though most of them knew that it would be weeks before the American Army would even be in Europe, let alone fighting and losing battles.

Captain Southard became privy to the secret of Captain Peterson's affair with Gladys Taylor. Matters became slightly complicated when Captain Smith began to flirt with the "stowaway." Haldor Smith himself was a married man and his flirting was more to get at his friend, Peterson. For his part, Captain Southard stayed out of the entire incident. Where von Luckner avoided ever using Peterson's name in writing to spare him embarrassment, Captain Southard's written account admits that he had changed the name of the captain to Roberts, ". . . for reasons of my own."

One thing was for sure: having the Americans on board the *Seeadler* was different than having European guests.

18

MOPELIA

July 10–August 2, 1917

The *Seeadler* was finding the Pacific to be less lucky than the Atlantic. The ship had been in the Pacific since April but had only captured three ships.

Not only was the search for prize ships not going well, but the raider was suffering other problems. The long months at sea had left her hull fouled with barnacle growth, which cut her speed. The problems with the fresh water supply had not gone away. The ship was becoming more dependent on an occasional rain shower to augment the fresh water reserves.

Adding to the problems, on July 23 Doctor Pietsch reported to Captain von Luckner that some of the crew were beginning to show signs of beriberi and scurvy. The limbs and joints of most of the crew were swelling, making the long voyage even more unbearable. The reduction in captured ships also made fresh fruits and vegetables scarce. The potatoes and other vegetables that the *Seeadler* carried from her previous plunders were spoiling quickly in the heat of the Pacific summer. The crew had been reduced to meals that consisted of hardtack (dried biscuit), salt meat, dried beans, and peas. The last good meal they remembered was the ham and fresh vegetables that had been taken from the *R. C. Slade*. Even when they captured ships, the food supplies for the small crews of eight or so men did not last long with the *Seeadler's* complement of Germans and prisoners.

The outbreak of scurvy and beriberi, the morale issues, and the lack of fresh water made it clear that if the *Seeadler* was going to continue her raid, she needed to provision shortly. Von Luckner hoped to find an isolated island and restock the ship, clean her hull, and give his weary crew much needed shore rest. Then he planned on sweeping to South Georgia Island and striking at the British whaling station located there. From there he would turn back to Cape Horn and the Atlantic, where he had enjoyed much better hunting.

Finding an isolated island was no small feat. The Pacific islands were dotted with colonies from Britain, Japan, and France. Many had small populations but were often equipped with wireless sets. He needed to find a place that had food and water, but a place that was isolated enough to avoid unwanted attention. Von Luckner and First Mate Kling settled on the Society Islands as a place to search.

On July 31 the *Seeadler* approached Mopelia (also known as Mopeha) Island. The coral atoll was little more than a thin ring of land surrounding a massive lagoon in the center. Fine white sand beaches and dense jungle growth on the eastern portion comprised roughly one third of the ring of the island formation. The atoll was nearly five miles across the green and blue water lagoon in the center.

Von Luckner hoped initially to take the raider into the lagoon, but he feared that it was not deep enough. He sent a motor launch into the lagoon. The opening in the coral was just wide enough for the *Seeadler* to enter, but checks of the depth of the lagoon showed that it was too shallow for the ship to take shelter there.

There was a strong current coming out of the lagoon, which was desirable. Captain von Luckner expressed some concerns over getting his ship too close to the coral formations. Even the steel hull of the *Seeadler* would be no match for the jagged coral. With the water of the lagoon pushing the ship away, his only real concern was the wind or changes to the weather that might move his ship.

Parties were sent to Mopelia and they found ample coconuts and ample plant life. Better yet, there was a small supply of fresh water. Kircheiß was disappointed when he learned the answer to the all-important question, "What about the women?" There were none.

The island itself was brilliant—emerald green with plant life and stark against the blue of the oceans, with white beaches that ringed the narrow strip of the eastern end of the island. The lagoon was filled with fish, massive eels, and rock lobsters. The beaches were covered with nesting birds, which meant ample eggs—a delicacy that the crew had not enjoyed for some time. There was a family of wild pigs running amok on the island, offering a chance at fresh meat.

There were three adult native Kanakas on the island, along with one young boy. They had come to Mopelia as workers for a French company out of Tahiti, to capture the turtles that lived on the island. Apparently, Mopelia was a well-known breeding ground for massive sea turtles that were highly prized for their meat. The Kanakas were friendly at first, but when they learned that the crew was German, they became quite nervous. The French company they worked for had done a good job of spreading fear among the local population. The company traditionally made runs every few months, dropping off the hunters and coming back at some point to pick them up.

At first glance, Mopelia had all of the makings of a lush tropical paradise. Despite his years of sailing through the Pacific, von Luckner knew that such small islands, with strong currents and dangerous coral, were tricky when it came to anchoring. According to several sources, he and First Officer Kling consulted with the members of the Captain's Club for their recommendations as to where to anchor. They concurred with the suggestion that von Luckner had made, counting on the currents to keep the ship away from the island.

For years following 1917 that short discussion would be the source of controversy.

The members of the crew who went ashore were recovered that first night and watches were posted on the *Seeadler*. When the morning of August 1 broke over the small island haven, the ship was much farther away. The *Seeadler* had drifted ten miles from Mopelia during the night. Her anchors had failed to hold on the coral, and the drift had been so smooth and so easy that no one on watch had noticed. From the captain's standpoint the slight embarrassment was mitigated by the fact that the ship had not drifted into the coral reef, but quite far away from it. That drifting would provide von Luckner and his officers a false sense of security. The *Seeadler* made her way back to the island and dropped anchor again.

The crew and some of the prisoners removed the fouling from the hull of the ship while other members were granted time to explore the island, gather fresh food, fish, and relax. It was exactly the kind of relief that von Luckner had hoped for, a release for his men.

On August 2, the members of the Captain's Club were to join Captain von Luckner for a picnic. Lieutenant Kircheiß took a small party out in one boat to the end of the island where the natives had set up their huts. Most of the crew had been sent ashore earlier in the morning, as had some of the prisoners. Lieutenant Pries had command of the *Seeadler*. Aboard the ship with him was a skeleton work detail, including Engineer Krause. If trouble arose, Lieutenant Pries was to fire off two rapid warning shots and run up a flag with double-stars on it as a signal for the rest of the crew to return to the ship.

The work crew aboard the ship noticed what was happening first. The crew and prisoners working on the side of the ship opposite the shore were sitting on planks suspended over the side of the ship, scraping barnacles and growth off the hull. The *Seeadler* was drifting—not to sea, but into the reef. The rest of the crew on the island got their first indication that something was wrong when the deck cannon barked out a series of warning shots in quick succession. The crew on board could feel the current nudge the *Seeadler* through the clear water; they could see the bottom and knew the ship they were hanging from was drifting toward the island. One of them muttered over and over, "Go, go, go," knowing that if the ship did hit the reef, he would not have to worry about being taken back to Germany as a prisoner.

A crewmember on deck was attempting to set the foresails. The stern anchor of the ship had lost its hold on the bottom. The aft of the *Seeadler* was swinging in a tidal surge—pivoting on the forward anchor, which was holding. Rather than swinging away from the island, the wind had apparently changed direction from northeast to northwest.

In one of the motor launches, von Luckner and a small party reached the narrow passage into the lagoon when they heard the sharp retort of the 4.2-inch cannon barking off two shots in rapid succession. The captain's first thought was they had sighted a warship in the distance. As the motor launch raced back to the raider, it was clear that it would not reach it in time to be of any help. It was 0925. He was 2.8 miles from his ship.

The stern of the *Seeadler* swung into the coral reef with a metallic grinding noise. The sound was different than hitting an iceberg. In the surge of warm tidal waters, it was a metallic puncturing noise— like a tin can being stabbed open with a screwdriver. As each gust of breeze and each rocking wave hit the ship, it ground the hull of the windjammer into the coral. For Captain von Luckner, it had to be the most sickening sound in the world.

By the time he reached the ship it was too late. Her hull was punctured in several places near the stern and she was taking on a great deal of water in the lower holds. Emergency crews went to work, but nothing was helping. The flow of water could be slowed; but with such a large number of holes, the raider was going to suffer a slow sinking death.

Belowdecks, Engineer Krause had been struggling to start the diesel engine. A crewman had contacted Lieutenant Pries that the anchor was losing its hold. Pries gave the order to start the auxiliary engine to control the ship's glide. On the assumption that the engine would be firing soon, he raised the forward anchor so the *Seeadler* could make way. When he didn't hear the rumble of the engine, he had opted instead to raise the foresails. This gave the ship some forward motion—but not in the desired manner, and not enough to save her. Combined with the raised anchor, Pries's actions only hastened the ship's drift into the reef. Krause had struggled to engage the diesel; but even in the best conditions, starting the engine took four minutes.

It took less than that for the raider to grind into the reef. Even after the hull had been ripped, the engine had stubbornly refused to start. After months of intermittent service, the low-grade oil that the engineering crew had been given had taken its toll. The temperamental engine was finally coaxed into action, but by the time it turned over, it served to only slap the propeller into the coral. It was too little too late. The aft anchor cable snapped.

The crew pulled everything they could from the lower holds, before they became contaminated with the incoming sea water. A few hours later, water seeped into the auxiliary engine room and it had to be abandoned. Near noon, the forecastle of the ship was ruptured as the ship continued to rock against the reef. The ship listed and then settled at an angle, imprisoned on the reef.

By mid-afternoon, it was over. After a trip of over 30,000 miles, after sinking fourteen ships, after the unfortunate death of Richard Page, after evading the Royal Navy's snare at Cape Horn, after sailing through a gale on Christmas to punch through the British blockade, after firing her guns in battle, after an iceberg sliced her hull, after scurvy and beriberi, it was over. The end of the last sailing ship sent into combat was not a glorious battle—it was bad luck.

At 1500 the order came to abandon ship.

As the *Seeadler* settled on the coral reef it was obvious that she was not a total loss. Much of the ship was still above the water, but the lower holds were submerged. For the crew and their captain, it had to be a solemn moment. But the prisoners must have felt a suppressed jubilation. They were stranded, but they were not going to be taken back to Germany as prisoners—which was one of the rumors that circulated on the ship as to their fate.

Von Luckner ordered that camp be established on Mopelia. The crew began the process of moving the supplies to the island. The first thing they took was the captured champagne and cognac from the *Horngarth*. From the prisoner's accounts of that first day, the German crew did not move much more. They opened the alcohol and in-dulged themselves. It was not a celebration; from the descriptions, it was a temporary release from authority. Von Luckner had never allowed his men to overindulge themselves with the spoils of al-cohol. As was the custom of most naval officers, he kept it carefully rationed.

There is no mention of Captain von Luckner attempting to stop them, nor is there any account of him joining the impromptu party.

19

DECEPTION IN PARADISE

August 2–August 23, 1917

The prisoners were kept aboard the *Seeadler* the night it became lodged on the reef, on the upper decks that were still above water. The raider's crew had taken food and the majority of the alcohol ashore and initiated a strange party—given that they had just become stranded in the Pacific Ocean.

The next day the crew began to systematically strip the *Seeadler* for anything and everything of value or use. There was no way the ship would ever become seaworthy again, so the ship became a supply base for a myriad of goods. The decking was not touched, but the sails and the interior of the ship became fair game for salvaging.

Of primary interest were the weapons and ammunition. These were secured by the Germans. Even though the prisoners shared the same plight as their captors, there was a need to maintain order and control of the captives. The Germans, despite the loss of their ship, had not given up hope. It was clear that if another ship came within striking range, they would attempt to seize her. The hope was that the ship's 4.2-inch guns could be removed and somehow reattached to a captured vessel.

The crew took the provisions off the ship to a small island just off of the main island, where they built a small jetty and carefully guarded their wares. The "provision island" was a staging point, an above-ground warehouse of goods necessary for the castaways to build some semblance of a life. Several prisoners commented that in the salvage of the crew's quarters, dozens of empty champagne bottles were discovered—evidence of the plunder of the *Horngarth*. In all, it took ten days to strip the *Seeadler* of the usable gear and supplies.

At first, Mopelia appeared to be a romantic tropical island; but as the reality of being shipwrecked set in, the paradise took on a darker side. The food provisions moved ashore tended to be used for the German crew while the Americans tended to scavenge the island. Food was plentiful, but the variety was limited after a few days.

On the shore, the crew and prisoners strung hammocks and constructed canvas tents from the sails of the *Seeadler*. The Germans struggled at first with making tents, but the American crews came over from their camp and assisted—having had more experience in camping out than the rugged sailors. The first few nights proved to be a challenge. Coconuts dropped from the trees in the night breezes, bombarding the crew as they attempted to sleep.

Some crewmembers tried sleeping on the beach to avoid the midnight thumping of the coconuts. But they discovered that an army of hermit crabs waded the shores of Mopelia at night. Those who slept on the beach usually awoke to dozens of hermit crabs crawling over their bodies in the night.

The crabs were seen at first as a wonderful source of food. The Germans had been at sea for a long time and the change of diet seemed to be a welcome invitation. The prisoners and crew spread pieces of sail along the beach at night and scooped up scores of crabs. The crew and the prisoners gorged on the crab meat for several days, but they eventually reached a point when even the *mention* of crab meat seemed to churn stomachs.

The coconuts proved to be a good cure for the Germans' scurvy and beriberi. The gull eggs that were so common on the island were welcomed by everyone as well. Hunting parties found the family of wild pigs on the island to be a hunting challenge, even for heavily armed Germans.

Fish were plentiful, but difficult to catch. The crewmembers improvised, using potato-masher hand grenades to fish. The concussion of the blast would kill dozens of fish in a matter of a second. This was permitted, but eventually von Luckner intervened out of fear of running out of grenades. His mind was on capturing another ship.

There were numerous problems with island living. Mopelia had an abundant insect population, which proved irritating. If you left a glass of water out at night, the glass would be filled with large cockroaches in the morning. The roaches were a constant problem that frustrated the crew and prisoners alike, crawling on exposed limbs during the night and waking them up.

The brilliant white sands hid another insect problem: ants. The tiny ants would creep along any surface—and it was not uncommon in the first few nights for crewmembers to wake up with hundreds of ants all over their bodies. They developed an ingenious solution. Once they built beds, the islanders put the legs in the cut shells of co-conuts. These were then filled with water. While it had an odd appearance, the small water-filled bowls served as a deterrent to ants.

The lush green island held another irritant that the crew and prisoners discovered soon after their arrival: rats. At night they scurried along the ground and managed to get into anything left out or open. They attempted to trap and kill them, but the population was simply too large to make a significant dent. Piperle, one of the ship's mascot dogs, did his part to try and wipe out the rats, but the task was far beyond one dog. In time, the dog—like the crew—learned to live with these natives.

Other nighttime annoyances such as lizards and flying insects made sleeping difficult. Engineer Krause commented that his sleep was constantly interrupted by lizards running over his arms. Mopelia was far from a paradise for the men trapped there.

Among the mix of groups and nationalities on the atoll, strange symbiotic relationships seemed to emerge. The native Kanakas taught the prisoners and crew how to harvest the coconut trees and eat the heart of the palm for nourishment. They showed them how to burn the dried husks of the coconut shells to smoke fish. The American crews, all with vast experience in the Pacific, taught the Germans how to fish the lagoon waters and how to harvest rock lobsters.

While it all sounded pastoral, there was an undercurrent of tension that emerged on Mopelia that didn't exist at sea aboard the *Seeadler*. The relationships were different. On the ship, the Germans were the providers: they had provided the food, the information—everything. That changed when they were on the island. When two of the prisoners went off in search of shellfish, von Luckner ordered

179

them to make daily expeditions to collect enough for the other members of the small colony. The Americans were quick to point out that the sharp coral cut at their feet, but Captain von Luckner did not relent. "This is your grave." The point was made—their responsibilities were not just their own well-being, but the well-being of everyone on the island.

The Americans and Germans constructed two camps side-by-side. Huts with tent roofs were erected in defined rows. Both crews worked on the camp together. The American crews took the liberty of naming the streets between the huts as Broadway, Pennsylvania Avenue, and the Bowery. The Germans allowed this but took the liberty of naming the small village Seeadlerdorf, or Sea Eagle Town.

The Germans stripped the wireless gear and antenna off of the *Seeadler* and brought it to Seeadlerdorf. They strung the aerial wire between two large palm trees. Power was provided from batteries that were brought to shore, and a pair of dynamos powered by portable engines that had been stripped from the ship. At night, the wireless operator listened for news of the world and provided a good form of entertainment for both the Germans and their prisoners. Strings of running lights were hung over the tiny makeshift village to provide some illumination in the night. These too were tied to the batteries in a festive arrangement that made the isolation seem a bit more civilized.

The portable engines and dynamos could recharge the batteries and only had to be run a short period of time each day. The *Seeadler* still had plenty of diesel fuel which was of little use and forced conservation. There were sixteen tanks that stored the fuel, all topped off when the ship left Germany. The temperamental engines had only been run enough on the voyage to empty five tanks.

The hospital tent did not see much service other than cuts and scrapes from the jagged coral. The ship's doctor, Rudolph "Beef-steak" Pietsch, had managed to salvage his considerable supply of cigars and his personal stash of alcohol. From more than one account, the doctor spent much of his time working his way through both during his time on the island.

Beefsteak also established a laundry for the castaways. Seeadler-dorf took on the trappings of a true village. The Germans took a shining to the young Kanaka boy. Some of them took him along as they explored or hunted for wild pigs. Others taught him folk songs, and at night, he would entertain the crew and the prisoners with his singing.

The Germans suffered their first loss of life to the crew during their exile. Schnäuzchen, the more ill-tempered of the ship's two mascot dogs, had declared open war on the crab population. The dog went after the crabs, yipping and barking at them. In one of her assaults against a large crab, she suffered some sort of seizure and died.

The other ship's dog, Piperle, had her own enemies on the atoll in the form of the gulls. Piperle would raid their nests for eggs and they in turn went after the small pup. Their beaks pecked and nipped at her legs, ears, and tail. After a short period of time, Piperle preferred to remain in the hut rather than venture out and face the wrath of the birds.

In his seven years of traveling the seas, Count von Luckner had faced difficult challenges before. While a mate aboard the *Flying Fish*, he broke his ankle. His ship had left him in Jamaica, without his possessions and without pay, to fend for himself. The young count was suddenly faced with the prospect of being a penniless tramp.

Von Luckner, as Phelax Lüdicke, lived on the beach, his leg still wrapped in a heavy plaster cast. His clothing deteriorated in the tropical climate and he was forced to clothe himself with coal sacks. Without living quarters, Phelax became a shabby shell of the young sailor he was.

One day he spotted the German warship, the *Panther*, arriving in port. Knowing that it was crewed by fellow countrymen, he went there to see a friendly face and hopefully get his feet back on the ground. The crewmembers were kind initially, sneaking him bread and spare uniform clothing when they could. He was sneaked aboard the ship one night, and an officer ordered him to be thrown off the ship.

Some of the crewmembers felt sorry enough for him to arrange a rendezvous with the young boy. They cut his hair, cleaned him up, and gave him enough clothing to make him presentable again. It was all that Luckner needed: a chance, an opportunity. With his new-found appearance, he was able to secure work on another ship—and once more, he was able to turn certain failure into success.

At some point during the early weeks on Mopelia, a realization came to Captain von Luckner that haunted him for years to come. The *Seeadler* was lost. Regardless of how that happened, the loss of a ship would result in a court martial—if only to investigate the cause of the loss. This was routine unless negligence was found.

The loss of the *Seeadler* was an accident, but it could have been prevented. He had ordered her anchored in a bad location. They knew the anchors did not hold on the coral bottom: their drift the first night had proven that. This thought nagged at von Luckner.

Ultimately the loss of the *Seeadler* would fall on his head as the captain. It was possible that upon return to Germany, the successes of the *Seeadler's* raid would be overshadowed with his own court martial. His solution was simple: he ordered the officers to lie.

After pulling them into a covert meeting, he told them he wanted them to say that a tidal wave had been the cause of the *Seeadler's* loss. The crew was to stick by this story. No blame would come to anyone in the crew for the shipwreck. They agreed. As far as Germany and the Admiralstab were concerned, the *Seeadler* was lost as a result of a freak tidal wave.

Only one person outside of the crew ever heard this story, a cabin boy from one of the American schooners. He never let on that he spoke German and was close enough to have heard the meeting.

The story of the tidal wave plagued von Luckner for many years. His own written account described it as a forty-five-foot wave on the horizon that literally overtook the ship. Researchers checked the tidal and weather conditions on the other nearby Society Islands and could find nothing to corroborate the story of a tidal wave. And the testimonies of the American crewmen and captains substantiate the story that the wind and a change of current doomed the *Seeadler*.

The crew of the *Seeadler* stuck to their word. In books or official documents, none of them ever spoke of anything other than a tidal wave as the cause of the ship's loss.

After three weeks on the island, it became clear that Mopelia was a small island with limited resources. Fresh water was not overly abundant, with two wells on the island that rose and sank with the tide. Worse yet, the water was often brackish and had to be heavily boiled before use. While the food was plentiful at the start of their forced seclusion, it was obvious that over time the population of the island would soon overcome the island's resources. According to rough estimates, there were four months' worth of food, if rationed. With spoilage, there would be less.

For weeks, von Luckner and the crew hoped that a ship would show up—so they could capture it. Mopelia's isolation had been one of the reasons that von Luckner had chosen it; now, that seemed to work against him. The native Kanakas informed him that the French ship that dropped them off came only twice a year to the island, and there was no way of knowing when the next ship might happen by. Removed from the major shipping lanes, a ready escape did not seem probable in the near future.

The *Seeadler* would never set sail ever again. She still packed potent firepower from her 4.2-inch cannons, but she was destined to remain on the reef forever. The crew was physically better, but they were a long way from home and surrounded by island colonies that were possessions of Germany's enemies.

From Von Luckner's perspective, the options were limited. They could remain on Mopelia until they were overtaken by a visiting merchant ship. That could take months, and there was no guarantee that the ship showing up was not an enemy warship. Also, the longer everyone remained on Mopelia, the more depleted the resources there would become.

The other option was to take to the sea, seek another ship of their choosing and capture it. For Captain von Luckner, this was the best possible course of action. He would split the supplies up, take to the seas, capture a ship, and come back to rescue his crew.

To do this, he was going to have to outfit another ship as a small raider. There were plenty of lifeboats from the *Seeadler*, but none of these would serve for a long sea voyage. That left the two large motor launches. These were twenty feet long, deep enough to weather moderate seas, and large enough for several crewmembers, making the chances of taking an enemy ship even better.

Of the two motor launches, one was in better condition and it was chosen to be the one outfitted for the voyage. It only had fourteen inches of freeboard above the boat's waterline so the crew fitted canvas along the sides. These could be extended upward to form a tent-like shelter for those aboard the tiny vessel.

The crew rigged a double jib and a jib boom and recaulked her. Despite three weeks of hard work, the ship still took on some water—even on idle seas. Engineer Krause overhauled the small motor, taking it apart, prepping it for extensive use, then rebuilding it.

Food and water supplies were going to be crucial. Hardtack, a side of bacon, the last of the pemmican, and fresh water were carefully packed. If rationed, it was enough for a crew of five or six for three weeks.

The boat would not travel unarmed. The sailors loaded one of the *Seeadler's* machine guns and ample ammunition along with rifles, pistols, and grenades. Those sent on the mission took their German naval uniforms as well as a German flag.

To keep the ammunition dry, they packed it in the buoyancy tanks of the small craft along with a camera, some of the food, a sextant, and a supply of tobacco. Sailing charts were taken as well. The crew brought a book for entertainment, *A Trip to Constantinople*, as well as other books, a coffeepot, a blowtorch, and a hand-accordion to help kill the idle hours at sea. The blowtorch was mostly for the crude but effective job of warming up the coffeepot. They also packed a carpenter's kit, signal rockets, and the logbook from the *R. C. Slade* in the hope that they might use it as a prop if pressed for documentation of their voyage. Four mattresses lay along the bottom of the vessel, along with enough fuel for five days. Von Luckner had some rum and a quantity of gold carefully stored aboard the boat. The *Seeadler's* cache was for use in neutral ports. According to von Luckner they had captured gold and jewelry from the *Seeadler*'s victims.

The crew made a test run with the boat on August 21. They took her outside of the lagoon for a sea trial, and the tiny vessel proved she was at least seaworthy on calm seas. How the vessel would handle a gale was yet to be seen.

Finally, the boat needed a name. Von Luckner chose *Kronprinzessin Cecilie*.

2 0

THE RAID OF THE
KRONPRINZESSIN CECILIE

August 23–September 22, 1917

Taking a small, open sailing ship into the Pacific in the middle of a war would be a daunting task for any crew. Von Luckner and his officers worked out a plan before their departure so those left behind knew what to expect, and when. He intended to sail first to the Cook Islands in search of a ship that they could commandeer. If they had no luck there, they would take an extended trip to the Fiji Islands in search of a target ship to seize. Von Luckner had sailed in the Pacific before but was by no means an expert on small boats on the open ocean. His best estimate was that he could travel sixty nautical miles a day.

Seizing a ship was the ultimate goal. Von Luckner would take five men with him and leave the rest of the *Seeadler* crew and the prisoners on Mopelia. While he was gone, they would be in charge of salvaging the 4.2-inch cannons so they could be remounted on the vessel von Luckner hoped to capture. His intention was simple: capture a ship, return to Mopelia, refit and rearm the ship there, and continue his original mission.

For his new tiny crew, he made careful and interesting choices: Karl Kircheiß, Friedrich Lüdemann, Heinrich Permien, Herman Krause, and Hermann Erdmann. Some of the reasons for his choices were easier to understand than others. Kircheiß had extensive sailing experience before the war in similar sized boats. The tiny engine might need repairs, hence the inclusion of the mechanic Krause. According to his own recollection of the selection, the captain chose men who had recovered the best from their bouts with scurvy and beriberi. Erdmann was one of the marines assigned to the *Seeadler* and hopefully would help provide some of the physical security for their mission.

Oddly missing from the list was Richard Pries, the burly and arrogant prize officer that von Luckner had personally recruited. His omission would have repercussions not for the captain, but for his first officer.

First Officer Kling was given specific orders. If he had a chance to capture a ship, he was to do so. He was to monitor the wireless to hear of their progress or capture. If von Luckner was captured or three months passed without a rescue by the *Kronprinzessin Cecilie*'s crew, they were to take the other motor launch and set off on their own to attempt to capture a ship. Three months was a critical time. The food supply on Mopelia that von Luckner was leaving behind was enough to last just over that amount of time. Beyond that, Lieutenant Kling would be forced to take off in search of a ship on his own or risk disease or starvation.

Von Luckner met with the crew and with the prisoners one more time to exchange handshakes and words of encouragement. As his final command, Captain von Luckner scribbled out a formal order. Alfred Kling was left in command of Mopelia. The prisoners and crew were to defer to him as the commanding officer. The *Seeadler*'s war diary and ship's log were left in the care of Lieutenant Kling.

The crew of the *Kronprinzessin Cecilie* sailed out of the shallow white sand lagoon of the tiny atoll. When passing through the inlet they passed the wreck of the *Seeadler*, straddled on the jagged coral. It was a sobering moment for the captain. One part of his mission was gone, another was now taking form. The *Seeadler* had carried him and his crew far—and now she lay permanently stranded.

The first leg of their journey was for the island Atiu. The crew found their small boat was prone to suffer under the waves of the high seas. Charts became soaked with sea spray and the mattresses they slept on were constantly dampened. It was difficult to take readings with a sextant during the day as the choppy seas tossed the ship about roughly. They had a regular pattern they tried to follow aboard the small ship: two men on each watch. From 8 to 12 AM Captain von Luckner and Permien stood watch; from 12 to 4 PM it was Engineer Krause and Lüdemann; and from 4 to 8 PM the ship was manned by Kircheiß and Erdmann. During the daytime hours, the men sailed. At night, they played the accordion, read out loud from the book they had brought, and plotted their course by the stars.

During their trip they plotted and refined a story that might explain a small boat wandering the Pacific. It was a thin tale at best, but it is apparent that they were relying on their acting skills more than their story to hold credible with anyone they met. In this ruse, von Luckner would claim that the crew were Dutch-Americans sailing the Pacific on a bet. If there were no ships available, they would ask one of the locals to provide them with a certificate to verify who they were, in hopes that it would be of use later in their journey. Von Luckner took the name "Van Houten," and Kircheiß assumed the role of Chief Officer "Southard," the name of the captain of the *Manilla*.

On the third day of their voyage they came across the first of the Cook islands on their course—Atiu, a British holding. They saw no ships in the tiny harbor and realized that they would need supplies, namely fresh fruits, vegetables, and drinking water. They landed and made their way to the residence of one of the British on the island. Von Luckner unfolded his tale. They were Dutch-Americans from San Francisco, sailing the Pacific on a bet. They were to sail from Honolulu to the Society Islands, then to the Cook Islands in an open boat, then back to Hawaii. Von Luckner pressed the resident for a certificate of some sort to verify that they had indeed been to the island.

The British resident was suspicious of the story and was too lazy to help the men out. "Well, a man must be a hell of a fool to go in for that kind of sport." He reluctantly scribbled out a note for the men indicating that they had been to Atiu. The Germans encountered a French missionary priest and convinced him that they were Dutch-Americans and had relatives in France . . . a lucky coincidence. The priest took them in, provided them with a meal, and caught them up on the war news. The Germans were careful to not reveal their true nature. He asked them where their next stop was going to be on their bet.

Von Luckner as Van Houten told him Aitutaki was their next probable stop. The missionary told them the name of someone to look up there and that there were plenty of Dutch settlers on the island. Playboys sailing the Pacific on a bet during a war would be something of celebrities there. It was a plain clue for von Luckner and his crew—they were going to have to come up with a different cover story for their next stop.

They took on mangoes, bananas, coconuts, and fresh water before they departed.

In Washington and London, another story was unfolding. An article in the *Washington Post*, on August 24, read as follows:

Teuton Raider Sunk in Fight at Sea. *See Adler* Surprised and Destroyed by a British Ship.

From an Atlantic Port: Surprised by a British warship, the German raider *See Adler*, which for a time roamed the seas with the famous raider *Moewe* in search of ships to destroy, has herself been sunk in the Atlantic Ocean. The news was brought to an Atlantic port by the British steamer *Harrington Head*, on board of which were part of the crew of the German ship. The vessel remained in an American port for two days, and then steamed to England to discharge her prisoners and cargo.

The raider, according to reports, went down fighting and part of her crew went down with her. The fight is said to have occurred more than 1,000 miles from this port several weeks ago . . .

The London papers ran the same article. The crew of the *Seeadler*, quite alive and in a different ocean, were now split into two groups: one trapped on a remote island, another desperately seeking another ship to use to continue their mission.

A few hours after leaving Atiu, the *Kronprinzessin Cecilie* ran into a storm. The mattresses that were laid in the bottom of the ship were soaked as were the blankets. The ship's cover was not enough to keep the torrential rains out, and at one point they were bailing over two hundred buckets of water an hour from the ship to keep her afloat. They struggled against nearby waterspouts that sprung from the storm—gray snaking monsters that tore at the ocean surface from the storm clouds above. The *Kronprinzessin Cecilie* had not been built for this kind of weather, but she somehow prevailed. As the storms subsided, the crew found themselves drenched, hot, and sore.

They planned to land at Rarotonga and approached the island in the evening, simply to take a rest. In the early nighttime hours, they spotted a large steamship at the entrance to the harbor seemingly parked in the darkness to guard the port. Immediately they assumed it was an armed merchant cruiser and smelled a trap. They continued on, fearful of being captured. In reality it was the merchant ship *Maitai* that had wrecked on the reef. In the dark, it appeared much more dangerous and menacing.

On August 31 the *Cecilie* arrived at Aitutaki at around 1100 hours. They did not attempt to conceal their arrival, apparently comfortable in the story that they had worked on during their cruise. They came to a small wharf and tied the ship up and debarked.

The arrival of a small open sailing ship with six white sailors attracted a great deal of attention. The Resident Agent Thomas Duncan, a British citizen, led the contingent that met with them—inviting them in for a meal and a discussion. Duncan was the ranking authority on the island.

Captain von Luckner had indeed spun a variation of the story he had crafted on Atiu. They were no longer Dutch-Americans; the Germans had once more become a group of Norwegians led by an American journalist. He once more became Mr. Van Houten and Kircheiß became the grizzled Mr. Southard. Van Houten was an American writer for *Harrod's Magazine* who was along to cover the adventure of the men on their bet.

The small band of Norwegians made a bet in the Dutch Club at San Francisco. As before, the $1,500 bet was that they were going to leave from Honolulu and sail to the Cook Islands and back. According to their background story, they had left San Francisco on the 28th of July aboard the steamship *Vancouver*. Once in Honolulu Van Houten had hired the crew he had with him. In Hawaii they had hired the *Cecilie* from a German firm, H. Hackfield and Company.

The story got more colorful and detailed as it was told. They had sailed to the island of Papeete where they had been picked up by a friendly French torpedo boat. Apparently part of this was to ease

Mr. Duncan's concerns that they were hostile—an ally of the British had picked them up. They had sailed to Maupiti and to Rarotonga and had conveyed their version of events at Atiu a few days earlier.

Mr. Duncan was beyond suspicious and asked for passports—which they could not provide. They claimed that they were surprised by his request, not sure why they would have brought them on such a trip. Their story didn't add up. Perhaps these men were escaped prisoners from another island, fleeing for their lives. To be sure, he needed more information. He invited them to dinner, but his quarters proved too small for the two men and him. His suggestion was that Southard dine with a friend of his. The ploy was fairly simple. Both men could be questioned separately and the British officials could compare notes later. If their story was a fraud, cracks should emerge.

They dined. Both of the Germans hung tight to their stories, enough so that all Duncan was left with were his suspicions. The next morning, Duncan had another plan to test their story. If he couldn't get them to crack, he could get them to let him aboard their ship.

Von Luckner purchased some canned fruit, cake, tobacco, and milk. It wasn't much, but it was some variety for their diet. He and Kircheiß retired for the evening. For them the evening had not been an entire loss. They learned that there were no guns on the island at all. If they wanted, they could have taken the entire island in one quick move.

The constant questioning and probing on the part of Thomas Duncan made one thing clear: he wasn't buying their story. Von Luckner inquired if there were any ships due in port, but Duncan either did not trust him enough to pass on that information or didn't know. Von Luckner later would say that he considered taking control of the island, but he knew that the locals would greatly outnumber them and eventually wear them down. It worked. Duncan provided them with the certificate that they asked for.

The next day, Mr. Duncan insisted that he go aboard the ship for a full inspection. He wanted to validate something of their story, anything. Kircheiß produced the logbook from the *R. C. Slade*; the British citizen couldn't have known she was one of the *Seeadler*'s prey. Kircheiß attempted to show that the dates in the log backed up their story, but it only seemed to create more questions than it resolved.

The adventurers claimed that it had been given to them by Consul Hackfield when they secured the *Cecilie*. The story didn't seem to hold water. At this point they said that he was the Consul of Honolulu—a title that didn't fit what Duncan knew. They claimed that they didn't even have a flag, which seemed out of place given the war that was raging around the world.

At one point, standing near the small launch, the Germans made sure he understood what he was facing. Growing weary of his nagging and interference, they made it clear to him that they had the upper hand. The canvas sidewalls of the ship were pulled back to reveal the stash of arms and grenades there, as well as the well-oiled machine gun. These were more than a match for the firepower on the island, which was nonexistent.

Duncan blanched at the sight. These were not escaped prisoners. He wasn't sure what they were, but they were not escapees—not with this amount of firepower at their disposal. He backed away. From that point on Thomas Duncan had one prime motivation: get these men away from his island.

In the end, by 1630, the Germans had bid farewell and had departed. Within a day of their departure, Thomas Duncan wrote a letter of query, detailing the events of the "mysterious foreigners" and asking the consulate of the Cook Islands how they could have possibly gotten past Papeete without passports in wartime. He omitted the guns and grenades, most likely afraid of the pressures he would receive for letting the men go. Let them be someone else's problem; that was his approach.

The letter of warning was transferred by ship. In the meantime, the *Kronprinzessin Cecilie* was on its way on the longest leg of its voyage—to the Fiji Islands.

The first leg of their voyage consisted of hundreds of miles. The trip from the Cook Islands to Fiji was well over a thousand miles across open seas. Almost immediately the voyage took a turn for the worse.

The skies filled with gray and purple storm clouds, erupting with violent winds and dousing rain. And the storms did not disappear, but seemed to hold onto the tiny *Kronprinzessin Cecilie* if only to torment her crew.

The wind was erratic and turned the deep cobalt seas into a churned white chop. There were clouds at night that blocked the stars, making navigation difficult. Even with the canvas covers pulled up, the rain soaked the mattresses and blankets again. Von Luckner knew that they were short of drinking water and ordered that the canvas be stretched like a giant funnel to catch the rain water. But the waves had soaked the canvas, so whatever water was captured was salty and worthless for drinking.

Navigation required help from most of the crew. Kircheiß performed the real work with the sextant, but for it to work, he had to see the horizon. In the height of the swell and the churn of the weather, he had to climb up on the shoulders of Permien and Erdmann, wrapping his arm around the mast for support. This propped him up high enough so that he could get an accurate reading.

The salt proved to be a constant irritant. The storms were not constant. They stopped during some of the days, enough for the sun to emerge and turn the seas into a hot sauna. The crew's clothing was soaked in sea water and when it dried it made them chafe and rubbed their skin raw.

At one point the crew came through what Captain von Luckner described as a sea of "brimstone," a sulfurous yellow grime floated on the surface and turned the azure waters into a sickening golden slop. Chances are this was really pumice on the surface, but it was not a happy find. The gritty substance reeked of sulfur, only adding to the misery of the men. When the storms came again, it splashed the material into the ship—and even with the bailing, it made their chafing even worse.

Since they had not resupplied on Aitutaki, their fruit was now gone or spoiled and their scurvy resurfaced quickly. The Germans' gums grew pale and their teeth became loose. Eating hardtack with their loose teeth only seemed to highlight their pain. Their joints swelled and ached and they were forced to cut their pants at the knee joints to relieve the pressure. They literally watched each other slowly begin to waste away.

After a few more days on the grinding seas, the reality of their water-supply problem was evident as well. Working only on their reserves, rationing was still not going to be enough. The rain water they gathered in the salt-laden sails was too tainted to drink but was clean enough for some bathing. When the storms did break and the sun came out, it made their tongues dry and swollen. In order to stir spit in their mouths, they would gnaw on their knuckles. Their lips became dark and painfully cracked. They still had a piece of salted bacon that they wanted to use for food, but they knew that it would only make their desire for water even worse.

For the six men in the *Kronprinzessin Cecilie*, the trip had to be something that pressed them close to the breaking point. They were in a microcosm on that tiny ship, living and slowly dying only a few feet from each other—day and night. When it wasn't storming they were baking in the sun. Every movement brought pain—and not moving even made their joints ache. Their headaches of starvation and dehydration, that throbbed with each battering rock of the waves, were a reminder of just how desperate their situation had become. Thoughts of suicide would have crept into their thinking—the sweet release that death might bright them. Such thoughts faded when the lookout spotted an island in the distance.

Katafangato was a populated island but had long isolated stretches. To the men aboard the small launch, it had to have looked like a vision of salvation. Locating a deserted lagoon, they landed the *Cecilie* and debarked. There were ample coconuts and bananas to help boost their vitamins and drive away the symptoms of the scurvy. More importantly, they found plenty of fresh water.

Inland on Katafangato they located an empty house that was apparently owned by a German. They opted to break into the house. For the seamen, it was a welcome treat; they slept on beds with sheets for the first time since the *Seeadler* had been wrecked. From the papers in the house, they determined that the owner was a man named Stockwell. Von Luckner raided the pantry the next day, taking foods for the rest of the trip. He left a note for the owner, apologizing for the intrusion, and signed it, "Max Pemberton."

Their plan, from what can be pieced together, was to sail on to Levuka island. Von Luckner hoped they might sneak into port, cut loose a sailing ship, and tow it out at night with the *Kronprinzessin Cecilie*.

On the night of September 18 a massive gale broke over the ship. The wind and waves were so strong that the *Cecilie* began to slip anchor and nearly repeated the fate of the *Seeadler*. They only narrowly avoided wrecking on a coral reef. The crew managed to get the ship into Wakaya Bay of Wakaya Island. In the shelter of the bay, they were able to drop and hold anchor. In the darkness and rolling of the storm, they could not make out any details.

When they woke in the morning they were surprised to find that the inner harbor had several ships at anchor. They immediately began to plan how they would seize a ship and which of the vessels would be their intended victim. They had been gone for a month from Mopelia. There was ample time to return, pick up the rest of the crew, and once again set out raiding.

Wakaya Island was unremarkable except for the fact that there were other ships available. The weary Germans began to see the potential of outfitting one of the ships with the *Seeadler*'s cannons. It would allow them to begin their cruise anew. The sight of other ships whetted the desire of the count to secure one and get back to the rest of his crew on Mopelia.

When they tied their boat up on the dock, two of the sailors stayed with the *Cecilie* while the rest went ashore. She was starting to show signs of wear. Her paint had been worn away in many places. Her sails were streaked with salt and the canvas sides were tattered at the edges.

Von Luckner and Kircheiß came across a native who told them that there was a wireless station on the island. More importantly, he told them that a recent warning had been posted about a small sailing ship filled with foreigners in the islands. The British had posted a reward of fifty pounds sterling, more than enough to motivate locals to keep alert. The warning coincided with newspaper articles already running in New Zealand, spawned by warnings that had been sent up from their previous encounter with Thomas Duncan. The native seemed more than inquisitive as to where the travelers were from and which ship was theirs.

The pair of German officers, still in civilian clothing, came across a British resident who invited them in. They went back to the ship and recovered some of their rum to share with the man. The story that they spun on Wakaya was that they were Americans from a ship called the *Hiawatha*. They had been hired to take a passenger from Suva and had been blown off course by a storm. The British resident seemed to be taken with their plight and offered them quarters for the night. Their focus had been on the native; they were still worried that the man might suspect their origins and try to turn them in for the reward.

That night some of the locals attempted to seize the *Kronprinzessin Cecilie*. They had waded out to where the ship was moored and untied it. What they didn't know was that two of the crew were sleeping on the ship and were awakened by the subtle splashes in the warm waters around them. They succeeded in scaring off the natives and anchored the ship farther out, where it was less prone to tampering.

The next morning a two-masted schooner arrived, the *Gleaner A*. She was relatively new and equipped with an auxiliary motor. From what von Luckner could see, she had all the potential of being the *Seeadler 2*. The key was to not raise a ruckus in the harbor. They would have to seize the ship farther out. Doing so in sight of the locals, who had access to a wireless, was bound to draw attention that none of the Germans desired.

Kircheiß came up with their lie. He told his story of being Americans to the schooner's captain. He added that their motor was giving them problems. When he found that the *Gleaner A* was bound for Levuka he claimed that was their destination. He negotiated that they would tie their ship up and take it in tow, and in return they would pay one pound sterling for passage. It seemed like a good arrangement. The captain arranged a time for them to rendezvous.

It seemed like a perfect plan. Captain von Luckner was worried about staying on Wakaya given the suspicion of the locals and the open reward on them. He ordered his crew to take the rifles, grenades, and pistols and hide them in their clothing, wrapping them in bundles. When they arrived on the *Gleaner A*, they would carry them aboard as their personal belongings. Then, once the ship was out of the harbor, they would seize it. Von Luckner himself carried a Luger pistol in his pocket. They had agreed to meet with the *Gleaner A* at 0730 in the morning.

The locals had traveled to another nearby island, suspecting that the *Kronprinzessin Cecilie* was the suspicious ship a reward had been posted for. The local authorities boarded the steamer *Arma* and set off for Wakaya to check out the mysterious foreigners for themselves. They arrived at the harbor at 0500 and surveyed the situation. The small sailing ship in question, the *Cecilie*, was anchored at the outer harbor.

As planned, von Luckner and his men set out for the *Gleaner A*. As they approached the schooner, they noticed that the steamer, the *Arma*, had swung over toward them and was lowering a boat. The inspector in charge of the police forces, Arthur Howard, prepared to inspect the small ship before it reached the *Gleaner A*.

It had to have been a challenging few minutes for the Germans. They had a machine gun, grenades, rifles, pistols, and more ammunition than would be found on five of the nearest islands. In the distance was the ship they wanted to seize, the magnificent schooner. But looming near them was the steamer—much faster and more threatening. Von Luckner ordered the *Cecilie* to swing wide of the approaching launch.

As they drew close in the launch, Sub-Inspector Harry Hills noticed that the occupants of the small ship seemed to be nervous and moving to evade them. He and Howard pulled their weapons, six shot revolvers. Aboard their launch there were six men: the odds were even.

Playing a bluff of his own, Sub-Inspector Hills called out that they had them under their guns. Von Luckner and Kircheiß looked up at the *Arma* and were not sure if it was a military patrol ship, a small auxiliary cruiser, or some sort of local militia. The portals on the side of the older steamer seemed threatening; Kircheiß suspected that they might conceal hidden guns.

The threat continued to close on the *Kronprinzessin Cecilie*. Captain von Luckner saw the ship approaching. He had enough firepower at his disposal to easily take out the smaller ship, but he was unsure of the threat that he faced from the steamer itself.

While it was doubtful that he had time to consider it, there was another factor von Luckner had to contemplate. He and his crew were wearing civilian clothing. Their German naval uniforms, a little worn from the journey, were packed away, as was the German flag for the *Cecilie*. If they did open fire, it would not be as German sailors but as potential spies or even pirates. They would not be entitled to being treated as prisoners of war. In fact, they could face trial as civilians. Worse yet, the stranded crew of the *Seeadler* might face the same label—pirates. In later years, von Luckner claimed that this was his prime motivation for his next actions, that he didn't want to doom his crew to being shot as spies or pirates. In reality, it was most likely the implied threat from the *Arma*. The grand bluffer had been out-bluffed.

"We surrender," he called out. "We are done . . . done. I am the commander. We are German Navy." The words had to have shocked the local police officials and had to have left a bitter taste in the mouths of the German crew.

When the launch came alongside of the *Kronprinzessin Cecilie* Captain von Luckner handed over his pistol to Inspector Howard. He and his crew were stunned to find that they were facing local police constables rather than armed troops. The *Arma* and her crew of local police had accomplished what the might of the Royal Navy and the United States Navy had failed to do.

But von Luckner's raiding days were far from over.

21

THE ESCAPE

September 22–December 1917

The captured Germans became something of an overnight sensation with New Zealanders. The authorities had to transfer them
to New Zealand because there were POW facilities there. The war
had been a world event that only seemed to pass their homeland and
was only evident when surface raiders operated nearby. Von Luckner
was the highest ranking German officer captured in some time and
he became the focal point for feelings about or against Germans.
While some attempts were made to suppress the news of his capture
until the fate of the rest of the crew and the *Seeadler* itself was known,
those attempts failed.

Things were tense for the prisoners at first. Protests by citizens
and irate guards made it clear that the Germans were not welcome
guests. It was widely believed that the Australian steamer *Wairuma*
struck a mine and sank, with a significant loss of life. Many of the
surface raiders, like the *Seeadler*, were equipped with sea mines and
laying equipment. When word of the capture of von Luckner and the
crew of the *Kronprinzessin Cecilie* was known, there were public out-
cries against the prisoners. Von Luckner was worried for his own personal safety and the safety of his men. While the *Seeadler* had nothing
to do with the sinking of the *Wairuma*, the perception was reality in
the eyes of many New Zealanders.

The SMS *Wolf* was another surface raider that, like the *Seeadler*, had
begun her life as a commercial merchantman. She was a steamer, burning coal—making her voyage somewhat trickier than that of the windjammer. Armed with six 15-centimeter guns and one 10.5-centimeter
gun identical to those mounted on the *Seeadler*, the *Wolf* even carried
an airplane—affectionately known as the Wolf Cub. She even carried
four torpedo tubes and started her cruise with 465 sea mines.

The *Wolf* had taken off at the end of November 1916 and cleared the Royal Navy's blockade without having to undergo inspection, as the *Seeadler* had. She sailed around Africa and into the Indian Ocean, striking at British ships at the same pace as the *Seeadler* had in the Atlantic. The *Wolf* was more along the lines of traditional raiders—prisoners were captured and held belowdecks only to be brought out a few times during the day to stretch their legs. The steamships that she struck were stripped of their coal so the raider could remain at sea.

Like any merchant ship that was converted into a raider, she had problems. When she fired her guns, they literally tore themselves loose from the deck. The prisoners reported that the living conditions in the hot, steamy lower decks were often unbearable. Like the *Seeadler*, she struggled to keep fresh water and food for both her crew and her prisoners.

The *Wolf* swung north toward India, then south of Australia. She swung up and around New Guinea. At the time that the *Seeadler* had run ashore at Mopelia, the *Wolf* was a mere three thousand miles away and the closest German ship. If the raiders had been provided rendezvous times and places, or they could have coordinated their efforts, the plight of the crew and of von Luckner might have been averted. As it was, the crews were unaware they were launching within a few days of each other and that they could have maintained radio contact during their operations.

The *Wolf* laid minefields in several ports and harbors, spreading fear with the Australians and New Zealanders. Mines were fearful weapons, they struck quickly without warning, and they could take down a ship before a lifeboat could be launched. The *Wolf* struck at ships in the merchant shipping lanes, capturing their crews and sinking the ships quickly. All that the locals knew is that ships went to sea and never returned.

The *Wolf* was one of a handful of merchant raiders that made it home. At the end of August 1917, she turned around in the Pacific and retraced her path through the Indian Ocean and then back around Africa into the Atlantic Ocean. Braving all odds, the *Wolf* returned to Germany—sailing back through the British blockade in February of 1918.

In her hold, unknown to the officials in New Zealand and Australia, were the forty-one crewmembers of the *Wairuma*.

Initially the crew of the *Cecilie* was taken to Devonport on Auckland. They moved again due to security concerns to a small prison island, Motuihe. The *Cecilie* was impounded and her contents reviewed by a board of inquiry that the New Zealand army had convened. At first the crewmembers said very little. The questions focused on the important issues—where was the *Seeadler* and the rest of the crew? Things changed when it was discovered that Engineer Krause had maintained a diary, dating back to his time aboard the *Seeadler*. The notes took some time to translate, but it provided the investigators with the names of several islands that offered potential as to where the crew of the *Seeadler* might be. More importantly, if the diary was to be believed, it indicated the fate of the *Seeadler*: "The ship was given up."

Krause's diary was damning when combined with the testimony of Thomas Duncan, which had been filed as a report. More importantly, the officials had the name of a location, Mopelia, and a place to check for the survivors of the shipwreck. This was what von Luckner feared most, that his capture would lead to the capture of the rest of his crew. It was now all in the hands of Lieutenant Kling and the hope that another ship wandered within striking distance of the *Seeadler* crew and was captured. If they did not capture another ship, their fates would soon be sealed. The Allied naval vessels now suspected that Mopelia was their hiding place.

New York Herald
October 10, 1917

Seeadler Wrecked
Lost Ship Succeeded by Two New Raiders

From Washington: A dispatch from the Naval Department from Tutuila (Somoa) announced the arrival there of an open boat containing the master of the American schooner *C. Slade*. He stated that the German raider *Seeadler* had ran ashore and was abandoned on Mopli (Lord Howe Island) on August 2.

> Later the commander and crew of the raider seized a motor sloop and the French schooner *Lutece*, which were armed, and put to sea respectively on August 21 and September 5 for the purpose of carrying out raids . . .

The article, which was published eighteen days after von Luckner's capture, continues to detail the capture of six Germans in an open launch near Fiji. While Captain von Luckner is not mentioned by name, his was one of the two ships mentioned in the article. Similar articles ran both around the world as the story spread slowly and methodically. Previous erroneous stories were quickly forgotten. The capture of Captain von Luckner did not end the threat of raiding in the Pacific. The remaining crew of the *Seeadler* was still at large and a potential risk.

Motuihe is a small farmed island between Motutapu and Waiheke islands just a little northeast of Auckland. Since the outbreak of the war it had served as an internment and POW camp. The prisoners sent there from New Zealand and Samoa were mostly German civilians or commercial sailors whom authorities had deemed security risks, as well as a handful of German POWs who had the unfortunate fate of being in the wrong place when the war broke out.

The authorities intended to keep the crew of the *Kronprinzessin Cecilie* on Motuihe for the duration of the war. The island was in command of Commandant Lieutenant Colonel Charles Harcourt Turner. As the ranking German officer, von Luckner essentially took on the role of being in command of the prisoner population of eighty men. He got to know the Germans on the island, and at the same time he became something of a regular in the office of Lieutenant Colonel Turner.

Given that the internment camp was on an isolated island, Turner did not foresee a great risk of escape. Prisoners were given some degree of latitude in their daily lives and had a wide range of duties, from working on the private farm land to acting as crew on the lieutenant colonel's private motor launch, the *Pearl*. Motuihe Island was not a traditional POW camp. There were two roll calls, one in the morning at muster and one in the early evening, but these tended to be casual in nature. The small number of prisoners and the intermingled guards made it more carefree. A form of the honor system was put in place for those on the island.

That wasn't to say that the camp was open. Lieutenant Colonel Turner did have armed guards patrol the island. He had a direct phone line with Auckland in case of an emergency. His small launch was considered safe at night because he had the spark plugs pulled from the engine and brought to his private quarters when the ship wasn't in use. He also kept an active dialogue with the Germans— especially Captain von Luckner.

By October, von Luckner had come to grips with the fact that Lieutenant Kling had managed to escape from Mopelia (the details of this are covered in the next chapter). For von Luckner, this meant that there was a chance of rescue from his fellow Germans. For his captors, the thought of the rest of the crew wandering the seas was nerve-racking. It worried Lieutenant Colonel Turner enough to question von Luckner if he were planning some sort of escape. No, the count assured him, he was not planning escape.

A formal inquest was held into the events of von Luckner's cruise aboard the *Kronprinzessin Cecilie*. Here again von Luckner waged his seemingly never-ending campaign of misinformation with his enemies. Now that the Americans had exposed the resting place of the *Seeadler*, von Luckner willingly told them that a gust of wind had wrecked his raider. This was a far cry from the tidal wave story that would dominate the media for years to come. When asked about the armaments of his ship, he once again lied, adding in torpedo tubes to the weapons at his disposal.

He told the officials about the ships he had sunk. Regarding the orders he had left with Lieutenant Kling for a potential rendezvous, von Luckner refused information. This only fueled the suspicion that the *Seeadler* crew might be coming to rescue their captain. For many New Zealanders, it was a romantic notion and added to the mystic charm of the charismatic German POW. Weeks before, the Great War was happening on the other side of the planet. Now it had come home. Given the daring of their celebrated POW, it was not hard to imagine his brethren rushing to his rescue.

Von Luckner and Kircheiß settled into a routine, mingling with a tight circle of other prisoners. They learned that some of the other prisoners on the island had been working on escape plans for some time. A civilian seaman, Walter Zatorski, had built a highly functional sextant and had been working with other prisoners on a plot to build several collapsible boats that could be used to flee the island. Kircheiß suggested that they consider taking advantage of the *Pearl*—the lieutenant colonel's launch. Kircheiß met with the prisoners planning an escape and suggested involving von Luckner in their plans, which they agreed to.

What they intended to do after capturing the launch was somewhat murky. The *Seeadler* crew was no longer on Mopelia and the chances of locating them in the Pacific were slim at best. The best plan that the Germans had was to make for a neutral country and be interned there, perhaps even be expatriated back to Germany.

Detailed escape plans were developed. By unscrewing the door hinges, they were able to gain access to the ammunition storage shed and steal some ammo for their venture. The stolen ammunition was used for the powder, allowing them to turn prisoner-issued tins of jam into ad-hoc grenades. Some guns were stolen as well, carefully hidden for when the escape might take place.

Seaman Erdmann had managed to get himself assigned to the crew of the *Pearl* and became not only familiar with her routine, but assisted the plotters with stealing extra fuel for their voyage. By siphoning off a small amount each day and storing it in empty food tins, the prisoners were able to gain an ample amount fuel to extend the range of the *Pearl*.

The escapees knew that the limited range of the launch was going to be a problem. They needed to sew an auxiliary sail, one that would allow them to conserve fuel if they had to. They needed a reason to create the sail, and for that, von Luckner proved his worth. In one of his many meetings with the lieutenant colonel, he suggested that the prisoners put on a Christmas play. He even went so far as to suggest that it might take their mind off of escape attempts. Turner agreed; in doing so, he gave a great deal of cover for the activities of the would-be escapees. Whatever they were working on could be attributed to the building of props or, in the case of sails, sewing curtains for the play.

Fresh water was easy to steal, but food was another matter. The escapees solved this by raiding the chicken coop in the camp and occasionally killing a chicken, then cooking it and canning it in their cabins. The loss of an occasional chicken did not appear to raise the suspicions of the New Zealand troops guarding them. Eggs were stolen as well, pickled and stored for the escape. They attributed the loss to the birds wandering off or dying of natural causes.

Von Luckner insisted that they have a German flag to avoid being treated as civilians. The circle of plotters took an old sheet and fashioned a Kriegsmarine ensign that could be hoisted up. They would need uniforms. New Zealand uniforms would have to suffice, stolen one part at a time and modified to pass as German naval uniforms. Even if caught, they could always claim that the uniforms were part of the Christmas play.

They knew that when the *Pearl* went missing, Lieutenant Colonel Turner would contact Auckland. Every military and civilian ship that could be mustered would be pressed into the search. They key was to cut off that notification. To do this, they enlisted the aid of a prisoner, Karl Grün, a radio and electronics specialist. He managed to trace the phone line from the camp to the mainland and made plans for cutting it when the escape came.

In late November, von Luckner injured his leg and took to walking with a cane, with a stiff leg. It was an exaggeration on his part, aimed at making Turner think that he was unable to escape. At the same time, it allowed him to smuggle goods that the escapees needed in his stiff leg. There were even articles in the office of the lieutenant colonel that he helped himself to.

Walter Zatorski's sextant was an ingenious and accurate piece of hand-crafted gear. But for the sextant to be of any use, they would need nautical charts—and accurate ones at that. Kircheiß solved this issue by using the small camp library. There was an atlas there with maps of the Pacific, albeit not at the level of detail he would have preferred. By cutting the two pages out of the book and pasting them together, Lieutenant Kircheiß felt he had enough of a map for rudimentary navigation. It was not perfect, but it was the best they would be able to muster.

Few of the prisoners were not at least aware of the escape plan. Only the New Zealand troops and their somewhat egotistical commander were in the dark as to what was happening.

That changed on the evening of November 29, 1917, when Lieutenant Colonel Turner received the prisoners' escape plan on a silver platter.

When the spark plugs came ashore that evening from the *Pearl*, there was a small broken-English note scribed in red ink addressed to Lieutenant Colonel Turner. The message was short and to the point: "Loock your Launch there is Proviant Benzin and Sail for Runaway to day. Don't mention this." The "Benzin" referred to benzene, the fuel the *Pearl* used.

Someone had betrayed the escapees.

A check was made of the camp and in the canteen, red ink was found where someone had recently written something and spilled some of the ink. Lieutenant Colonel Turner had been provided with not just a warning, but the means by which the prisoners planned to escape—his launch.

It would be child's play to now capture the escapees. For any officer other than Turner . . .

No escape attempt was made on November 29 and the Germans involved with the plot began to suspect that some of their fellow prisoners may not be so loyal. It was two more weeks before the Germans felt they were ready. There were to be eleven prisoners total that would take part in the escape, over ten percent of the population of Motuihe Island—a sizeable escape from any POW camp.

On December 13, Lieutenant Colonel Turner returned from Auckland in the *Pearl* and had it tied at the dock. He retired to his cabin as he always did, safe in the knowledge that his security measures—the pulling of the spark plugs—would happen later on in the evening. Nightly roll call was done at 1800 hours and all prisoners were accounted for. For all intents, it appeared to be a typical night on Motuihe Island.

The prisoners implemented their plan with precision. Karl Grün severed the telephone communications in an innocuous location, isolating the island from further aid. Erdmann and another prisoner moved the gear aboard the *Pearl* as they unloaded the supplies and mail. They didn't start the engines but pushed the launch out into the deep waters by hand to avoid attracting attention.

At 1910 the camp sergeant major contacted the lieutenant colonel. "Your dinghy has got away and is going along the back of the barracks in a sinking condition and your launch has gone to pick it up." The dinghy was fine; this was an assumption on the part of the sergeant major as to why the *Pearl* was leaving her slip. It was logical—why else would the *Pearl* be sailing away?

When he got out of his cabin, he realized something was wrong. He asked the sergeant major, "Where is that count?" No one had seen von Luckner since before dinner when he and Kircheiß had taken tea with another prisoner. In fact, there were several prisoners missing.

Turner attempted to raise Auckland by phone, but the line was dead. In the pit of his stomach, he knew what he was facing and who was behind it. The most widely known prisoner in New Zealand, if not all of the Pacific, had escaped from his camp.

In a fit of desperation he ordered kerosene brought up and a signal fire lit. While he couldn't call Auckland, he was determined to get the attention of someone off of the island and warn them. There was still time to stop von Luckner and the other prisoners. There was still time to save his career.

The escapees fired up the *Pearl* and headed out into the Hauraki Gulf and then between Motuihi and Motutapa islands. They proceeded through the night. The next day, they sailed to the Mercury group of islands and took shelter near a small island where some of the crew set up a watch for approaching vessels. There were none. They had gotten away from the camp without so much as a shot being fired and had gained precious hours of time.

The food situation, despite the planning, was limited aboard the *Pearl* so they decided to head to the Kermadec Islands. Von Luckner knew from his previous trips that the New Zealand government had several shelters set up along the rocky coasts with supplies set up for shipwreck survivors. There they planned to replenish supplies, courtesy of the people they were escaping from. They were 600 miles away, a staggering distance in such a small launch.

For two days they did not encounter any sign of pursuit or threat. The seas were rough and choppy, but the men were now former prisoners and happy with their fate. While they rested in the shelter of a small island, a lookout on the high ground spotted two ships in the distance. Von Luckner ordered everyone back aboard the *Pearl*. The question of how they would reach the Kermadec Islands had been answered—they would do it in a captured ship.

Both sailing ships were loaded with timber and von Luckner opted for the closest one. The *Pearl*, still flying the New Zealand flag, approached the ship. On her stern, he could make out her name, *Moa*. As he pulled close, the *Moa*'s crew thought it was some sort of government ship. Von Luckner hailed them with his deep booming voice, "Heave-to. I wish to communicate."

Just as the *Pearl* came alongside, the New Zealand flag went down and the German flag went up. The Germans scampered up over the sides of the *Moa*, their homemade bombs in hand, surprising the crew. The captain, a former member of the Royal Navy, William Bourke, saw that he was outmatched.

"Surrender!" von Luckner warned. "You are now prisoners of his Imperial Majesty the Kaiser!"

Captain Bourke was stunned. "I am the master of this vessel and it's hard luck to be taken like this."

Captain von Luckner did not demure. "I have to inform you that you and your crew are civilian prisoners of the kaiser. You must strictly obey my orders and make no resistance. You and your crew will be paid for the time you spend in the kaiser's service."

In the distance, the other schooner, the *Rangi*, had watched as the events unfolded on the *Moa*. While the crew of the *Moa* had no idea what was happening, the *Rangi* had heard word that a launch filled with escaped German POWs was loose. Before she too became a victim, the *Rangi* swung away from the scene, heading for the nearest place they knew of with a phone—Port Charles on the Colville Peninsula. From there, they could let the authorities know that they had spotted the suspected Germans and that they now had control of a sailing ship.

The *Pearl* was tied off of the back of the *Moa* and taken in tow. Captain Bourke and his first officer were assigned to watches along with the Germans who had commandeered his ship. The sails were raised and the *Moa* got underway. Von Luckner realized that the load of lumber on her deck was going to slow her down and ordered that it be dumped overboard.

The *Moa* plowed on toward the Kermadec Islands uneventfully for two days until a strong gale passed through. The *Moa* endured the sudden squall with no problem, but the *Pearl* being towed behind her was not as lucky. The small ship capsized and sank in the churn of the deep green waters.

Finally, on December 21, the *Moa* reached the Kermadec's lonely Curtis Island. Von Luckner ordered that the *Moa* anchor in MacDonald Cove and that Lieutenant Kircheiß along with three other sailors were to raid the supply shed that the government had placed there. Thanks to the loss of the *Pearl*, Kircheiß was forced to take the men in a tiny rowed dinghy from the *Moa*. They reached the corrugated iron shed and found tins of food, medicine, blankets, butter, tools, a new sail, and dried meats waiting for them.

Von Luckner had hoped to drop the prisoners off on Curtis Island along with a note of thanks to the New Zealand government. Loading up, they headed back to the *Moa*. As soon as they arrived and started unloading the provisions, one of the sailors called out a warning, "Smoke in sight!"

The wind was painfully light and even with full sails the *Moa* could only manage five knots or so. The ship that was approaching was coming fast, and it was clear that she was a steamship intent on getting to the captured schooner. The strange ship ran up signal flags, but Kircheiß could not make out the flags. Von Luckner didn't care regardless, something told him in his heart that he knew what they were signaling: Heave-to.

The *Moa* limped along, each minute bringing the steamer closer and closer. The *Moa* was unarmed, except for the handmade grenades and the small arms stolen during their prison break. In defiance, the Germans ran their flag up the mast. Their primary concern was if the ship facing them was armed. If it was, there would be very little fight.

They got their answer a few minutes later in the chase. A shell hit the water and exploded some fifty yards from the *Moa*, sending a column of white frothing sea water up into the air. The ship chasing them was the *Iris*, a ship of the Pacific Cable Company that had been pressed into service as an armed auxiliary cruiser. The *Iris* was armed with two six-pound naval cannons, one fore and one aft—both crewed by members of the Auckland Garrison Artillery.

They had been intercepted at Port Charles by the schooner *Rangi* and had heard the entire story of the capture of the *Moa* from their perspective. They had witnessed the capture of the *Moa* and had, only by a quirk of fate, avoided being captured themselves. A marine on board the *Iris* had correctly guessed that the Germans might be planning to raid the provisions at Kermadec Islands, and the ship had moved to intercept them. It was pure luck that they had come across the *Moa* at the right place, at the right time.

Ironically, if they had managed to keep the faster launch *Pearl*, von Luckner's men could have raided the supplies much faster and might have been gone by the time the *Iris* arrived.

The shot across their bow sent a blast in the water into the air. It was something that von Luckner himself had done many times before but now he found himself on the receiving end. It was a dark moment for him. There had to be a temptation to try and flee, but the chances of success were slim—especially against an auxiliary cruiser.

"We're done," he said to the crew. "We cannot help ourselves further. Bring the ship into the wind, Herr Lieutenant, and haul down the headsails. At least we surrender to superior forces."

Lieutenant Kircheiß, dejected by the turn of events, complied with the commands of his superior officer. The *Moa* lowered the German flag, a signal of surrender. The men tossed their weapons overboard into the Pacific. One of the items that went into the water was a sword that had come from the internment camp at Motuihe Island. That moment had to give von Luckner some degree of satisfaction.

The escape of Count von Luckner from his command had turned the life of Lieutenant Colonel Charles Harcourt Turner into turmoil. He was forced into a court martial to review the evidence to see if he was incompetent in his handling of affairs on Motuihe Island. The people of New Zealand were outraged that the most famous and flamboyant German prisoner in their custody had managed to escape. It was an embarrassment to the military, and at the same time it served to turn Captain von Luckner into something of a folk hero with the local population. The average New Zealander didn't feel at risk with him on the loose, his reputation being one of not killing prisoners but treating them well. At the same time most of them agreed that if the circumstances were the same, they might have escaped as well.

One day Lieutenant Colonel Turner went to wear his dress sword that he wore in his office for one of the proceedings. The sword was usually kept in a canvas scabbard tucked in the corner of the office and used only for formal affairs.

When he grabbed the sword he found only a wooden stick and an empty tin can for the scabbard. It dawned on him then that all of those times Count von Luckner was in his office walking with a stiff leg and with a cane, he was stealing from him. In at least one case, he had taken his dress sword.

The *Iris* pulled alongside of the *Moa* and one of the New Zealand officers with a megaphone leaned over and yelled to the sailing ship. "Where are you from?"

Von Luckner offered a short and somewhat humorous reply. "From Auckland."

"Are there any Germans on your boat?"

One of the captured *Moa* sailors on the deck smirked. "I should say so."

Von Luckner replied with a smile. "Yes."

They ordered him aboard a dinghy and brought him aboard the *Iris*. The cruiser kept her guns trained on the wooden schooner, wary she still might pose a threat. Von Luckner was hauled to the deck at the point of bayonet and searched. The New Zealanders were nervous and heavily armed, unsure of how to deal with the ostentatious count who had eluded them for so many days. For his part, von Luckner tried to keep matters in perspective during the rather humiliating search.

"You left your door open. You cannot blame me for walking out."

22

THE JOURNEY OF THE *FORTUNA*

August 23, 1917–March 1918

Polar exploration at the turn of the nineteenth and into the early twentieth century was considered the pinnacle of bravery and daring. Anyone who was literate carefully studied the heroic expeditions that went to the north and south poles. Going to the poles was like a race to the moon. Such expeditions were matters of national pride. This was not lost on the Germans who mounted several expeditions themselves.

The problems with the German Antarctic expeditions is that they often brought failure. The first expedition in 1901–1903 of the steamship *Gauss* managed to reach Antarctica but did not result in the teams reaching the South Pole. The *Gauss* failed because of inadequate planning and preparation.

When Wilhelm Filchner was forming the second major German expedition, the kaiser wanted to try and cross the pole with a zeppelin rather than a ground-based team. Filchner went with private funding, only obtaining government help in the crewing of his expedition's ship, the *Deutschland*, mostly with naval reservists. A handful of these sailors also had been aboard the first expedition's ship, the *Gauss*, and had the experience Filchner sought.

The planning for the Filchner expedition was meticulous, covering every possible contingency. He even brought along eight Manchurian ponies, noted for their sure-footedness and tolerances to cold climates. On May 7, 1911, this expedition left Bremerhaven for the South Pole. The captain of the *Deutschland*, Richard Vahsel, was a man who did not follow orders well nor did he carry the respect of his crew. Problems arose by the time the expedition reached South America and Filchner found that he needed to replace Captain Vahsel. For that replacement, he sought out a young officer aboard the ship who had sailed before on the *Gauss* and who had experience in Antarctic waters, Alfred Kling.

He was a young officer in the naval reserve, and for him, the temporary command of the *Deutschland* was his first taste of true authority. His command of the expedition was short-lived. Captain Vahsel managed to regain his command, though his drinking and the drinking of the crew was a constant irritation to Wilhelm Filchner. Eventually the Filchner expedition hesitantly reached Antarctica and the team built a station house on the glacier while the *Deutschland* held off the coast in the frigid waters. The location of the station house was chosen by a self-proclaimed expert on the glaciers. The completion of the station house would allow the expedition to have a staging area for deeper attempts at the South Pole itself. For a short time it appeared that this might be Germany's long-hoped-for success in Antarctica. Those hopes were dashed when the warming of the glacier literally ripped the station house apart in a violent upheaval of the ice.

The Filchner expedition was yet another German failure. The failure was not in the planning, but in the cooperation of the men on the trip. And despite the disappointment, the people of Germany saw the men of the ill-fated expedition as heroes.

With the departure of the *Kronprinzessin Cecilie*, Lieutenant Alfred Kling obtained something that had eluded him most of his career: command. Mopelia, the crew there, the prisoners—they were all under his command, his leadership. For Kling, the man who had taken his lessons from the Antarctic expedition and had planned so well for the cruise of the *Seeadler*, he now had the formal authority to lead. If Captain von Luckner managed to return with a ship, he would be content to depart. If not, Kling fully intended to lead the crew out of their isolation on the tropical island on his own. It would be his one chance to demonstrate his command capabilities.

The fifty-five crewmembers and three officers of the *Seeadler* that were still on Mopelia were probably the most heavily armed force in that region of the Pacific. They had thirty-four carbines, thirty-four personal sidearms, twenty-three Luger pistols, a machine gun, and a hundred hand grenades. Kling had over 3,000 rounds of ammunition for the carbines, three thousand pistol rounds, and twenty-eight explosive charges.

Almost immediately, things began to go wrong. A sudden tidal surge rose one evening and when the Germans woke up, they realized that their tiny provision island and the landing had literally disappeared with the wave, taking with it the sundries and supplies that had not already been transferred to the village. The loss of supplies was damning, leaving them with only a one-month supply. Right from the start Lieutenant Kling was facing his own life-threatening crisis.

The wreck of the *Seeadler* became a concern for him. The masts poking up into the brilliant blue sky could be seen for fifteen miles. While they may lure in a ship that could be captured, they just as well could draw in a military vessel hoping to rescue shipwrecked survivors. On August 30, Lieutenant Kling ordered Lieutenant Pries to return to the *Seeadler* and use explosive charges to take the masts down. He and a small crew boarded the windjammer and placed explosive cartridges at the base of the masts. They were lit and went off with a deep thudding blast. The masts teetered for a moment, then came careening down as the cable rigging whipped and snapped.

What Lieutenant Pries had not foreseen was that the diesel tank exhaust vents had been left open. From his own description, the wooden deck had been littered with debris from the systematic looting of the ship and the downed masts. While the guns had been fired on the deck many times during her voyage with no problems, the vents had always been closed in battle. Now the remaining diesel fuel caught on fire as did the wooden deck. As Pries and the rest of the boarding party attempted to put out the roaring flames, it was apparent that the fire was already out of control.

Pries made a good quick decision: get away from the *Seeadler*. In her forward magazine were still some 4.2-inch cannon shells. Within a few minutes, the flames cooked off the rounds, blowing some of the hull plating free with a muffled underwater blast.

The flames and billowing smoke from the teak and oak formed a funeral pyre of the once proud ship. Yes, the masts were down as

Lieutenant Kling had hoped, but the result was that the ship was a complete loss and was serving as a signal that could be seen miles away. The *Seeadler* burned for five days, casting an eerie orange and red glow on the horizon at nightfall as the shipwreck survivors watched. The varnished oak and teak went up as did the lower decks—slowly, almost painfully for her crew who hopelessly watched the hulk ripple with the heat of the fire, day and night. The dark smoke billowed upward and was visible for miles, the very situation that Lieutenant Kling had hoped to avoid.

As the fire finally burned itself out days later, Kling inspected the ship and discovered that the guns had been badly charred by the intense heat. Fearful that they might have been damaged, he realized that salvaging them and using them again might be risky. A final command was given to spike the guns. Explosives were placed in the breaches and the guns were blown. The *Seeadler* would no longer use the proud deck guns in battle.

Some facts were not in dispute. The man who had burned the ship was Lieutenant Richard Pries, the bully who intimidated the prisoners. He was the man von Luckner had handpicked for his prize crew. Pries was the man who had been in command of the *Seeadler* when it had slapped into the coral reef. Now he was the man who had burned the *Seeadler*. From the surviving records, it is clear that the destruction of the ship was a turning point for the burly prize officer.

A few days later the tensions between Kling and Pries reached a boil. There is a notation in the war diary by Pries, almost obscure. He indicated that he was no longer going to follow the orders of Lieutenant Kling. Moreover, he involved other members of the crew and an officer—the ship's doctor. It was a challenge to authority that could not be ignored. There are no other records of conflict between the two men, but it is obvious that Pries was now ignoring the authority of the commanding officer, refusing to serve under any vessel that Lieutenant Kling commanded. Kling went so far as to record the events such that Pries was in violation of following the orders of a superior officer. He was charged with inciting rebellion with the officers and crew. In a word, mutiny.

✠ ✠ ✠

Every night they listened to the wireless set under the purr of the engine that powered the dynamos. The strung deck lights provided some semblance of civilization as did the radio traffic. The Associated Press reports were favorites, telling about the latest news from the war—none of which seemed to please the Germans as much as the American prisoners. Lieutenant Kling kept waiting, hoping to hear some sort of news about his commanding officer.

The first of September brought about some worries. The wireless had picked up a signal that the *A. B. Johnson* was overdue and there were worries that she may have fallen prey to a raider. It was a sobering thought for Kling. If the American Navy began a search for the ship, it was really only a matter of time before they came to Mopelia. Even with the impressive stash of arms they had, they would be no match for an armed ship.

On September 5 at 0520, a lookout spotted a sail on the horizon, heading for Mopelia. Kling assembled a boarding party and had them man the remaining launch, the sistership to the *Kronprinzessin Cecilie*, armed with rifles, pistols, and grenades. He ordered canvas pulled over most of the men and set out toward the approaching sailing ship.

The ship, the *Lutèce*, was a 126-ton island trader. As the motor launch rapidly approached, the captain of the ship became suspicious and attempted to get away. When he saw armed Germans aiming rifles at his unarmed ship, he realized escape was impractical and hoveto. The Germans swarmed out from under the canvas cover and climbed aboard the ship. The mostly Polynesian crew were stunned at the thought that Germans had captured their ship. Kling anchored the vessel and took quick stock of what he had seized.

Initial looks were deceiving. The *Lutèce* seemed to be a perfect ship. She carried a menagerie of goods for island trade including food, clothing, bolts of cloth, butter—a department store on the sea. There was enough food for the Germans to last for several months. His decision was made quickly. The time had come for the crew of the *Seeadler* to leave Mopelia.

But where would they go? The *Lutèce* was unarmed other than rifles and pistols, making return to their original mission of raiding difficult at best. Lieutenant Kling came to the realization that the best hope for the crew was to get back to Germany. And the best way to get back to Germany was through a neutral country. The plan he developed was to sail to Chile. From there, they could hope to be expatriated back home.

A similar effort had been waged by the crew of the cruiser SMS *Emden*. When their ship had been lost, the crew, under command of the first officer, used a smaller craft and a great deal of guile to make their way past the British and her colonies in the Indian Ocean. Once on land the *Emden* crew made their way across the Arabian deserts, through the Ottoman Empire, and eventually back home to Germany. The voyage of the *Emden* crew was mythic in nature. When they had returned back to Germany they were heroes. Kling had mentioned it to the American prisoners on several occasions and while he never told the prisoners where he intended to go, most thought that he was headed along the same route through the Indian Ocean and back home.

September 5 was a busy day. The Germans packed camp and prepared for departure. Kling ordered the wireless set smashed so they couldn't use it to signal for help. He was going to leave them with the single motor launch. From his estimate, it would take two weeks to get the small craft in condition to travel between islands. The excess ammunition the Germans didn't need was taken into the lagoon and dumped into the water. Some of the Germans left letters with their American counterparts—messages for families back in Germany. If something happened to them aboard the *Lutèce*, they wanted to ensure that some word would one day reach their loved ones.

Lieutenant Kling packed up the war diary for the *Seeadler* and the log of the ship to take with him. It was the only official record of the voyage from start to end. Some of the pages of the log were left behind in his hut, to be recovered later by the Americans. They listed some of the victims of the *Seeadler*'s earlier voyage.

By evening, the *Lutèce* was loaded and ready for departure. Lieutenant Kling gathered the prisoners and gave them a short speech. "I leave you in charge of Captain Southard. Don't quarrel and keep yourselves in good discipline. Try and do the best thing under the circumstances and the best for the welfare of all of you and show yourselves to be good Americans."

His last words may have seemed strange coming from a German officer, but Kling had ties to the United States. His brother and mother lived in Ohio.

He also told them that they would be paid, as promised, for their service to the kaiser. Each was offered sixty pounds sterling compensation. Almost all of the Americans turned the money down. They preferred to be treated as prisoners rather than employees of the German Navy. The prisoners made no fuss and the Germans respected the defiant gesture.

As Kling and the others departed, one of the American crewmembers, a Swiss named Charles Julius, went to his cabin. Inside he found a clock that Kling had conspicuously left behind. Julius kept the clock the rest of his life. On the back of the clock was inscribed, *Pass of Balmaha*.

The Americans would have been wise to heed Kling's parting words. Perhaps he saw some of the personality conflicts brewing on the atoll. Captain Southard ordered the immediate repair of the motor launch so that he could set out for help. Captain Smith, apparently irritated at command being turned over to Southard, constantly scorned him and his efforts. Southard, Captain Porutu from the *Lutèce*, and Polynesian crewman Pedro Miller left after only three days' repair to the launch. Captain Southard hoped that taking Porutu with him, someone raised traveling the islands, would help his navigation.

Their voyage was supposed to take them only a day's travel away. They encountered gales that tossed the small launch about. They had brought small supplies of food and water and found themselves lost for several days on the choppy seas in an open ship that had been ill-prepared for the voyage. They finally made their way back to Mopelia, having failed to reach any of the islands. The men were blackened from the sun, badly dehydrated, and sick from starvation. It only seemed to add fuel to Captain Smith's argument as to who should have been left in command of the island.

With Southard ill and too weary to lead, Smith assumed command. He ordered the prisoners to repair the boat and prepare her properly for a much longer sea voyage. Along with his first mate, Baer, and two crewmen from the *Manilla*, he dubbed the small launch *The Deliverer of Mopelia* and set off on September 19.

He undertook a trek shorter than that of von Luckner and his men, but one that faced all of the same risks. They arrived in Pago Pago ten days later and contacted the American naval station in Tahiti. The word of what they had been through, where the *Seeadler* had been shipwrecked, and the fate of the crews was finally known to the world. Newspapers around the globe covered the story over the next two days. Captain Smith was hailed as a hero—a role that he wrapped himself in.

A few days out from Mopelia, Lieutenant Kling had renamed the *Lutèce*, the *Fortuna*. But the trading ship that had seemed such a perfect find a few days earlier proved to have a few problems—mostly in the form of wood rot. The masts had signs of rotting, which prevented him from raising full sails, and the ship leaked. Every day they had to pump water from the hold for several hours. One day, the leaking was so bad that even with the pumps running all day, they still had to hand bail the water out of the hold.

The ship itself, while loaded with goods, was also infested. Cockroaches, scorpions, and rats made sleep as difficult as the first nights on Mopelia. Keeping the *Fortuna* afloat required all of his skill and kept the crew busy.

On October 3, the ship reached Easter Island, a possession of Chile. They anchored the ship and met with the government representative who allowed them to stay on the island while they repaired the ship. The wood on the hull was filled with wood borers and was not repairable. On October 5 the ship bumped a coral reef and within a few days it was taking on water steadily. It was going to be impossible to keep the ship afloat for any period of time.

The realization set in for the Germans. For the second time in two months, they had become shipwrecked. The men amused themselves on Easter Island by inspecting the huge face-statues on the island and relaxing on neutral soil. Once more they raided their floundering ship for supplies and set up a second Seeadlerdorf village on a hill slope overlooking the wreck of the *Fortuna*.

They had to wait until January 25, 1918 for the Chilean government to send a ship, the *Falcon*, to pick them up. With the help of the local authorities, they negotiated with the captain and were eventually dropped off in March in Talcahuano, Chile.

Many people wanted to make sure that the *Seeadler* was indeed on Mopelia and no longer posed a threat. The Australians sent a ship to the island in 1919. They climbed aboard the burned-out wreck looking for some salvage or evidence from the ship they might be able to recover—but they found none.

The American governor to Tahiti organized an expedition to the *Seeadler* as well. Climbing aboard the grand old dame of the seas, they took photographs of themselves standing on the support metal that once held her deck. They took photos of the deadly guns, pointing upward, forever silent. For them, it was more like a tourist visit. The ship that had terrorized two oceans was now a rusting hulk, tipped at an awkward angle, slowly settling to her ultimate demise in the warm waters of the Pacific.

23

GLORY

December 1917–1928

At the other end of the Pacific Ocean, the capture of the *Moa* and her renegade crew brought a collective sigh of relief from the people of New Zealand—as well as criticism of the government and the military. The German sailors were initially taken to Mt. Eden prison where they spent three weeks while the government figured out what they would do with them. Von Luckner assumed that he would return to Motuihe Island, but there were concerns about putting this flamboyant officer back to where he had fled from. The officials were worried about keeping the prisoners together and facing the potential of another, even more embarrassing escape. Instead they were split up—at least in the short term.

Captain von Luckner and Lieutenant Kircheiß were sent to the tiny internment camp at Ripa Island in Lyttelton Harbour. The other prisoners were disbursed to other camps so they would not be able to coordinate their efforts. The isolated little speck of land that made up Ripa Island was run much differently than von Luckner's first internment camp. This was a more traditional camp, with tough guards, tough prisoners, and few of the freedoms he had on Motuihe.

Von Luckner began a campaign of complaining, both in letters home and to New Zealand officials. His celebrity status with fellow prisoners only brought scorn from the guards. His complaints about the conditions and his treatment eventually got both of the officers transferred back to Motuihe—once the locals were sure there was no way that he could repeat his flight. It was there they remained until the end of the war in November of 1918.

While still a prisoner, the German Navy had asked him to assist them in straightening out the affairs of his former crew in Chile. He had written his first real account of the cruise of the *Seeadler* at that time, attempting to explain the state of his former crew as shipwreck survivors. His was a compelling account of the voyage, though it is unknown if it swayed any of the Chilean authorities.

According to the captain's memoirs, he spent the last few months of his time as a POW plotting another escape. It was one that he would never get a chance to try. In May of 1919, von Luckner and the other Germans in camp were put on a ship to begin the voyage home.

The rest of the *Seeadler* crew initially found Chile to be a wonderful place to spend the end of the war. The German community welcomed them openly, with parties and celebrations. According to newspaper reports, the *Seeadler* crew lived like kings. The crew was quartered for a while aboard the *Dresden*, a German ship that had become interned in Chile, and there the two crews mingled well.

When the war came to an end, problems arose immediately. Lieutenant Kling claimed that the crew were survivors of a shipwreck on Easter Island—the slow death of the *Fortuna*. Chile considered them sailors who were taking advantage of the internment in a neutral country—and thus Germany was responsible for paying for their fare. Much of this was due to the fact that with the end of the war, many countries were preying on Germany, sucking what money they could from the bankrupt country. Articles ran in many Chilean newspapers, questioning the status of the *Seeadler* survivors. Some even claimed that they were technically fugitives from the British since their captain had already been captured, technically making them escaped POWs.

Chile was not just touched by greed, she was also being prodded by other governments. The United States and Italy were intercepting the mail from Lieutenant Kling and other Germans, translating it, and sending it back to Chile in hopes that it would solidify their case for the Germans to foot the bill for the internment of the *Seeadler* crew. This was against international law and protocol, but it showed the interest that governments had at keeping the crew of the *Seeadler* where it was. Memories of raiders like the *Möwe*, returning to Germany only to set sail again, must have resonated with them. With the war over, it was an act of diplomatic spite—an attempt to gouge a beaten enemy.

On May 1, 1919 the Chilean authorities announced that the *Seeadler* crew would be returned to Germany. One crewmember did not return. Doctor Pietsch, the hard-drinking, cigar-smoking medical officer of the *Seeadler,* became downtrodden when he learned of Germany's surrender in November. He died of a heart attack and was buried in Chile, making him the only human loss of the entire cruise.

The crew returned home under the command of Lieutenant Pries. Lieutenant Kling turned over the command to the mutineer and opted to remain in Chile. While turning over command to someone that he planned on court-martialing may seem out of the ordinary, it was within proper naval doctrine.

At the time, Kling thought he would stay in Chile and have his wife join him there. Perhaps his thoughts were of settling down, that his time on the high seas was over. From the newspapers and radio, he knew that the Germany he had left was gone—and what was left was turmoil and change. But Chile would not be his home forever.

Scapa Flow in Scotland was the homeport of the British Grand Fleet and even today remains a key naval port for the Royal Navy. The port was accustomed to the sight of the massive dreadnoughts, the coal-powered, steam-driven battleships and cruisers that were the backbone of the Royal Navy. What *was* a novelty was the presence of the German High Seas Fleet.

Eight months after the end of the Great War, Rear Admiral Ludwig von Reuter stood on the bridge of the German flagship, *Friedrich der Grosse,* as the ferry *Flying Kestrel* brought another shipload of school children for a sightseeing tour. It was June 21, 1919, a clear day. Most of the young boys pointed in amusement and amazement at his ships and vessels, which were the pride of the German Navy: the fleet they saw had held the Royal Navy at a standstill for years. Now, Reuter's twelve-inch guns were impotent. During the Great War, he had hoped to be in Scapa Flow, guns blazing, cordite and steel burning. It would have been glorious—the type of battle that every German sailor dreamed of.

It was a dream that had almost come true. When treaty talks were in the early stages, the German Navy command drew up plans for a glorious battle. In their minds, the army was facing defeat, but not the navy. The naval command hoped to launch one more battle, a glorious fight. When successful, they would be able to demand better terms from the Allied forces facing them.

The problem was that Red communists had infiltrated the navy. The sailors were weary of the war and were convinced by agitators that one more grand battle was nothing more than a suicide run. Why fight when peace was only a few weeks away? Quite literally the command of the German Navy dissolved overnight in a massive mutiny. It was not the glorious roar of battle with the Royal Navy, but a dull whimper of fear and disillusionment.

Now, months later, Admiral Reuter's powerful fleet had been reduced from fearsome machines of war to a tourist attraction for British children. It ate at his very soul.

The Armistice with the Allies in November of the previous year had called for the surrender or internment of the German Navy in a neutral port until peace negotiations were over. They had disarmed, their crews had been stripped to skeleton-levels. The German flag had been lowered as they entered the port and had not been allowed to be raised since. It was the British alone, out of the Allies, that had insisted that a neutral port would not do—that the fleet must be secured in a Royal Navy facility.

Now the British were making overtures that they were not satisfied only with disarmament. If the German agents and U.K. newspapers were right, the British were planning on simply seizing the remains of the German fleet, and in turn, expanding their own navy to new levels of strength. His own crews were talking about mutiny against their officers. Some of it was simply communist agitation, but there was a genuine risk that his ships might be used one day against their builders.

Admiral Reuter had waited for the bulk of the British vessels to put to sea that morning. It was 1030 hours. His plans had been in place for several days. Germany had lost the war, but its navy had never been soundly defeated. They had spent most of the war at dock. A few ships, a handful of them, had gone to sea as raiders and had caused a great deal of turmoil to the British. What he was doing, he was doing for all German sailors, no matter where they were.

He contacted the wireless room. He sent a message to the entire fleet. "Paragraph eleven. Confirm." He looked over to his own bridge crew and gave them a firm nod. They had not heard him wrong. The signal had been sent.

While the ferry of school children swung past the fleet, the order went up and down the line of proud German ships. One by one, they opened their flood valves. The witnesses saw something unprecedented in the history of naval warfare—an entire fleet committing suicide. The order he had sent had been the code to scuttle the pride of the German Navy.

From ships' vents oil, some smoke, and a spray of salt water shot into the air. The sea filled with lifeboats and anything that would float. The British ships that were in port reacted as best they could, pushing some of the ships out of the shipping lanes as they sank by their own hand.

From his own lifeboat, Rear Admiral Reuter heard the sounds of men in the water, suddenly interrupted with the sound of rifle shots. He closed his eyes. The British marines were shooting at his men in the water. Reuter did not panic but let a calm come over him. He had beaten the British plans. He had denied the Royal Navy his precious ships. Like many brave sailors before him, Reuter had placed the needs of his people above his personal desires.

He watched as the ships disappeared. The *Seydlitz*, the *Von Der Tann*, the *König*, and the *Kronprinz Wilhelm*: with proud names and histories in battle, each slid under the waters within an hour after his order had been sent.

On that day, the last shots of World War One were fired and the last men died—nine German sailors. And everywhere, regardless of their country of origin, naval men and sailors paused for a moment when they heard of the suicide of the fleet. German sailors the world over felt a bond with those who sacrificed their ships that day. They sought their own release, they wanted one moment when destiny was in their own hands.

✠ ✠ ✠

Von Luckner returned home to Germany just in time to spend a last few weeks with his father. Three weeks after his return, the elder von Luckner died. According to his eldest son, he complained up until the end that he had been denied a chance to fight for the kaiser. Heinrich von Luckner had seen his son make the family proud in the uniform of his country, and perhaps that had been enough for him.

Germany after the war was a place of revolution, turmoil, social and political upheaval, and breathtaking inflation. For a naval officer, it was particularly hard to return. The navy had a blemish that was hard to shake—the rebellion and mutinies at the end of the war. Some honor had been gained with the "grand scuttle" at Scapa Flow, but it was cold comfort in light of the loss of the entire German Navy.

In the midst of this there was one bright light—and that was the return of von Luckner and eventually his crew. They had been spared the darkest hours of the German Navy. They were heroes from a war that had few grand moments. The exploits of the *Seeadler* had been played up in newspapers and the gallant captain was a character that played well with the commoners as well as the middle and upper classes. He was not at all like anyone else—but at the same time, he was everyman.

Von Luckner submitted a request that his crew be awarded the Iron Cross, which was granted enthusiastically. Several of the civilian Germans who had escaped with him were granted, at his request, the military rank equivalent of chief petty officers. While he was awarded the illustrious Pour Le Merite, known more commonly as the Blue Max, he made sure his former crew were acknowledged for their risks and daring.

That wasn't to say there weren't problems with his former crew. Lieutenant Pries had executed a mutiny against Lieutenant Kling's command and the event was documented in the war diary. This was a court-martial offense. At the same time there would need to be a court martial to investigate the circumstances around the loss of the *Seeadler*. Neither of these episodes were destined to paint the crew of the heroic ship in a positive light. And if the court martials were held, it was not going to change anything except to smear the names of men to whom the common citizens looked during a time of catastrophic national loss. The Admiralty had to find a solution to this problem, and they did so with military precision. They covered it up.

The investigation into the loss of the *Seeadler* was shelved permanently. Von Luckner communicated with his former first officer and the charges were dropped, but more by the count than by Kling. It was a decision that the Admiralty fully endorsed. The crew of the *Seeadler* were given their Iron Crosses on January 7, 1920 in a grand and glorious ceremony. Admiral Pohl, former commander of the German High Seas Fleet presented the medals to the men and gave them a stirring speech. Bands struck up martial chords. For a few minutes, German pride in their navy returned.

He was given a new command, one he was aptly suited for. He took command of a three-masted ship that was to be used to train a new generation of sailors in a new German Navy. The ship had been a Danish cargo schooner named *Thyholm*. The vessel was registered as the *Niobe*, a name that stirred his passion for his youth.

The task was challenging. The navy yards had been looted of supplies after the collapse of order following the mutiny and there was no money left to fund the military. He had to scrounge for parts to keep the *Niobe* afloat and operational. For a crew, he recruited young men he couldn't afford to pay. What he could offer them was three meals a day, and in a ravaged post-war Germany, that was a powerful incentive. He enjoyed the assignment. It was a chance to sail again, and in the eyes of the young men aboard the *Niobe*, he was something of a living legend.

It is no small note that none of his former crew served under him aboard the training ship. The crew of the *Seeadler* did not stay bound together after the war, but went their separate ways. They too were heroes, but the spotlight was clearly focused on their former commanding officer.

Military marches were written about all of the great German naval leaders or their ships. The *Atlantis* and *Gniesenau* had songs composed about them. Admiral Spee had his own song as well, hopefully to inspire a new German Navy. Lyricists wrote two songs about the events of the *Seeadler* and her commander, the "*Seeadler* March," and the "Graf Luckner March." One is a serious toned military march, where the other is more light, almost peppy. It was an indication of how much the German people and the navy thought about the cruise of the *Seeadler*.

Von Luckner found himself to be a celebrity in high demand. In his grandmother's hometown, Halle, at the Saalschloss Brauerei, he gave his first public lecture and was surprised at the size of the crowd that gathered to hear him recount the story of the raid and his early childhood. He had been contracted to write several "yearbooks," which really consisted of stories of his recent travels or people he had met. The books served to keep his name in the public's eye and sold quite well.

But the count had a tendency to spend money almost as fast as he could earn it. Some of his expenses were simply wasted extravagance, such as elaborate parties. Others were more personal gifts—such as the anchor monument that he purchased and had placed over the grave of his mentor, Old Peter.

Eventually he became convinced that his story would sell and he undertook his autobiography. The book, *Seeteufel, abenteuer aus meinem Leben* (The Sea Devil, The Adventure of My Life), became a stunning best-seller in Germany. The nickname "Sea Devil" was something he claimed he had been called by his former prisoners— and it played well with audiences. The government was so pleased with the positive images of Germany and the chivalry this new role model provided, that the book became required school reading for the youth of the war-torn country. Children playing in Germany pretended to be "Seeadlers," sailing the seas and taking prisoners.

The book set the stage for the myth of Felix von Luckner and his epic cruise. In the book a handful of fundamental truths were changed. Whether these were changed by his publicist/agent Frau Schneider-Lindermann, his editor, or the count himself, we cannot tell.

The most staggering mistruth he wrote was that he never took a life during his raid. The death of the young wireless operator aboard the *Horngarth* was not just glossed over, but ignored. He often used a quote in his stage appearances and in written accounts, "I had the courage to sink ships but I had not the courage to deprive a mother of a child. I fought the war without killing anyone." He even went so far as to say, "I thought of my mother and imagined what tears and sadness I would cause if I called the son of some other mother." He stood by these written versions throughout the remainder of his life. While it is doubtful that Richard Douglas Page's family would have agreed with his words, to an adoring public, it was sentimental and patriotic.

Von Luckner also hung close to his story that the *Seeadler* had been wrecked in a massive tidal wave that hit the ship and shattered the masts. This seemed to be backed up with photographs, from the *Seeadler* crew after the war, showing the ship with toppled masts. These masts of course had been blow up by Lieutenant Pries in the incident that had burned the *Seeadler* up—but this did not seem to matter. This is a dramatic change even from his sworn testimony while in prison in New Zealand. There were dozens of other alterations to the true story.

To a war-weary Germany, it didn't matter. The people, especially the youth of Germany, needed a heroic figure—and the dynamic captain gave them just what they desired. The German Navy encouraged him to step down from the command of the *Niobe*. The Admiralty realized that von Luckner could do more good for the navy by being a public role model rather than an instructor on the high-seas. On May 31, 1922, Felix von Luckner retired from the German Navy at the rank of commander. The *Niobe* was the last military vessel he would command.

Felix von Luckner married his second wife, Ingeborg von Engestrom of Sweden, the daughter of a wealthy industrialist. He had been married before the war from 1913 to 1914 and even had a daughter from that first marriage. It had ended in divorce, which was not uncommon with young naval officers prone to long assignments overseas. Ingeborg von Luckner proved to be a good match for him. She was a miserly woman, counter to his free-wheeling approach to spending. She understood the social graces of high society, where her husband, thanks to seven years on the high seas, was always rough around the edges.

On one of their trips they met American reporter and author Lowell Thomas at an airfield. Thomas had read some of the newspaper exploits of von Luckner during the war and was an adventurer himself—having spent some time riding with Lawrence of Arabia during the war. The two men became good friends and Thomas convinced von Luckner to take his story to the English-speaking audience.

The book, *The Sea Devil*, was written by Thomas but for the most part was the work of von Luckner. In most respects, it was a very close translation from *Seeteufel*, but in English. There were parts that had been cut from the American version, minor paragraphs here and there. Likewise there were parts that were added, either by von Luckner's active imagination or by Lowell Thomas. The misinformation originally in *Seeteufel* took on a broader life with an English-reading audience. Thomas's book sold 250,000 copies its first year in publication. Americans who learned about the chivalrous German count in newspapers during the war now could read his action-packed story.

The American version of *Sea Devil* had been written in first person by Thomas. Coupled with Thomas's own reputation as a reporter and commentator, it created the illusion that the information in the book was totally factual. In reality, there is no evidence that Lowell Thomas ever checked or verified any of the count's version of events. For hundreds of thousands of readers it was a true story, whereas in reality it was full of holes, mistakes, misrepresentations, and at least a significant lie or two.

The holes in the story were challenged. Magazine and dime novel accounts by prisoners who were there, aboard the *Seeadler*, offered a glimpse of the truth. But the media didn't seem to care, nor did von Luckner. Many of the former prisoners received letters from the count and considered themselves his friend. He did not bear them ill-will and that seemed to be enough for the press who was more satisfied with the glorified account of events.

As the royalties from books came in, the count gave more public speeches. People were willing to pay to see him, to hear his booming voice and his accounts of his infamous raids. They reveled at his enlarged telling of his brilliant escape from New Zealand custody and stared in wonder as he related stories of his childhood at the mast.

Along with several friends, he came up with the idea of taking a sailing ship and traveling around the world. He could host speaking engagements and make a good living doing what he loved most, traveling on the seas. Yacht clubs fondly made him an honorary member wherever he went. He joined the Freemasons and rose to the rank of Grand Master of the Templar. This membership was one that he cherished, but later on in his life it would have great repercussions.

He wanted to go farther than just Germany and Europe, where he was known. The United States was ripe for him, as were some of his old haunts in the Pacific. There was only one way for the infamous Sea Devil to go on such a trip—at the helm of his own ship. In 1926 he purchased a refitted sailing ship, renaming the vessel the *Vaterland*. The count and countess equipped the ship with the best of everything. The German government approached the count and presented him with funding in exchange for von Luckner's promotion of German goods during his travels. He was to be an informal emissary for a new Germany, one that hoped to recover from the weight of the Treaty of Versailles and the losses during the war.

He sailed the *Vaterland* on a tour of America and was stunned by the reception he received in the United States. The sales of *The Sea Devil* had turned him into a celebrity long before his arrival in the country. He spoke at places such as Carnegie Hall, where he filled the venue to capacity, and even at high school events and auditoriums. He thrilled audiences with his magic tricks, the tricks learned in the ports of his youth that turned him into a court jester of sorts for the kaiser. People thrilled to his stories, and with each telling and each audience, the story of the *Seeadler* and her cruise grew more and more, morphing into a story that was all based on truth, but factually changed.

He autographed everything he could lay his hands on—from ticket stubs to photographs, which he sold for a nickel. The business was so brisk that at times he hired others to sign his name for him. The count, when questioned about his strength, tore a phone book in half on a stage. It was a hit and he included the stunt in many performances for cheering crowds. It didn't matter that a few years before, Germany was an enemy. Women adored him because he painted himself as a pirate—a bad boy who in his heart of hearts was good. The beautiful countess at his side helped cultivate a proper image as well.

He was made an honorary citizen of the United States of America and of twenty-five American cities on his tour. Henry Ford gave him a new automobile as a present. When the tour eventually reached San Francisco, he was made an honorary citizen of the city at the same time as Charles Lindbergh. Factories gave him guided tours. The Niagara Falls Power Plant showed him and the countess the wonders of the falls and the generators. The Boy Scouts made him an honorary scout master. The citizens of Miami granted him local citizenship, welcoming him with open arms. He was made an honorary member of the Rotary Club International. Even President Calvin Coolidge met with him. As one writer put it in later years, von Luckner was the most popular European in America.

In New Jersey, he stayed with his friend Lowell "Tommy" Thomas. Along with Thomas's millionaire friend Burt Massee, they sailed down the East Coast on a wedding party that turned into a wild party and drinking binge that lasted several weeks. Massee hired the ship and its infamous captain for a honeymoon cruise. Von Luckner loaded the wild group aboard the *Vaterland* and sailed down to Florida and into the Caribbean drinking, vandalizing, and generally partying every mile of the voyage. Thomas convinced him that given the anti-German sentiments still in the world, he would be better off renaming the *Vaterland* something else—something less Prussian. Around drinks, the men agreed on a new name for the yacht, the *Mopelia*. Given the nature of the party cruise, the new name was initiated over champagne. It was short-lived. The Wall Street crash devastated Massee, cutting his cruise dramatically short.

The cruise of the *Mopelia* ended when he returned to Germany. The count and several of his crew boarded a launch and left the *Mopelia* to go ashore. A short time later the ship burst into flames and was gutted with fire. The local newspapers swarmed the charred ruins of the deck and a search for the count resulted in no luck. The assumption was that he had died in the fire. The next morning he had the honor of reading his own obituary in the paper. While outwardly he chuckled at the incident, the loss of the *Mopelia* meant that once again the Sea Devil was land bound.

Oftentimes the crews of ships hold reunions. They come together in later life to retell their stories. Some of the men of the *Seeadler* sold their stories, Karl Kircheiß and Heinrich Hinz, for example, both sold books—none reaching the popularity of the count's book. But there were no reunions of the *Seeadler* crew, even after all they had been through together during those long romping months on the seas. Perhaps it was the fact their former captain altered the truth, or that the limelight seemed to focus on him and him alone. Few ever came out and said anything cross about von Luckner, but by the same token the bonds of their long voyage together seemed to have frayed.

Von Luckner received word that the Pope wanted an audience with him. He and the countess traveled to Italy and he was awarded the Cross of Saint George for his humanitarian services. He was said to have waged war without taking a life. It was a lie, but the story had taken on a life of its own. From 1920 on he never recanted this version.

For years he traveled between Europe and America, providing lectures, writing additional books, and wrapping himself in the legend of his exploits aboard the *Seeadler*. He even secured a radio show in the early 1930s on the NBC network. While popular, it lasted only a few years, the victim of his thick German accent. Besides, von Luckner was a visual man; his sweeping arm gestures and sheer physical presence often drove his stories and made the audience a part of his adventures.

Money became tight and he was forced to divest himself of the family holdings in Hamburg, settling with his mother and wife in his grandmother's house in Halle. Most people would have thought that his moments in history were over, that his fifteen minutes of fame had already run their course, but some of his most daring adventures and greatest controversies were yet to come.

✠ ✠ ✠

The German Navy training ship *Niobe* had seventy-nine crew aboard; mostly young men, ensigns, and first-time sailors. The ship was a true training ship, painted white or gray. During wargames, the cost-strapped German navy had the *Niobe* simulate a steam ship by draping canvas tubes over her masts so that they appeared in the distance to be thick smokestacks. It was embarrassing that only a few years before, the navy had been the second largest in the world and was the one true threat to Britain's Royal Navy. Now it was humbled.

The boat was a source of pride for her sailors. She had been the ship of Count Felix von Luckner—the Sea Devil. He was a legend in the navy. Most of the men working on that deck must have wondered what it had been like to serve under such a man in that fantastic cruise. Most aspired to the greatness that he represented. They had read his story as children in schools, and no doubt some of them had seen or heard him speak.

On July 26, 1932 a white squall broke on the Baltic, catching the *Niobe* before she could make port. The ship was ripped apart, then capsized in the sudden and violent storm. Sixty-nine of the cadets, ensigns, and instructors aboard the *Niobe* were killed in a matter of moments. Only a handful on the weather deck survived, swept into the sea to be later recovered.

In 1924 the advertisement ran for the cruise of a yacht called the *Seeadler*. With four masts and two engines, she was a luxury ship owned by a firm in Hamburg. The promoters heavily advertised for the few people in Germany and around Europe who could afford the cruise. The ship would take them north around Helgoländ, through the fjords of Norway, and up near the Arctic Circle. Guests would take tours along the promenade deck and attend feasts in the plush dining quarters; the men would have a chance to hunt whales.

The captain of this venture was someone with polar experience and world fame: Alfred Kling. Already renowned for his work on the Filchner expedition he fully leveraged his fame as the architect of the original *Seeadler* cruise during the war.

Kling had put on a great deal of weight from his time in Chile, that much is evident from the brochure for the trip. He was back home, in Germany, attempting to make a name for himself—but at the same time was still tied to the events of his past. One thing, however, was for sure: This *Seeadler* was his to command. This time, the ship was his own.

24

THE VALLEY OF DARKNESS

1929–April 1966

Count von Luckner always had problems managing his finances. He provided well for his daughter from his first marriage, but he found it hard to keep the current countess in the lifestyle to which she was accustomed. The unstable German economy after the war, complete with rampant inflation, only added to the problem. At one point he found himself nearly broke, but some unknown benefactor provided him with funds. Speculation has pointed to several sources over the years, including Lowell Thomas or even the kaiser himself.

The rise of the National Socialist Party to power in Germany was not lost on the count. He, like many Germans, was proud to see a unified and strong Germany rising again on a world stage. The darker aspects of the Nazis were glossed over or simply ignored. Although the Nazis had asked him to join, he had no use for them, and to do so he would have to surrender his most cherished honors, his foreign citizenships and his membership in the Freemasons, an organization despised by the party. It was a move that did not endear him to the Nazi leadership, but at the same time they calculated that the count was a highly respected and well-known figure. In reality, they could not have picked a riskier spokesperson to represent a new Germany. Von Luckner was quick to point out that he was not a politician. He was a storyteller, a common sailor. He did not have the savvy for political drama. All he wanted to do was to write, speak, and live a life of luxury. If someone was willing to fund that, so much the better.

The Propaganda Bureau found a way to achieve both of their goals. The proposal surfaced that the government would help von Luckner fund a trip around the world to help spread "German ideals" and a positive image of life under Hitler. They would help him purchase a new ship. He would be able to take the countess and sail around the world. All that he was formally asked to do was to present Germany in a positive light.

There is a certain amount of naiveté in the count's interpretation of this series of events. He did not see himself as working for the German government, the Nazis, Hitler, or anyone else. His perception was that the German Reich was treating him to a cruise around the world. And why not? He was a hero of the realm, idolized by Germans young and old alike. Every time he spoke in public, in his mind, he was expounding upon what was good about Germany. The count's ego, along with his almost immature thinking about the intentions of his financial backers, was risky. The Countess von Luckner, however, saw the potential of currying the favors of Hitler and the Nazi party. She encouraged the trip for her own motivations.

On the surface, this appears to be a win-win where all parties could and would benefit from such a cruise. In reality, it was a recipe for a diplomatic nightmare.

Hitler and Himmler both donated token contributions for the trip, as did the Reich government. The rest of the money was raised from private resources and paid for by the count himself. The Reich purchased a ship for the tour, named the *Seeteufel* (Sea Devil).

She weighed in at 177 tons, was 88 feet long, and had an auxiliary engine. At von Luckner's specifications, the figurehead on the bow of the ship was said to be that of his wife, Ingeborg. The ship had a small movie screening room and was ornately decorated. Pictures of Nazi officials hung in the forecastle and dining areas. Paintings of von Luckner's grandfather were displayed as well. The ship had a modern refrigeration system, an extensive galley, and a new electronic depth-finding system.

There were seven crewmen aboard the ship, in addition to the count and the countess. At least one of them was a gestapo agent, sent along to report on his activities. The ship set sail April 19, 1937 with the count's eighty-one-year-old mother waving to them from the dock. In almost every respect, the tour appeared just like any one of the other trips the count had made to America, his first stopping point. He arrived, gave lectures, signed autographs; there was no hint of propaganda or hidden political messages. Transcripts of the lectures reveal that he spoke fondly of his home country in the way that anyone might.

The tour passed through the Panama Canal and then set sail for the Pacific, with the final intended destination being Australia. The count had made it clear that he wanted to visit Mopelia, intent on recovering some buried treasure that he had left there—which was more myth than reality. He also wanted to visit New Zealand, to show his wife where he had been interned and where he had escaped. The propaganda tour was in reality nothing more than a government-funded trip for the von Luckners.

Where the Americans had welcomed back the count with open arms, the New Zealanders and Australians were infuriated and argued among themselves as to whether he should be allowed to visit their country—let alone speak publicly there. Hitler's Anschluß (the annexation scheme to seize the Rhineland, Austria, and Silesia) was underway in Europe, and anti-German and anti-Nazi sentiments were on the rise. The thought of sending a widely known German public figure out to a member of the British Commonwealth at such a time was folly on the part of the Reich.

Many groups claimed that the heroic count was a spy. They claimed that his depth-finding gear was intended to map out possible future attack routes where he visited. There were fears that he was going to try and sway the youth of the Pacific to become Nazis. German nationalist groups and veterans countered that he was a great war hero and had always treated the people of the Pacific rim honorably.

The tour of Australia and New Zealand was a debacle at best. Two of his old internment camps had been turned into military bases and he was not granted permission to visit. He claimed this resulted from the mistaken perception that he was a spy; at the same time, those who suspected him of covert activities pointed to his attempts to infiltrate sensitive military bases as proof of their version of events. He did manage to see some of his old prison camp on Motuihe, showing his wife where they had hidden their supplies and how they had stolen the *Pearl*. His travels had all of the trappings of an old veteran visiting a battlefield of his youth, rather than a trip to convert New

Zealanders to become Nazis. Still, some groups and unions staged protests against him when he spoke in public.

Worse yet, when he did speak, von Luckner did not necessarily tow the official Nazi line. He commented that Stalin was a fool—at a time when Hitler was courting Stalin over the imminent joint invasion of Poland by Germany and Russia. He made ill remarks about the Japanese. He claimed he did not fully support Hitler but respected what Hitler had done thus far for Germany. He spoke proudly that the Germans were becoming a powerful force in Europe—all truthful, but tough words to a nervous people. Almost everything he said was blown out of proportion and twisted against him. For the nonpolitical von Luckner, this only made matters worse each time he hosted a lecture.

There were problems with the crew as well. Their pay, which von Luckner was responsible for, was withheld. He was said to have a heavy hand with his crew, threatening them and berating them in public. The countess kept supplies locked away and was miserly even with meal portions. The crew complained that he had turned the *Seeteufel* into a party cruise and wasn't pushing propaganda enough. All of this at the same time the Australians were claiming that he was pushing too much German ideology.

For his part, the count seemed to stumble his way through matters with as much grace as he could muster. He visited former officers and whispered to them that he knew that gestapo agents were among the crew, but that he wanted nothing to do with propaganda. At the same time, his wife openly flaunted her support of the Reich.

The German Foreign Office did what it could to repair some of the damage from his statements, but the injury had already been done. There were concerns about how to handle von Luckner. If pressed too hard, there were concerns he might speak out against the government—an act that couldn't be tolerated. It was decided that the key was to silence the count.

Upon his return to Germany, von Luckner assumed that he was going to be welcomed back by the Reich with open arms. The reality couldn't have been further from the truth. The Reich filed charges against him, thanks to the gestapo agent hidden in his crew, and sales of his books were suspended. Furthermore, he was told not to speak publicly until the matter was resolved. The effect of this was to cut off his means of making a living.

On July 5, 1939 Hitler signed an order calling for a Court of Honor against Count von Luckner. Being called up for such a court was a serious issue. Given the Night of the Long Knives, the legal system in Germany had ceased to be a judicial branch of the government but instead was a platform for inflicting harm on citizens.

The prosecution's charges were inaccurate and inflated, such as the false claim that the count had tossed all of the printed propaganda materials for the cruise overboard. The chief charge leveled at von Luckner was that he used the cruise for his own personal indulgence rather than for generating goodwill about Germany.

Fortunately for von Luckner, witnesses for the prosecution were out of the country. With World War II having started by the time the court was called, it would be impossible to hold formal testimony.

The gestapo had placed a number of trumped-up charges into the mix as well, to ensure the count's silence. He was accused of molesting his daughter from his first marriage. He was accused of making disparaging remarks about other high-ranking Nazi officials. Also brought into the mix of accusations was that he would not renounce his foreign citizenships or his affiliation with the Freemasons. The loading of false and potentially embarrassing charges in such cases was not out of the ordinary.

Both sides entered a lopsided legal battle that was destined to end in some sort of a plea bargain. Almost all of the charges were dropped, as was the intention all along. Von Luckner did plead guilty to misuse of the Reich funds. He did not recant his membership in the Freemasons or his foreign citizenships. In return for having the Honor Court charges sealed, he was banned from public speaking. He was not to travel without permission—and when he did, the gestapo shadowed or validated his moves. His books were pulled from library shelves and were not allowed to be sold in stores. He would later claim that his books were publicly burned.

For von Luckner this had to have been the darkest hour he had faced since the war. His livelihood was taken from him. His books, his stories, his legend was being erased from a generation of Germans. At one point his books were required reading in schools: now they were scorned as contraband. He was still a hero to Germans, which is probably what kept him alive—but that was all. He had maintained his honor and integrity.

He returned to his grandmother's former house in Halle and settled in for the duration of the war, forced into obscurity, almost forgotten, until the Reich found another use for his name. In 1942 the German Navy issued a press release that caught the attention of Allied intelligence officers. "Count Felix von Luckner was leading twenty-four merchant raiders into the Indian Ocean to wage war on the Allied shipping." Initially the report caught intelligence planners off guard and caused considerable worry. Was it possible that the Sea Devil might actually be in action once more? The prospect of having von Luckner once again on the high seas was alarming enough to cause some investigation of the matter. The last that Allied naval planners had heard, the count had fallen out of favor with the Reich and was living a life under virtual arrest.

How the intelligence was gathered or confirmed is unknown. But in a short period of time, a relieved Allied command learned that von Luckner was living out the war in Halle and that he was only alive because the German people deeply respected him.

By 1942 the German Navy had sought out the best of the officers from the previous war and had recommissioned them for active duty. One of those men was an officer of the *Seeadler*—Karl Kircheiß. Given command of a torpedo boat, this experienced and grizzled sailor once again sailed under the German flag for his country. It was a small command but he did see action in the war, proving that his skills were not merely a piece of the von Luckner myth, but his own.

He survived the Second World War and traveled again around the world on a sailing ship. He wrote several books of his exploits, but none of them seemed to equal the months aboard the *Seeadler*.

In 1943 the count went to the Kaiser Willhelm Memorial, most likely to rekindle memories of another time, to meet friends nearby, or to simply get away from his imposed house arrest. His trip was approved by the government and he found himself in Berlin on a frosty morning after a nighttime British air raid. He was stunned to see so much carnage and destruction. Halle had been spared bombing attacks. Berlin was pummeled at night by the British and in the day by the Americans.

At one recently destroyed home he asked the crew cleaning up the mess if the occupants had survived. They had not, but their papers had. He flipped through the pile of paperwork, identification papers, and passports and found the name of one of the female victims—Frieda Schäfer. She was a young woman, attractive, now a victim of war. He absentmindedly tucked the woman's passport in his pocket and continued on his business.

Shortly thereafter he was approached by a young sobbing woman asking for his help. She was Jewish and the SS was looking for her. Her entire family had been taken away. Her name was Rose Jansen and she turned to this tall burly stranger for help. Von Luckner whisked her away to a friend's apartment. He gave her Frieda Schäfer's passport and told Rose that she must forget who she was before and assume this identity. His friend took the woman in as her maid.

The count left and never inquired as to what happened to the woman after that day. He believed he had saved her life and that seemed to be enough at the time.

The American 104th Infantry Division was nicknamed the Timberwolves, and the name was appropriate. They fought with a vengeance and a fury that was highly regarded among the Allied armies. Part of that was due to the men and their spirit; part of it was due to their leader, General Terry Allen.

General Allen had commanded the First Division, the infamous Big Red One. He was known for his tenacity and his tendency to not follow military norms in terms of discipline. To a certain extent, his removal of command of the First Division was a testimony to the high command's regard of his leadership style. It didn't shake him. Even hard-line generals like George Patton held Allen in high regard. If anything, his change of command hardened Terry Allen.

By April of 1945, the western front was collapsing. Pockets of fierce and determined German defense still hoped for some sort of victory. Units such as the 104th Division were sweeping forward, shattering the hold-outs, blasting the last vestiges of the Third Reich in their wake.

On April 14, the Timberwolves encountered a fierce pocket of German soldiers in Halle.

Halle had been spared the carpet bombings that had razed most of the Reich's major cities. It had been hit, but only lightly. As the tenth-largest city in Germany, and still relatively intact, it was naturally defended. Before the war it was where the first spark of communist revolution took hold in old Germany. Hitler suppressed it by subjecting the town to hard-line Nazi efforts. This old town, the birthplace of George Frideric Handel, was fortified. There were fifteen military hospitals in the city and large numbers of Allied prisoners of war were held there. As the Timberwolves approached, they slugged it out in the suburbs with the defenders, and one thing became clear to General Allen: taking it would kill countless men, German and Allied. There had to be another way.

The Count and Countess von Luckner, along with Felix's aged mother, huddled in a nearby apartment. Oddly enough, the slight Allied bombing that had hit the city had damaged the family home. The count knew that the Americans were near, and he knew that they would be forced to fight their way into that resistance. Given the orders of Hitler, he knew the German defenders under General von Edelsheim would be forced to fight to the bitter end.

General Allen wanted to find a solution that could spare the city. He met with the prisoners of war and asked if any of the captured officers would take a surrender offer to the Germans in Halle. None accepted. They knew that the SS contingent in Halle would execute any officer who negotiated surrender terms. The options were running out. Allen was under orders to take the city and he knew he would be forced to act soon, regardless of what that meant to civilians and POWs there.

It was then that two war correspondents from *Stars and Stripes* stepped forward. Al Newman remembered that von Luckner lived in Halle. If he could be located and brought through the lines, he might be able to serve as a good negotiator with the German defenders.

Newman offered to infiltrate the enemy in search of the count. He began to cut through the enemy lines along with fellow journalist G. K. Hodenfield and a small contingent of troops.

The mission was fraught with risks. They took fire on several occasions as they dodged house-to-house, snaking their way forward. A German civilian gave them the count's address and the small group made their way through the dark streets of Halle. They came across a car painted with the symbol of the Red Cross, moving through the streets. A husky man in the back seat burst out and rushed forward to them, arms open.

"By Joe, I'm so glad to see you. I haven't been so happy since I broke through the British blockade in 1916!" Von Luckner carried a scrapbook of articles about himself, almost as if it were proof of his identity.

Mortar rounds rained down and they withdrew back to the American lines. When they eventually got back to the command post, von Luckner met with General Allen. The situation was grim for the city. A menacing total of 700 bombers and 260 fighters were awaiting his order to take off. They would raze Halle in order to take it. The general laid out maps for the count and outlined the situation . . . the Germans' position was untenable.

Von Luckner agreed to take an offer of unconditional surrender back to the German general. He was also told that time was running out. He had a day. After that, General Allen would be forced to unleash the full might of the Allied military.

While von Luckner took the message, General Allen did some checking on his own with his G2 intelligence office. Count von Luckner was a man considered by American intelligence to be trustworthy. His prestige had kept him alive against the desires of the Reich, and he had refused to give up his honorary citizenships with the United States and other countries—which was something that made him trustworthy in Allen's eyes.

Von Luckner returned to American lines at 0230 on April 15. The German general had refused to surrender, not because he didn't desire it, but out of fear of what the dreaded SS would do to his family.

It was not all bad news. Von Luckner and a handful of brave German citizens had managed to negotiate that the hospital areas were to be declared neutral, as were certain safety zones, for civilians. This limited the areas of combat and allowed the Germans to withdraw much of their force from the city to the south. More importantly, the German withdrawal gave the high ground to the Timberwolves. Von Luckner had given the people of Halle, his adopted hometown, the gift of survival.

While Halle was spared and the Timberwolves pressed on, they expressed their thanks to the count by making him an honorary colonel of the division. Word spread to other war correspondents that Newman and Hodenfield had managed to reach von Luckner, and that von Luckner had acted to save Halle.

When Lowell Thomas heard that the count had been recovered, he was on duty in Germany reporting on the war effort. He arranged to join his old friend in Halle and they spent several days together. Thomas coordinated with General Allen to arrange a meeting between von Luckner and General Patton.

The von Luckners spent a week with General Patton in the last days of the war. Patton himself was an avid sailor before the war, having taken his family on a sailing voyage to Hawaii before the war. At the behest of Lowell Thomas and General Allen, Patton arranged for the von Luckners to be taken to Sweden, where they could join the countess's family. He even called Patton after the war ended, offering his services to the general to assist training the German people in the ways of democracy. It was an offer politely refused. For the remainder of the war and the new peace, the count remained an expatriate of Germany.

The end of the war should have been a happy time for the count. The end of the Nazi regime meant that the bans and restrictions placed on him were gone. His books could be sold and he could perform his public lectures. Oddly enough, it was not a time of joy for him. Circumstances had turned against the count in a way he could never have foreseen.

Halle, his ancestral hometown, fell into Soviet control and what would become East Germany. People with Imperial title were not welcome: going home was not an option for the count.

His books, now available, were no longer popular reading. People around the world didn't want to read about courageous Germans. Years of war had left them weary of speaking or reading about Germany in general. The devastation in Europe left him few venues where he could speak—and very few where he could hope to make any money doing so.

In Germany, there was an uneasy bitterness with some people toward the count. Some saw him as a traitor who had betrayed his own people to the Americans in the last days of the war. His actions in Halle had been touted widely in the few newspapers running in Germany at the time, and the label traitor proved hard to shake. In written accounts and interviews, the count was quick to say that he was not a traitor and that he acted to save both American and German lives, and that that had been his motivation all along. Despite this, some of his countrymen still saw him as a betrayer.

The count turned to America, hoping that his support there would be strong enough to look past the events of the last few years. But in post-war America, the concept of a German coming to speak was not as popular as he had hoped. There were fans, but the packed auditoriums of the past were diminishing in his twilight years. He traveled back and forth from the States and Sweden, where he took up residence.

In one such meeting in New York City, he stood on stage and was rushed by a middle-aged woman. She wrapped her arms around him, thanking him for saving her life. Her name was Rose Jansen. The last time he had seen her, he had told her to use the name of Frieda Schäfer.

Rose Jansen's entire family had been killed in the concentration camps. Von Luckner had never tried to follow up with the young woman he had given the passport to in Berlin. Now he knew. She had survived the Holocaust because of him and he provided the stunned audience with the full story of their encounter. The tale instantly became part of the von Luckner mythos.

In 1953, the aged Count was awarded the Federal Grand Cross of Merit by the German government. It seemed to be a turning point in his life, putting an end to whispers of treachery as he was once again embraced by this people.

In November of 1959 the count was invited to New York to help surprise an old friend, Lowell Thomas. The television show *This is Your Life* had told him that he would be one of the featured speakers for Tommy, and he and the countess traveled to the United States to honor their old friend. The truth of the matter was that von Luckner himself was the guest of honor.

Some of his former captives were brought out to speak for him, as was Lowell Thomas. The count spoke with his German accent and constantly turned away from the camera, evidently unaccustomed to appearing on television. He struggled with some of the words and his giant hands quaked from time to time during the broadcast. A hearing aide was visible. There was a glint in his eyes, a hint at the spirit that had earned him the title of Sea Devil—but it was fading with age.

There were touching moments. Rose Jansen came out and held him, fighting for words to express her gratitude. His first female prisoner, her honeymoon interrupted by the *Seeadler*'s raid, spoke about the champagne liberated from the *Horngarth*. The grand old man was clearly moved as he fought to bring up the memories of the events of his life.

At the end of the show, Ralph Edwards announced that the Revell model company was going to be making a model kit of the *Seeadler*. A percentage of the profits from the kit would be donated in the count's name to the Boy Scouts of America, one of his favorite charities. Once more, the count would be inspiring young men to think of boldness and daring—and perhaps remember the days when a single man could run away and become the captain of a grand sailing vessel.

In 1964, when his brother Karl died, he made his last trip to Halle. Many turned out to catch a glimpse of the hero. He maintained a small flat in Hamburg but spent much of his time traveling to and from Sweden. Gone was the vibrant energy he had always displayed. Age was overtaking him. After the funeral he and the countess returned to Malmo, Sweden, where he lived until 1966.

On April 13, in a hospital bed, with his beloved Ingeborg at his side, Count Felix von Luckner died. His obituary ran around the world, many times as page one of the newspaper. In every small town where he had spoken, he was still remembered for his visit. For the major cities, he was a celebrity and an icon from another age. Most focused on the raid of the *Seeadler*. Others spoke of his saving of American lives in Halle.

His body was brought to his parents' plot in Hamburg's Ohlsdorfer churchyard for final internment. Thousands lined the streets to pay homage to him as he made his final review. He was the last commander from a major government to take a sailing vessel into combat. Gone was the age when a young boy could run away from home and have a grand adventure, then return to gain fame, honor, and glory. His passing marked the end of an era but left a glimpse at what we could all be, and especially so in the message that he wrote thousands of times on the autographed photos he sold for a nickel: "Never say die."

EPILOGUE

Was the raid of the *Seeadler* successful? Her crew was responsible for the capture or destruction of eighteen ships. The value of the ships and cargo, at the time, was $25 million in 1918 dollars. Tons of war material that would have been used to take other lives was destroyed. Lloyd's of London, at least for a short period of time, raised its rates—though it is hard to attribute that to the *Seeadler* alone. The raid diverted resources from the Royal Navy and the American Navy in a vain effort to track and capture the ship.

Her crew received Iron Crosses, some both First and Second Class, for their gallantry. Many went on to serve as officers and even captains in World War II. They were bound to a period in their lives where a single man, with a strong wind at his back, could make a difference in not just the war, but the world. They were the last of a breed, sailing men in battle. They fired the last shot from a sailing ship in battle ever.

The Great War was a horrible prelude of things to come. Battlefields ate tens of thousands of victims in a day. It was a war that introduced poison gas, aerial bombardment, flamethrowers, torpedoes, submarines, and tanks into warfare—turning it into a bloody stain on the history of mankind. Out of that mire came one story about a man and his crew. If nothing else, it was something bright, something admirable in a war that brought horrors and suffering to so many.

The silent hero of von Luckner's cruise rests on the reef to this day, though the distinction between the reef and her hull has all but disappeared. A part of her bow had stabbed upward into the sky over the surface of the warm Pacific Ocean until the early 1970s, when decay and gravity took their toll. Her body is fragile now, crumbling as the reef overtakes her in a slow death.

Divers have explored the *Seeadler* for years for both casual recreation and for the mythical treasure that the count is said to have left on the island. Her warm grave is in shallow waters, though the currents are said to be strong and tricky to navigate. Settled in thirty feet of water, visitors find her to be a quaint dive, well illuminated against the white coral in the shallow water.

The locals have set up a small community on the grounds where Seeadlerdorf once stood. Some artifacts from the ship are still in use. Pieces of chain and cable from the ship are used on some of the local fishing boats. In the 1960s, one of the antique dynamos that once powered her running lights and wireless set was still rusting in the village. The inhabitants of the island had long ago forgotten what it was or where it came from, but it remains a monument to the ship.

One of the *Seeadler*'s 4.2-inch deck guns stands in a park in Papeete, Tahiti. People walk by it all of the time and never give it a second thought, like so many military cannons in so many parks around the world. It has been silent for decades, and yet it eventually points out toward the sea.

The cruise of the *Seeadler* reads almost like an early twentieth-century version of *Star Trek*. You had the ship operating far from its base, on a daring military mission. The dashing, Horatio Hornblower-style captain was the product of his own audacity and daring. There was the intellectual first officer who was considered by many to be the brains behind the operation. There was the rough-and-tough engineer who did what he could, with sweat and swearing to keep the auxiliary engine of the raider running. There was the grizzled older doctor who smoked cigars, drank, and kept the crew alive through scurvy and other ills.

They had a mission where long odds were stacked against them from the start. The age of the windjammer for the most part had already come to pass years before. That didn't stop the crew of the *Seeadler*. They'd set a sailing ship up against cruisers. They dared to test the might of the Royal Navy, and the French and American navies, and they won. Even when faced with defeat, they turned that defeat into a fighting chance for survival.

The men are all gone now. All that is left is their story. Count von Luckner managed to keep that alive for many years, managed to make the raid of the *Seeadler* more than a fading memory in the his-

tory of the Great War. He refused to let the raid of the old windjammer simply fade away, and in doing so, he provided us all with a legend and inspiration.

As he signed on some of his autographed photos, "Who doesn't
dare in life, doesn't win."

By Joe, he was right.

POSTSCRIPT

The Myth versus the Reality of the Seeadler*'s Cruise*

The myth of the voyage of the *Seeadler* and the other elements of the life of Count Felix von Luckner have arisen from a variety of sources. In some cases, as I've stated earlier, the count simply lied. In some cases, he altered the facts intentionally to tell a better story in his written accounts and at public speaking events. He'd told the story of his cruise so many times in his life that over the years it tended to evolve and grow. These are unintentional exaggerations—but they made getting close to the truth difficult and sometimes outright frustrating.

This chapter dissects some of the more common elements of the von Luckner legend. For those of you who have read some of the previous histories of the count, either by him or by other authors, you will notice some changes throughout my book. This section will help you understand why your previous accounts and my own do not match up. I have omitted the fact that the count (even in his written version) often confuses what day he captured which ship and who captained each vessel. These are mostly attributed to bad memory and a lack of reference materials.

What was the name of *Seeadler* when she sailed the blockade?

It has been the claim for decades that von Luckner named the *Seeadler* the *Irma* when he sailed through the Royal Navy's blockade on Christmas of 1916. He claimed it was named for the love of his life. This version of the story played well to female members at his public speaking events, adding an air of chivalry to his version of events. The *Seeadler* was eventually renamed the *Irma*, but not when it passed through the blockade. This is mostly an exaggeration on the part of the count.

The name *Hero* was used because it appears most commonly in the war diary in the interview accounts from the *Seeadler* crew. The *Hero* had a homeport out of Arendal. The name *Hero Arendal* is

referenced in Heinrich Hinz's version of events. His book has a photograph of the crew around a life preserver painted with "*Hero Arendal*" on it, which helps to validate his story. Chances are the use of
Hero was simply a shortened form for the full name, as Hinz reported. With all of the contradictions presented, the most realistic and
neutral selection was to use *Hero* for this book.

Absolutely no other accounts support von Luckner's alleged naming convention other than he did use the name *Irma* after the prisoners were discharged and sent to Rio. His insistence that the ship used
that name while running through the blockade is simply a distortion
of facts to make his story much more romantic.

Which ship stopped the *Seeadler*?

In von Luckner's and Lowell Thomas's account of events, the ship was
identified as the auxiliary cruiser *Avenger*. In later lectures, during his
1938 tour of Australia, he referred to the vessel as the *Adventurer*, a
name change that could be attributed simply to the count's fading
memory. According to the official British version of the war, they are
unsure which ship it was; but they assume it was the auxiliary cruiser
Patia, claiming that the *Avenger* does not exist. The crew of the
Seeadler claim in the war diary and in their personal accounts that the
ship was the *Highland Scot*, but also the *Highland Laddie*. This of
course only muddies the waters even more.

I was granted access to the archives of the Imperial War Museum
in London in May 2003 and found a diary from an officer aboard an
auxiliary cruiser named the *Avenger*. Without listing coordinates,
times, or anything specific, the diary claims that the ship stopped a
sailing ship on Christmas Day. It is entirely possible that this ship had
changed its name in the same manner as the *Seeadler* had.

Did seaman Schmidt really put on a dress to pass as the count's wife?

Some historians point to the war diary and say that no details exist
that describe anyone dressing up as the captain's wife to fool the

British at the blockade. The war diary is a very light-reading ship's log and details were often simply not recorded. There are immeasurable details that it does not go into regarding the voyage, which are corroborated by other sources such as Kircheiß or Hinz's works. Hinz doesn't specifically mention the event, but does say that every effort was made to make the crew appear to be a normal band of sailing Norwegians.

The photographic evidence does show Josefeena with von Luckner in the correct style of uniform that he had with him on the cruise. There are photographs of Josefeena half-dressed, wig in hand, and another with Luckner and Pries. Hence the incident is included in this book with the assumption that the *Seeadler* crew spared Schmidt the embarrassment of recording his cross-dressing in official records.

The auxiliary engines of the ship

Count von Luckner, in every written account and every lecture about his voyage, has declared that the *Seeadler* had two 500-horsepower auxiliary engines in her hull for back-up propulsion. The truth of the matter is that it was a single diesel engine. This has been confirmed by Krause and by the evidence from the German World War I Naval Archives.

The count probably did not fully understand the configuration of the engine. Its shape, when installed, may have led him to believe it was indeed two engines. He may have been deceived by the bulkheads in relation to the engine and thought it was two. There was no reason for him to lie about this aspect of the raid preparation, so you have to assume that von Luckner did not fully understand what he had in the lower decks.

Who was the brains behind the cruise of the *Seeadler*?

By all written accounts, the idea for the cruise originated with Alfred Kling. This is backed by a wide range of evidence in the German archives. Von Luckner was picked as captain after the refit of the *Pass of Balmaha* had commenced under Kling's guidance.

When the American prisoners were rescued they provided detailed interviews and transcripts of their time with the *Seeadler* crew. Many of the men spoke very highly of Kling. Most addressed him as "the brains of the outfit," and one even went so far as to say that von Luckner was "a figurehead, there for looks."

The leadership capabilities of Kling were in question from day one. His commanding officer had him slated to be first officer or executive officer on the cruise—not the captain. Lieutenant Pries rebelled against him openly on Mopelia. He did not seem to have the leadership qualities that made him stand out in the eyes of superiors, aside from von Luckner.

At the same time, there is no doubt whatsoever that without Kling, the cruise would have been a failure. He brought with him, from his polar exploration days, the kinds of preparedness and logistics skills that made the *Seeadler*'s raid as successful as it was. Von Luckner brought about true leadership skills. Without the dashing and daring captain, the cruise would have been a failure in the hands of Kling alone.

The two officers most likely had a symbiotic relationship. When they separated at Mopelia, neither enjoyed great success on their own in terms of raiding. For those who claim that von Luckner was a figurehead, they need to review the voyage of the *Cecilie*, the capture of the *Pearl* and the *Moa*, and his exploits in the Second World War. Even without the *Seeadler*, the count was destined to do great and daring things in his life.

Taking the *Pinmore* for a joyride

In his first accounts of the cruise of the *Seeadler*, the count discusses going aboard his former ship, the *Pinmore*, then leaving her to be sunk. Oddly enough, in lectures starting in 1937 he began to tell another story—one that was much more than adventurous.

In the new version of events, the count took a prize crew aboard the *Pinmore* and sailed to Rio, impersonated Captain Mullen, purchased additional supplies, then returned to the *Seeadler*. He put his arm in a sling, to explain why his signature did not match Mullen's signature when in port. This multi-day mini-voyage has some romantic elements and has surfaced in other historical books as fact; in reality, it never happened.

The origins of the new version of this story began in 1918 when von Luckner was captured in New Zealand. In a testimony with a Captain Thompson of the Royal Navy, who was attached as an advisor to the New Zealand government, he told this new version of events for the first time. It is assumed that he did so to deliberately throw off the Royal Navy officer. Why it surfaced again in later years is unknown.

There is no evidence of this mini-cruise. Mullen was known in Rio and someone impersonating him would have been quickly spotted. And if von Luckner had returned with a cargo hold full of supplies, the *Seeadler* crew most likely would not have faced scurvy a few months later.

The death of Richard Douglas Page

The count always maintained that he never took a life during his cruise. But even his own records and testimony at the time of his first capture in New Zealand point to the fact that he did indeed take the life of Richard Douglas Page. By and large it is the greatest lie of the raid of the *Seeadler*.

It is possible that he felt shameful about this in what was otherwise a very successful operation. He often expressed that he could not have faced his mother if she knew that he had taken the life of another mother's son. Another possible answer is that it was not his idea to alter these facts but came from the publisher or his agent. What remains is the truth. The count *did* take a life; he did so honorably and in full accordance with military law. How he dealt with the death of the young boy was more compelling and realistic than his humanitarian version.

It was not a well-kept secret. Articles and interviews provided by former prisoners and crew in the 1920s and 1930s reference the death of the boy, in some cases by name. What is different is that people did not want to tear down their heroes as they would today. Even in these few published accounts, the people spoke so highly of von Luckner that it was clear they did not hold him personally account-able—which is a view the public must have adopted as well. The count was able to simply stick with his version of events without a public forum or an attempt to discredit him.

Was there champagne aboard the *Horngarth*?

The official manifest of the *Horngarth* says the vessel was carrying corn and other assorted cargo. Some historians have challenged if there was indeed a large quantity of champagne aboard the ship. Was this part of von Luckner's grand story of events or a reality?

It was reality. This has been confirmed in two ways. The testimony of one of the prisoners in 1959 during the television show *This is Your Life* validates the large quantity of champagne taken from the *Horn-garth*. Also testimonies of American prisoners about the wreck of the *Seeadler* refer to hundreds of empty champagne bottles scattered in the lower decks, evidence of her earlier raids. Photographs I recov-ered also show the crew band nestled in with many bottles taken from the ship as booty.

The prisoner count

Like so many details of the cruise of the *Seeadler*, the number of pris-oners released aboard the *Cambronne* for their expatriation in Rio has been distorted over time. Von Luckner's written accounts put the numbers at 265. His oral presentations of history place the numbers at well over 285. This number is seemingly substantiated by the Na-tional Archives of the United Kingdom, but this is apparently based on his testimony to New Zealand authorities, which he is known to have exaggerated. Similarly, he exaggerated the tonnage of the ships he sank, their sizes, and the number of the crew.

The war diary of the *Seeadler* places the number of transferred prisoners at 203 men. The assumption is that the women were always counted separately in the war diary, so their inclusion would have increased this number by two. This number does not include the crew of the *Cambronne* herself, which was not recorded but had to have been more than twenty.

The sighting of the *Otranto* at Cape Horn

In the count's version of events, the crew spotted the auxiliary cruiser *Otranto* in a gale as the *Seeadler* rounded Cape Horn. For some odd reason, the cruiser did not see the *Seeadler* and the windjammer managed to get away.

In the official British naval war history, Henry Newbolt explained that it was impossible for the two ships to see each other. The course of the *Seeadler* and that of the *Otranto* were (on paper) never closer than eighty miles apart. According to Newbolt, it is technically possible to see between the ships, if you stood on top of the mast and if the weather was clear. But the reality is, it was impossible.

So did it happen? According to Kircheiß's notes in the war diary, the *Seeadler* did see the vessel—at least they were convinced it was the *Otranto*. The *Seeadler* spotted a ship in the distance, as described in this book, and moved to avoid her. How did that happen if Newbolt is correct? Most likely bad navigation was the culprit. In the war diary of the *Seeadler* the storm is described as worse than a hurricane. It is entirely possible that the recorded coordinates of the raider were incorrect, thrown off slightly by the raging storm. The ship they saw may or may not have been the *Otranto*. It may have been another ship, or none at all.

Did the *Seeadler* hit an iceberg?

When racing around Cape Horn and around the British blockade, did the *Seeadler* hit an iceberg? The war diary mentions water coming into the ship and pumping during that period. But did the water come from an iceberg against the hull or water from the torrential rain of the storm?

The war diary on many instances did not record the appropriate detail to make a determination. Von Luckner's and other accounts speak of the iceberg incident and at least one other account refers to hitting ice in the run around Cape Horn.

The wreck of the *Seeadler*

The wreck of the *Seeadler* is controversial even to this day. The accounts of the American captains indicate that von Luckner did indeed consult with them as to how to anchor the *Seeadler*. Two of the captains, Peterson and Smith, claim they deliberately misled von Luckner, tricking him to anchor in such a way that would ensure that the raider would eventually ground itself. Was this simply false bravado on their part or did they fool the count?

Von Luckner's version was that a tidal wave slammed the *Seeadler* into the reef. This version grew over time. The wave grew to forty-five feet (enough to swamp all of Mopelia) in later renditions. In one version the count is on the *Seeadler*, in another version he is not. The crew maintained it was a wave because that was the lie that was agreed upon, period.

The absolute best written source on this material is Professor James Bade's book, *Von Luckner: A Reassessment*. For anyone wishing to compare and contrast the wide range of conflicting versions of this story, I highly recommend this book.

What can be said is that von Luckner was negligent in the anchoring of the raider at Mopelia and that this negligence resulted in her loss. It seems unlikely that the American captains really had a role in this because they might face repercussions from the Germans, and they had no way of knowing at the time if Mopelia could support them. Any attempt to mislead the count into stranding the vessel might have proven to be a death sentence.

The treasure of the *Seeadler*

The *Seeadler* set sail with some gold and a large quantity of German marks and British pounds to be used at neutral ports to purchase supplies. When the ship became lodged on the reef on Mopelia, von

Luckner claimed to have buried this precious material on the island. He took most of the marks with him and some of the gold coins. The rest, most likely, went to Lieutenant Kling on the *Fortuna*, though it was not documented.

During his tour of the Pacific in 1938 the count had his ship stop at Mopelia but did not go ashore. He told the Australian press that he had gone ashore and had recovered money that was now-worthless German marks, some coins, and the documentation that the kaiser had given him authorizing his cruise. He was able to see the remains of the *Seeadler* poking out of the water still, rusted and hardly recognizable as a ship.

In the late 1950s, in messages to author Ralph Varady, von Luckner indicated that the ship's log and confiscated treasure had been put in 1918 in a waterproof container and hidden underwater in the reef. According to von Luckner, the map of the exact location was tattooed on his leg. Varady was convinced, as were many individuals, that the treasure was hidden on Mopelia and sought it out. With the death of the count, there was no way to validate the story—but it is widely considered that no treasure is still buried on Mopelia.

The exaggerated voyage in the *Cecilie*

When you read the count's version of the cruise of the *Kronprinzessin Cecilie* it had numerous elements that were added. Given the long hot trip, it is entirely possible that the count and his small crew had invented many of the additions to the story simply to pass time. They did distort somewhat a dangerous voyage where such additions were not necessary.

During the portion of the trip to Fiji, he concocted a trip to an island along the way, Niue, complete with a dangerous encounter with natives. In reality, the *Cecilie* passed one hundred miles away from the island. In his fictitious version, the crew came upon the island and were confronted by dozens of natives. Von Luckner, fearing they were cannibals, ordered the decks, "Cleared for action!" Heavily armed, the weary German sailors were prepared to go down with a fight.

But in the end the natives turned out to be against the British consul on the island and provisioned them with water and fresh fruit.

It was an incredible element of a more complex story of their cruise in a small open ship across the Pacific, but in reality it never occurred. Chances are it was simply a fond thought created to pass time as the men made their way to New Zealand.

Events on Aitutaki

On Aitutaki the count claimed that the way he handled the British official was to draw grenades and threaten him, slowly forcing him to let them leave. The official report that Thomas Duncan sent to the other Fiji islands makes no reference to the weapons.

Duncan's story changed a few weeks later, with the capture of von Luckner and his crew. He filed official reports claiming that there was a cache of weapons aboard the tiny *Cecilie*. Oddly enough, this version matches von Luckner's for the most part, which is why it made its way into the book. It is still entirely possible, though improbable, that the event never happened at all.

The boyhood exploits of von Luckner

Did the count really sail aboard the *Niobe* as a boy, slopping pigs? What about the wreck of the *Caesaria*; did that happen? Commercial-ship crew records from that era are difficult to find and hard to validate.

What we are left with is the count's version of events and those few times that former crewmembers emerged and sold articles to validate elements of his stories. In the end, these are minor elements of a much broader story. But there is little we can validate or disprove from these early years of his life under sail.

Richard Pries—An accident waiting to happen

Lieutenant Pries is something of an enigma. His involvement with the cruise of the *Seeadler* proved tragic. According to the prisoners he was arrogant, cocky, and something of a braggart and a bully. Of all of the crew, he was the only one who had ties to the count before the war. He was in command of the *Seeadler* when she ran aground. Despite their friendship, the count did not take him with him aboard the *Kronprinzessin Cecilie*. It was Pries who had set fire to the *Seeadler* when blasting her masts. Pries refused to follow the orders of Lieutenant Kling when he had taken command of the *Fortuna*.

Was this man a loose cannon, a rebel? Was he responsible for the loss of the *Seeadler*? Where were his loyalties? Out of all the crewmembers we would have expected to see more of in later years, Pries seems to have disappeared. He managed to avoid court martial after the war for his mutiny, but that doesn't change who he was and what he did. Oddly enough, it was his good friend, the count, who helped suppress that court martial.

In Lieutenant Kling's letters to his wife from Chile, he noted: "Unfortunately our brave *Seeadler* went aground; whose fault it was, you can guess." Kling did not like Pries, but was he pointing the finger at this other officer or at his captain? No additional clarification was provided—and while others saw him as the "brains" of the raid, he did not seek to expand his own role or seek to obscure von Luckner's limelight.

The truth of the matter is that we may never fully know his intentions or culpability in the affairs of the *Seeadler* and her crew. While much has been said about von Luckner's responsibilities in the loss of his ship, few historians have looked at this officer and his role.

Were Count Luckner's books ghostwritten?

Some historians have implied that von Luckner's accounts may have been ghostwritten. The count lacked a formal education—he was after all, a runaway from school. Among the suggested authors: Alfred Kling, Karl Kircheiß, and Professor Fritz Kern. Is it possible? Yes. Is it probable? No. Kircheiß wrote his own books and was not in need of von Luckner's name to profit from the events of 1916 to 1920 while aboard the *Seeadler*. Kling did not seem to be close to the count, certainly not close enough to have written his books for him. His role on the cruise seemed overshadowed by the count, and ghostwriting the epic story would have only added to that.

Another factor is that the books after *Seeteufel* matched the same writing style, format, tone, and feel. The lack of hard evidence in this matter seems to imply that it is not a realistic possibility. Any claims made in later years may have been an attempt for some of the men to ride the coattails of their now-famous former captain.

DEDICATION

This book is not about just one man. No one man could have sculpted such a story. This book is about a group of people who became much more than a footnote in history: they defined heroism and daring. To the brave crew of the SMS *Seeadler* and her captain.

Officers

Captain Graf Felix von Luckner
First Officer Lieutenant Alfred Kling
Navigator and Artillery Officer, Lieutenant Karl Theodor
   Friedrich Kircheiß
Prize Officer Lieutenant Richard Pries
Medical Officer, Rudolf "Beefsteak" Pietsch

Crew

Hermann Bahrs
Ewald Barten
Hans Datzmann
Willy Draheim
Gustav "Chips" Dreyer
Ernst Dreyer
Walter Esch
Hermann Erdmann
Theodor Feldmann
Heinrich Feth
Richard Friebel
August Frühling
Albert Hanke
Fritz Hanke
Heinrich Harms
Ernst Harzmener
Otto Heitmann
Paul Henning

Heinrich Hinz
Paul Hühmer
Adolf Jacob
Karol Kawohl
Johann Kohlenberg
Fritz Kolberg
Herman Krause
Fritz Langkopf
Alfred Lindenau
Arthur Lohaus
Friedrich Lüdemann
Fritz Matthießen
Otto Pallaske
Reinhold Karl Paschold
Heinrich Permien
Johann Pfrang
Teophil Puwezyk
Karl Ratzlaff
Werner Reichenbach
Walter "Adolph" "Sparks" Renz
Heinrich Röhling
Karl Sachse
Friedrich Schaumann
Hugo Schmidt
Otto Schmidt
Walter Schmidt
Hugo Schultz
Otto Schultz
Robert Schulz
Helmuth Segelitz
Herman Seidler
Friedrich Silla
Maximilian Sliwa
Christian Sörensen
August Sottmann
Wilhelm Sprengel

Albert Spulsen
Heinrich Stührk
Franz Thieme
Peter Wehner
Gustav Zemke

Honorary Crewmembers—From the Escape of
the **Pearl** *in New Zealand*

Albrecht Von Egidy
Otto Freund
Karl Grun
Ernst Klohn
Friedrich Mellert
Walter Schmidt
Walter Zatorski

And, to the One Victim of the **Seeadler**

Richard Douglas Page—Wireless Operator, *Horngarth*

ACKNOWLEDGMENTS

The hardest part of writing a non-fiction book like this is that the participants have been dead for years. I always have believed that real-life stories far surpass fiction—and that is the case in the story, myth, and legend that is Felix von Luckner and his crew.

As much as there is a general knowledge of von Luckner, there is not a great deal written about him in book form. His own autobiographical work written after the war in Germany was adopted for the most part by Lowell Thomas in his book, *The Sea Devil*. Thomas did not fact-check the storyteller, so many of the details in his book are suspect. Thomas's book itself is a good source of information for the conversational elements of the story—and I have used that book as a primary source for most discussions presented herein, since they are the only possible references to things that were said during the raid of the *Seeadler*.

The problem seems to surface because Count von Luckner was a storyteller in the grandest traditions of sailors on the high seas. As such, the truth was a good starting point, but over the years he embellished the tale of his cruise aboard the *Seeadler*. Much of this myth was complicated when prisoners added their accounts to the stories that von Luckner told, further confusing the distinction between events and a good story. Research, logic, and a touch of luck have come into play, allowing me to ferret out elements that are fictional or just downright inaccurate. I have detailed most of these in the last chapter of this book. Sometimes the legend is not nearly as entertaining as the reality.

The naming of the Pacific islands seems to have changed numerous times. Mopelia was also known as Lord Howe Island, Maupelia, and Mopeha. Ripappa Island went by several different names. I've had to pick a single way of addressing each island and have remained with that convention.

Likewise the naming of the German sailors involved with the crew of the *Seeadler* appear different in multiple official records as well as in the various secondary resources. I have tried to go with the most official spelling available, from the war diary of the *Seeadler*.

This book would not have been possible without a few resources on the Web. eBay introduced me to a community of people on the web interested in the same subjects I was researching, and a number of those people proved to be good sources.

Alibris.com, the used-book Website, proved invaluable in tracking down books that libraries were unable to help me with.

A number of people assisted me either directly or indirectly in the writing of this book. These individuals are not listed in any particular order but they all have my appreciation and gratitude.

Thanks to Alan Andrews, veteran of the 101st Airborne Division in Vietnam, who loaned me a battered copy of the Lowell Thomas book when I was fourteen years old and delivering newspapers. He got me hooked, damn it—and now I've brought this full circle.

Rebecca Livingston and Robin Cookson from the National Archives of the United States deserve thanks. Rebecca was a masterful guide to the First World War U.S. Naval records, most of which are still indexed manually. Robin Cookson in the College Park facility helped me track down the German World War I Archives records, which were invaluable.

Keith B. Mickle's father served with Lieutenant Colonel Turner in New Zealand during the First World War. He helped confirm the story regarding the sword stolen from the colonel. He met Graf von Luckner during the count's trip to Australia in 1938 and was able to give some firsthand insights into the count's insistence that he was not a Nazi spy.

Matthias Maurer, writer and attorney in Halle, Germany, was a great help. He helped steer me to a number of resources and people on top of writing an excellent book, *Our Way to Halle*, during the last days of the Second World War.

At the Mariner's Museum Library in Newport News, Virginia, the author's hometown, special thanks go to researchers Josh Graml and Leanette Dillabough and the volunteer staff working there. Anita Smith was a tremendous help in tracking down several photographs.

The Archives of New Zealand was a wonderful resource and Adrienne Burgess was a great help.

Paul Johnson of the National Archives of the United Kingdom helped track down some of the previously unpublished photographs taken from von Luckner.

The Royal Navy of New Zealand Museum's Paul Restall was very helpful in this process.

Other people provided me great assistance in this effort. Peter Branton of the 104th Infantry Division (the Timberwolves) Official Historian provided contacts for researching von Luckner's role in the surrender of Halle. Master Chief Petty Officer Andrew Moeller, office of the Naval Attaché of the German Embassy, Washington D.C., helped guide me through the maze of German World War I military records. Michael Hofmann, a bookseller in Germany, helped me track down several critical reference tools.

Klaus Füst of the Deutsches Schiffahrtsmuseum was quite helpful in going through their archives of images of the *Seeadler* and pulling out some photographs that, up to this point, had not seen press.

MacKenzie J. Gregory, who runs the Ahoy Mac Website, was instrumental in helping keep the von Luckner legend alive all of these years and was a great way to get to people who had stories to tell of their encounters with the count. Special thanks to Jay McCullough at The Lyons Press.

Finally, this book would not be possible without my wife Cyndi, my children Alexander and Victoria, and the rest of my family—both in Virginia and Michigan. Thanks also to the Journalism Department of Central Michigan University, for motivating me to be a writer so many years ago.

If, after reading this book, you find that you too have a bond with the man who was Felix von Luckner, feel free to join us at the von Luckner Society. We are attempting to build a museum in Halle, as a tribute to a man and a time that is now past.

http://luckner-society.com/

Victims of the Seeadler Crew

Date Sunk:	Ship:	Location:
January 9, 1917	*Gladys Royale*	Lat. 37° 51' N. Long. 21° 11' W.
January 10, 1917	*Lundy Island*	Lat. 35° 12' N. Long. 22° 11' W.
January 21, 1917	*Charles Gounod*	Lat. 6° 41' N. Long. 28° 41' W.
January 28, 1917	*Perce*	Lat. 3° 00' N. Long. 28° 00' W.
February 3, 1917	*Antonin*	Lat. 6° 35' N. Long. 33° 26' W.
February 9, 1917	*Buenos Aires*	Lat. 5° 22' N. Long. 32° 26' W.
February 19, 1917	*Pinmore*	Lat. 8° 05' N. Long. 35° 26' W.
February 25, 1917	*Viking* (neutral ship. Searched and released)	Lat. 6° 24' N. Long. 33° 48' W.
February 26, 1917	*British Yeoman*	Lat. 4° 56' N. Long. 31° 56' W.
February 27, 1917	*La Rochefoucauld*	Lat. 4° 35' N. Long. 32° 15' W.
March 6, 1917	*Dupleix*	Lat. 1° 10' N. Long. 26° 50' W.
March 11, 1917	*Horngarth*	Lat. 1° 59' N. Long. 26° 10' W.
March 21, 1917	*Cambronne* (captured not sunk)	Lat. 20° 10' S. Long. 25° 50' W.
June 14, 1917	*A. B. Johnson*	Lat. 1° 00' N. Long. 150° 00' W.
June 17, 1917	*R. C. Slade*	Lat. 2° 00' N. Long. 150° 00' W.
July 8, 1917	*Manila*	Lat. 9° 00' N. Long. 150° 00' W.
September 5, 1917	*Lutéce* (captured and renamed *Fortuna*)	Mopelia Island
December 13, 1917	*Pearl* (lost at sea while in tow)	Motuihe Island
December 21, 1917	*Moa* (captured by the *Iris*)	Curtis Island

SOURCES

The difficulties in researching this book stem from a number of areas. None of the participants in the cruise of the *Seeadler* are still alive so live interviews often necessary to distinguish fact from fiction or myth were not possible. Also, German military records are available but many are written in "old German," making the use of many contemporary translators difficult.

Archives and Libraries

- The Imperial War Museum Archives, London. *Access to the journal of an officer aboard the* Avenger *helped resolve the issue over the name* Seeadler *sailed under when she passed through the blockade.*
- The Bundersarchiv/Militararchiv in Breisgau, Germany, Federal Archives, Military Division
- The Mariner's Museum Library, Newport News, Virginia. *Perhaps one of the best naval libraries and museums in the United States. The museum's exhibit of artifacts from the wreck of the USS* Monitor *are stunning.*
- Militärgeschichtiched Forchungamt (German Military Research Center)
- Deutsches Schiffahrtsmuseum in Bremerhaven, Germany. *Excellent source of German information on the* Seeadler *including exclusive photographs of the* Seeadler *painted as the* Walter *in dock.*
- Ralph Edwards Studios. *Their archives proved most useful for the viewer's copy of* This is Your Life
- The Archives of New Zealand
- The National Archives of the United Kingdom
- The Royal Navy of New Zealand Museum

Books

- *1,000 Jahre Seefahrt.* Unton Maner. Berlin: Paul Frante Berlig, 1934, pages 5–6. *Foreword by Count von Luckner.*

- *A Boy Scout with the Sea Devil.* David P. Martin Jr. New York: G. P. Putnam's Sons, 1930. *This book covers Count von Luckner taking a crew of Boy Scouts on his personal yacht, the* Mopelia, *and sailing with them in the Caribbean.*
- *Castles of Steel.* Robert K. Massie. New York: Random House, 2003. *An outstanding book of the naval war during World War I. A must-read book for anyone who is interesting in this period.*
- *Count Luckner, The Sea Devil.* Lowell Thomas. New York: Double-day, Page, and Company, 1927. *For most Americans this is considered the definitive account of the life of von Luckner and the* Seeadler *cruise. It has some erroneous accounts and in some places is more story than fact.*
- *Count von Luckner—Knight of the Sea.* Edwin P. Hoyt. New York: David McKay Company Inc., 1969. *Excellent book dealing with the facts of the* Seeadler *cruise.*
- *Count Von Luckner, The Famous German Raider.* Captain Fred Southard, Edited by Joseph Kaye. Buffalo, New York: Reed Publishing, 1932. *This dime novel was written by the captain of the* Manilla, *one of the ships captured by von Luckner. It gives a firsthand account of the sinking of the ship, life of the American captives, etc. It is a wonderful insight into facts around the sinking of the* Seeadler *that were not revealed in later books.*
- *Cruise of the Kronprinz Wilhelm.* Alfred von Niezichowski. New York: Doubleday, 1929, pages xiii–xiv. *Foreword by Count von Luckner.*
- *Der I. Weltkrieg 1914–1918 in Word Und Bild. Der Kreig zur See, Bands 1–4.* Peter Körner. München: Welhelm Heyne Verlag, 1968. *This is the official account of the German war at sea.*
- *German Exploration of the Polar World—A History, 1870–1940.* David Thomas Murphy. University of Nebraska Press, 2002, pages 65–106. *This book provides some insights into the first officer of the* Seeadler, *Alfred Kling, prior to his service aboard the ship.*
- *Good Evening Everybody: From Cripple Creek to Samarkand.* Lowell Thomas. New York: William Morrow and Company, 1976. *Book covers some details of the relationship between Lowell Thomas and Count von Luckner in the early years.*

- *Graf Luckner's* Seeadler. Hans D. Schenk. Hamburg: Die Hanse, 1999. *This book essentially takes the handwritten war diary of the* Seeadler *and translates it to contemporary German. Having struggled with the archived copy of the war diary, Mr. Schenk has done an outstanding job of making translation to English possible and practical.*
- *Great Hoaxes of All Time.* Lowell Thomas and Count Felix von Luckner, Edited by Robert McBride and Neil Pritchie. New York: Robert McBride Publishing, 1956. *Chapter included in book on the* Seeadler's *sailing through the British lines.*
- *Il Pirata della Guerra Mondiale del Coute Felix von Luckner.* Italy: Adriano Salani, 1930. *Italian variant/version of* Seeteufel.
- *Jane's Fighting Ships of World War 1.* Random House Reprint, Studio Books, 2001. *Most useful for its maps of German ports, rank systems, gun calibers, and penetration charts.*
- *Last Cruise of the* Emden. Edwin P. Hoyt. Guilford, Connecticut: Lyons Press. *This book covers the extraordinary cruise of the* Emden *and the eventual escape of the crew back to Germany.*
- *Liberty's Victorious Conflict.* The Magazine Circulation Company, Inc., Chicago, Illinois, 1919, Page 58. *Photograph of the wreck of the* Seeadler.
- *Ludner-Jahrebuch 1925.* Sans Severin Schroeder. Germany: R. F. Koehlers, 1925. *The interviews with von Luckner and several previously unpublished photographs were useful in filling in some gaps regarding the postwar wedding of the count and the cruise through the blockade.*
- *Many Lagoons.* Ralph Varady. New York: William Morrow & Company, 1958, pages 61–111. *Interesting look at the wreck of the* Seeadler *and some of the artifacts still present.*
- *Our Way to Halle.* Matthias J. Maurer. Leipzig, Germany: Fliegenkopf Verlag, 2001. *This book details Halle during World War II and has an outstanding photographic record of the count during the surrender talks.*
- *Out of an Old Sea Chest.* Count Felix von Luckner, Translated by Edward Fitzgerald. London: Methuen and Company Ltd., 1958. *Best account of the World War II events in the count's life . . . from his perspective.*
- *Seeteufel* (Sea Devil). Graf Felix von Luckner. Germany: Köhlers Books, 1921. *This is the autobiography of Count Luckner's cruise. It is a*

good source of material for not just the cruise but his early life. There are elements in this book that do not appear in the English-language version of this book by Lowell Thomas.

- *Seeteufel erobert Amerika.* Felix von Luckner. Leipzig Germany: Hafe & Koehler, 1928. *Written by the count of his first tour of America in 1927–1928.*
- *So Long Until Tomorrow.* Lowell Thomas. New York: William Morrow and Company, 1977. *This sequel to* Good Evening Everybody *provides some details associated with Count Luckner's meeting with General George S. Patton.*
- *Stories of the Famous Sea Raiders.* Len Ortzen. London: Arthur Baker Books, 1973. *Mr. Ortzen really provides some good context for the* Seeadler's *mission as part of an overall surface raider campaign.*
- *Terrible Terry Allen—Combat General of World War II—Life of an American Soldier.* Gerald Astor. New York: Ballentine Books—Presidio Press, 2003. *Provides a good background into the general that von Luckner treated with over the surrender of Halle in World War II.*
- *The German Pirate—His Methods and Record.* Ajax, C. London: Arthur Pearson Ltd., 1918. *This small propaganda book reveals a great deal of the military code that the Germans were exploiting in their raiding program.*
- *The Great War—Stories of World War 1.* Edward Jablonski. Racine, Wisconsin: Whitman Publishing, 1965.
- *The Kaiser's Pirates, German Surface Raiders in World War One.* John Walter. Annapolis Maryland: Naval Institute Press, 1994. *Excellent book on each raider. Mr. Walter's research with Lloyd's of London into each ship sunk by the* Seeadler *was incredibly useful.*
- *The Official History of the War, Naval Operations, Volume IV.* Henry Newbolt. Originally published in 1928, reprinted with permission of the Imperial War Museum by Battery Press, Inc., 1996, pages 181–225. *This is the official British account of naval operations and covers not only how the* Seeadler *slipped the blockade, but all actions in response by the Royal Navy to capture her.*
- *The Patton Papers.* Edited by Martin Blumenson. New York: DaCapo Press, 1995, page 279. *Reference to a phone call from von Luckner to General Patton with an offer to teach the post-war Germans about democracy.*

- *The Sea Devil Came Calling.* Howard Henry. Auckland: Sovereign Pacific Publishing, 2001. *This small-press book is a narrative of von Luckner's cruise in the Pacific aboard the* Cecilie.

- *The Sea Devil, The Controversial Cruise of the Nazi Emissary Von Luckner to Australia and New Zealand in 1938.* Carl Ruhen. Australia: Kagaroo Press, 1988. *A heavily slanted book (as the title implies) on the count's tour of the Pacific in 1938.*

- *The Sea Devil's Fo'c'sle.* Lowell Thomas. New Jersey: Garden City Publishing, 1929. *This was a series of add-on tales and memories recorded from the count to Lowell Thomas. Most of these incidents deal with the youth of von Luckner after his fame had been established.*

- *The Windjammers.* Oliver Allen, Alexandria Virginia: Time Life Books, 1978, pages 120–135. *This book has a number of inaccuracies perpetuated by years of story-telling on the part of Count von Luckner. It does, however, have some hand-drawn images of the refitting of the* Seeadler *that are interesting and accurate.*

- *Tin-Pots & Pirate Ships.* Michael Hadley and Roger Sarty. London, Ontario: McGill Queens University Press, 1936.

- *Unter Graf Luckner als Obermatrof.* Heinrich Hinz. Hamburg: Eente Verlag, 1922. *Written by one of the crew of the* Seeadler *within a year of Count von Luckner's published account. This book provides insights into the events surrounding not only the* Seeadler's *cruise but the crew's internment in Chile.*

- *Uuf Kaperfurs (The Raiders).* Walter Von Schoen. Berlin: A.G. Ullstein, 1934. *German perspective of the World War I raiders including a chapter on the* Seeadler.

- *Von Luckner: A Reassessment. Count Felix von Luckner in New Zealand and the South Pacific—1917–1919 and 1938.* Professor James N. Bade, Germanica Pacifica Volume 3. Frankfurt, Germany: Peter Lang Books, 2004. *Perhaps one of the best researched pieces dealing with von Luckner's Pacific years. Great detail. Provides a translated transcript of Engineer Krause's Diary.*

- *Wasser-Wind und weite Welt.* Kapitan Karl Kircheiß. Germany: Umschlag und Einband S. Kortrmeier, 1953. *Written by one of the former crew of the* Seeadler, *this book offers insights into the background of Karl Kircheiß and several aspects of the cruise of the* Seeadler.

Articles

- "Auf der Fährete des *Seeadlers*," *Der Landser*, Number 21, November 1996, pages 3–33. *Excellent article on the cruise of the* Seeadler. *This is a reprint of the Otto Mielke article from SOS Schicksale Deutscher Schiffe.*
- "Captured, Shipwrecked and Marooned: the American Schooner *Manilla* and the German Raider *Seeadler*, the Experience of F. J. Williams, Mate of the *Manilla*," *U.S. Naval Institute Proceedings*, Captain Edward T. Pollock, U.S. Navy, Retired, Vol. 53, No. 290, 1927, pages 427–435.
- "Cook Island Mystery," *The Herald* (New Zealand), September 22, 1917. *Tracking of a boatload of foreigners traveling through the Pacific— possibly Germans.*
- "Count Felix Von Luckner," *Nautical Brass*, Ian A. Miller, Volume VI, Number 1, January/February 1986, pages 6–7.
- "Count von Luckner and the Voyage of the *Seeadler*," *Strategy & Tactics*, Kenneth I. Roy, Number 93, Summer 1983, pages 9–10.
- "Count Von Luckner, The Sea Devil," *Sea Classics*, William McKee, March 1995, pages 14–19, 67–70. *An outstanding article on the voyage of the* Seeadler *that makes use of the National Archives resources.*
- "Coursair *Seeadler* Survivors," *El Mercurio* (Chile), September 7, 1918. *Article about the* Seeadler *survivors living on the Dresden at the expense of the Chilean government.*
- "Des 'Seeteufels' große Reise," *SOS Schicksale Deutscher Schiffe*, Otto Mielke, Number 114, 1957. *Excellent article on the cruise of the* Seeadler.
- "Discovered: The Wreck of the Sea Pirate Von Luckner," Garland Roark with Ralph Varady, *Argosy*, Volume 366, Number 3, March 1968, pages 52–57, 90. *The authors' correspondence with von Luckner offers a fanciful explanation of what happened to the logbook and the gold bullion of the* Seeadler.
- "Fighting Uncle Sam in the Pacific," *World's Work*, Lowell Thomas, November 1927, pages 59–75. *Thomas recounts most of the content from* The Sea Devil, *but he offers some additional details not previously released.*
- "Hilfskreuzer MS *Seeadler*—Legends und . . . ?" *Das Logbuch*, Dirk Nottelman, 33, July 1997, pages 15–22. *An outstanding source not only*

debunking the myth of von Luckner, but at the engineering feat of the Seeadler *itself and some of the problems that the shipwrights must have faced in mounting an engine in the ship.*

- "Mysterious Launch," *The Star* (New Zealand), September 19, 1917. *Interview with Duncan Thomas on the suspicious visitors to his island and a warning for other islands to be on the lookout for them.*
- "Sailing Raider's Exploits," *London Times,* April 2, 1917.
- "She Was Von Luckner's Captive," Jessie Neilson, as told to Harold Bradley Say, *Liberty,* January 7, 1933, pages 12–13. *The best-documented evidence that von Luckner did take a life during the cruise of the* Seeadler. *This article, by a female captive, recounts in exacting detail the death of a young boy from the capture of the* Horngarth.
- "Thank God for Blohm & Voss," *Naval History,* Russell Drumm, Vol. 11, Issue 1, January/February 1997, pages 20–21. *Background information on the* Niobe *and her fate after von Luckner's outfitting of the vessel.*
- "The Pirate of the Pacific: German Naval Officer's daring Escape from his Prison Island and Recapture in Mid-Ocean," *The Wide World Magazine,* James Cowan, July 1918, pages 253–260. *A detailed account of von Luckner's escape from custody and recapture from New Zealand sources.*
- "The Sea Devil," James Powles, *Our Navy,* Volume 59, Number 4, April 1964, pages 24–25.
- "The Sea Devil," Lowell Thomas, *Argosy,* Volume 364, Number 4, April 1967, pages 66–72, 92.
- "The Unexpected End to the *Seeadler,*" *The American Neptune,* Robert L. Clifford, October 1976, pages 266–275. *Excellent account of the sinking of the* Seeadler.
- "Von Luckner's Pirate's House Party," *The* (Washington) *Sunday Star,* David Carter, January 30, 1927. *Newspaper article on von Luckner's relaxed method of raiding—coincides with his tour of the United States in 1927.*

Other sources

- National Archives, US Navy Subject File 1910–27 *JT-Enemy Ships other than U-Boats.* Also, *JP-Enemy Raider Activities.* Navy Area File-

South Pacific Area 1911–1927, Naval Intelligence Communiqués, Boxes 267–269. *NA-6 Key German Naval Officers Profiles. By and large the most lucrative source out there on the* Seeadler *and her cruise, interviews with numerous prisoners, as well as naval intelligence information on the raider. The reports of the Consulate in Tahiti proved to be a wealth of primary material on the Pacific journey of the* Kronprinzessin Cecilie *and the rescue of the American prisoners.*

• National Archives, Microfilm T10-022 KTB Role 375, Ships Records, SMS *Seeadler. Includes full handwritten copy of the war diary of the vessel, ship's records, etc.*

• National Archives, Microfilm T10-022 KTB Role 719. Admiralstab records July 16, 1917–December 20, 1918. *Records of intelligence information on the* Seeadler *and her crew's internment in Chile. This includes von Luckner's letter of appeal to the Chilean government to release the crew back to Germany and his first written account of the cruise of the* Seeadler.

• National Archives, Microfilm T10-022 KTB Role 193, Admiralstab and ship reports, 1916–1917. *This includes telegrams and personnel records of the crew. Also included are news clippings from a number of newspapers, including* Berlin, *the* London Times, *and others once the* Cambronne *arrived in harbor.*

• Transcript Testimony, Fred J. Williams, *Manilla*, to Governor J. M. Poyer, American Samoa, June 7, 1919. Filed in the Mariner's Museum, Newport News, Virginia.

• Nordland Fahrten. 1924 Advertising brochure for the cruise of the yacht *Seeadler* under the command of Captain Kling. *Excellent photographs of Kling during his Arctic era and post-war.*

• Kreigsmarine Volume 2, CD of Marches of the German Navy. *Includes the "Seeadler Marsch" and the "Von Luckner Marsch."*

• The Archives of New Zealand, Archives Reference Files G-41/30, 2660a. *Photographs of the count during his stays in New Zealand were invaluable.*

• The National Archives of the United Kingdom, Reference Boxes ADM137/3909, ADM137/1431, and File MPI1/483.

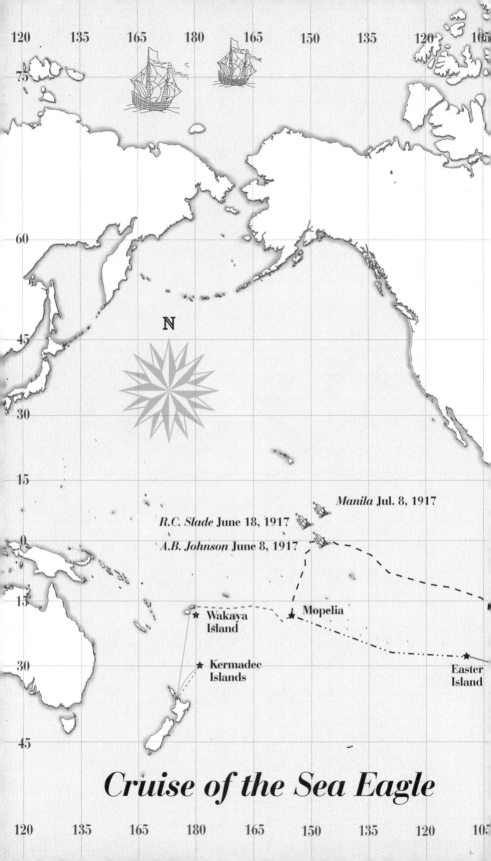

120   135   165   180   165   150   135   120   105

75

60

N

45

30

15

0

Manila Jul. 8, 1917

R.C. Slade June 18, 1917

A.B. Johnson June 8, 1917

15

★ Wakaya
Island

★ Mopelia

30

★ Kermadec
Islands

★ Easter
Island

45

Cruise of the Sea Eagle

120   135   165   180   165   150   135   120   105